D1430193

WE HAVE YOUR HUSBAND

WE HAVE YOUR HUSBAND

One Woman's Terrifying Story of a Kidnapping in Mexico

JAYNE GARCIA VALSECA

WITH MARK EBNER

BERKLEY BOOKS, NEW YORK

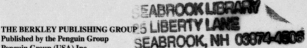

THE BERKLEY PUBLISHING GROUP
Published by the Penguin Group
Penguin Group (USA) Inc.
375 Hudson Street, New York, New York 10014, USA

Penguin Group (Canada), 90 Eglinton Avenue East, Suite 700, Toronto, Ontario M4P 2Y3, Canada
(a division of Pearson Penguin Canada Inc.)
Penguin Book Ltd., 80 Strand, London WC2R 0RL, England
Penguin Group Ireland, 25 St. Stephen's Green, Dublin 2, Ireland (a division of Penguin Books Ltd.)
Penguin Group (Australia), 250 Camberwell Road, Camberwell, Victoria 3124, Australia
(a division of Pearson Australia Group Pty. Ltd.)
Penguin Books India Pvt. Ltd., 11 Community Centre, Panchsheel Park, New Delhi—110 017, India
Penguin Group (NZ), 67 Apollo Drive, Rosedale, Auckland 0632, New Zealand
(a division of Pearson New Zealand Ltd.)
Penguin Books (South Africa) (Pty.) Ltd., 24 Sturdee Avenue, Rosebank, Johannesburg 2196,
South Africa

Penguin Books Ltd., Registered Offices: 80 Strand, London WC2R 0RL, England

The publisher does not have any control over and does not assume any responsibility for author or third-party websites or their content.

WE HAVE YOUR HUSBAND

A Berkley Book / published by arrangement with the authors

PRINTING HISTORY
Berkley mass-market edition / May 2011

ISBN: 978-0-425-24178-3

PRINTED IN THE UNITED STATES OF AMERICA

10 9 8 7 6 5 4 3 2 1

This book is dedicated to Eduardo and my children—Fernando, Emiliano, and Nayah—and to all the families who go through what we did. May your loved ones make it home safely.

ACKNOWLEDGMENTS

My husband's kidnapping and all that followed was one of the most challenging times of my life. I could not have gotten through it without the help and support of my family and close friends. Eduardo, my soul mate: I thank you for giving me strength and unwavering encouragement in my most desperate moments. Thank you for your contagious love of life that makes my every day a fiesta! I adore you.

Cielo, Leti, and Verita, you were my absolute pillars. I could never have made it through this without you. Thank you from the bottom of my heart and soul.

Mom, you have always been there for me in the best of times and the worst with your unconditional love and support. I love you.

My father, Dalbert Rager: Although you are no longer with me in the flesh, you are with me always. Thank you for the wisdom you shared with me in life.

Fernando, Emiliano, and Nayah, you are my life. You brought smiles to my face when I thought my face couldn't smile anymore. There is no possible way I could have made it through all of this had it not been for the joy you instill in me. You give me strength, fill my life with light, and are my inspiration for being.

My dear brother, John Rager, I will never forget you offering me everything you had and crying with me on the phone. I love you, little brother.

The gratitude that I feel for those individuals who loaned me what I needed to pay the ransom is beyond words. Although I will not mention you by name, I want you to know that for as long as I live, I will never forget what you did.

Thank you to Lupe, Uncle Ted, and John Robert Garman for sharing your wisdom and support, as always.

Thank you to Mary Jordan and Kevin Sullivan for your valuable guidance in my moment of crisis and the inspiration and encouragement to write this book.

A special thank-you to Barbara Feinman Todd for the time, wisdom, and experience you so generously shared with me, and for telling me that my story needed to be told.

Thank you to David Montgomery, Kira Zalan, and Carol Gable for your outstanding work in journalism, telling the stories that change the world.

My sincerest thanks to Michael Wright, Joel Gotler, and Laura Dail for making this book a reality.

Thank you to Mr. Richard Stephenson of Cancer Treatment Centers of America, the man who created the place that helped me to heal on every level when I was told by others that I may never get well.

My deepest gratitude to Dr. Michael Barry, the man who taught me about forgiveness. It was you, Wendell Scanterbury, and your team who brought me to my turning point. Thank you to Dr. Les Darroff for treating us even when you were no longer on the clock. If it were not for you, I would have never found the strength and courage to use my voice.

Thank you to Cindy and Mark Ross for providing guidance and rooms with views in which to write. Camp Ross will always be our favorite destination.

Thank you to Ruth and Max Suberi for so generously sharing your frequent-flier miles with us.

Thank you to Kris Carr. You inspired me to find healing when all I could see was a deep, dark hole in the ground, waiting for me to get in it.

Mark Ebner, it is an honor to know you and to have had the opportunity to write with you. Thank you for the support, encouragement, and friendship. There is so much of your own heart in this book, and I can't thank you enough. A special thank you to Paul Cullum as well.

I would also like to express my profound thanks to the people of San Miguel de Allende and around the world who have prayed for us, lit candles for us, and held my family in their thoughts throughout our time of pain and crisis. So many came to my aid, and did so selflessly. Thank you to Glenn Davis, Jennifer Grega, Aidan Lines, Jorge Septien, the late Felix Batista, Michael and Erika French, Judith Tomamichel, Elsanne Barrows, Dr. Beverly Nelson, Ivy Ana, Eduardo Morales, Cofe Fiakpui, Raul, Cal, Greywolf, Jim and Vicky Flood, Arturo Vidales, Jacqueline Farrington, Richard Leet, Lynn James, Meriget and James Turner, Mr. and Mrs. Don Bosie and everyone at Unisono, Iñaki Garcia Gioricelaya, Rafael Loret de Mola, Lucy Nuñez Zavala, Javier Zavala, Alma and Luis Alberto Villarreal and the entire Villarreal family.

Mark Ebner thanks Paul Cullum, Wendy Loo, Jenny Pool, Elizabeth Schwartz, Joel Gotler, Laura Dail, Lisa Ullmann, Lisa Derrick, Cat Noel, Mr. Bruce, and Dexter.

CONTENTS

PROLOGUE

What would you do if the sky fell? If the moon became unhinged and crashed to the earth around you? Everyone— mothers and fathers, husbands and wives, caretakers and providers—has their plans and contingencies, but no one really knows how they'll react when the most fundamental things in life are suddenly called into question, or what strengths they'll find in reserve. A shift of weight, a sudden stillness in the air, a momentary sound or flash, and then it's upon them. The best they can do is act on instinct and try to get out from under.

This is how it happened for me.

I was thirty-six years old and living a charmed life. Married to a man eighteen years my senior, a storybook romance that had brought me to the most beautiful place in the world—San Miguel de Allende, in the high desert of central Mexico—I was living a dream. I had just given birth to my third child, my daughter Nayah, a strong-willed spitfire who even later, at ten months old, would let me know exactly the way she liked for things to be. My other two children—Fernando, seven, my charmer, and Emiliano, one and a half, whose heart I feared would burst sometimes, so much did he seem to care—were both great kids, and every day they filled me with a mixture of pride and awe that these little engines of exuberance could have come from me. After two decades in Mexico, my love affair with my husband had expanded to include my adopted home, the land of his birth, and through his eyes I saw its spectral wonders, its incandescent pleasures and fusillades of color and flavor, and learned to cherish them as my own. We had good friends and a beautiful ninety-acre ranch on the outskirts of town where we grew alfalfa and raised horses, with a natural hot springs and a Chichimeca ruin just down the hill. It was a postcard existence, a movie poster, a travel brochure—the retirement you imagine for yourself at the end of your life, except that I was still relatively young, and we were all discovering it together.

The first sign that something was wrong was when Nayah refused to nurse on one side. Six months after that, I developed an acute pain and then a lump in the breast she rejected. My doctor assured me it was nothing—even after I went back to him ten months later with what seemed like a low-grade infection. A standard mammogram turned up nothing. When I went to see him the third time, my lymph nodes throbbing, I could see his face turn red during the examination. I immediately got on a plane to the Washington, D.C., area where doctors at the hospital diagnosed me with inflammatory breast cancer. Although my mother had breast cancer, I led what I considered a healthy lifestyle: I exercised, did yoga, kept an organic garden, and was very discerning about my diet. It just never seemed like a possibility to me.

On doctors' advice, I started on chemotherapy immediately. A pernicious strain of cancer had dug deep into my right breast—it was spreading so quickly that I could watch it day to day in the mirror growing red and more inflamed. In quick succession, I went in for surgery and then started on radiation. It was now two and a half years since I'd first noticed something was wrong, and it was almost too late. It left the whole family shaken. But by any measure, it could have been worse, so I made plans to return for checkups every three months, and we all tried to put it behind us. With a clean bill of health, I could go in for reconstructive surgery in another year. It was now March 2006. The doctors assured me they had gotten it all and everything would be fine.

But it wasn't fine. It had set loose something in the spirit—some acrid vapor that curled about the five of us and hung unspoken in the air, staining our outlook and suppressing the possibilities we had earmarked for the future. Now anything could happen to us. Our life was no longer charmed.

First, my father died of a heart attack just before Christmas. We were unusually close, and it was completely unexpected. He had also recently become very good friends with my husband, Eduardo, and so it was doubly hard. There was a land deal that ended in litigation, and we got sucked into it because we had sold a parcel of land to one of the aggrieved parties. And then Eduardo—always upbeat, positive, a life force you could physically sense whenever he walked into a room—was stricken with some mysterious intestinal disorder. Within a matter of weeks, he was paralyzed with intense heartburn, stomachaches, chronic diarrhea. He couldn't digest food or keep down liquids, making him almost a prisoner in our home, which left him riddled with anxiety and then insomnia, and the tranquilizers he took to sleep made him more or less a zombie. He started to check out of our life and then from life altogether. I could feel him slipping away.

On a day trip with the kids to see the monarch butterfly migration, I called him on the way home and he sounded awful—despondent, barely able to speak. I felt helpless, hours from home, with nothing I could do. I later learned that he came close to committing suicide that day—he had the note written and everything. It was only by imagining the kids finding his body that he was able to snap himself out of it. Three days later, I put him in the car and drove him to the British hospital in Mexico City, which finally identified the problem as an absorption problem in his digestive tract. We designed a special diet for him, and within a matter of weeks his condition started to turn around. He had been uncomfortably thin, fragile, unable to exercise, in terrible shape—and then suddenly he was better.

I remember one night in particular: We met for drinks with another couple, Sandy and Derek, some of our oldest friends in San Miguel. A developer had come from the States and wanted to buy some of our land for a golf resort he and his partners were planning. It was enough money that we could do the things we'd always talked about—travel, see the world—and we were keeping it close to the vest for fear of jinxing the deal. This was the first time we had told anyone else about our good fortune, and we were celebrating over dinner. After tapas and wine, we walked down to the central gardens where the mariachis stroll and play.

From the first time I visited Mexico, Eduardo would take me to the main square on the weekends and he would call the mariachis over to serenade me. Mariachi music can reflect a whole range of emotions—you see the bands at weddings and birthdays but at funerals too—and he enjoyed the music so much that it came to symbolize Mexican culture for me: the happiness but also the bittersweet that creeps in at the edges—the constant fiesta that celebrates everyday life, even the sad parts. It's completely alluring and more than a little addictive. You get so caught up in it, and your senses are so stimulated—I felt so alive in Mexico—that you don't see the darker undercurrents of reality. So when I fell madly in love with my husband, I fell madly in love with his country at the same time. I planned on growing old there. When he asked me one day, "If you go before I do, what do you want me to do?" I said, "Bring the mariachis, cremate me, and scatter my ashes around the playground at the school"—the one we'd founded on our property, which I'm happy to report is still going strong.

Eduardo walked right over to this favorite group of his, in his signature poncho and wide-brimmed hat, and started singing with them. He knew them, they'd been to our house many times, and the song they were singing was our song, "Solamente una vez": "Only one time I have loved in my life/Only one time, nothing more . . ." Suddenly, it changed the whole atmosphere of the square: People started gathering around, and it became a party. One of the friends we were with said, "Look—the old Eduardo is back!" and we raised a toast to him with our glasses. He had returned from the dead. I had beaten cancer. We just had to sign the papers on a deal that promised us financial independence. We were looking forward to the summer, when I would have my reconstructive surgery in Washington, D.C., and then we would drive cross-country with the kids. That moment, the lights of the square sparkling in our champagne glasses, mariachi music filling the air, was when I knew we had finally gotten through it.

The darkness was lifting. We really were going to be all right.

ONE

The Abduction

It was a morning like any other.

Eduardo was padding about in his pajamas. I was getting the kids' lunches ready for school. Although the Waldorf school we founded was located on our property, no more than a half mile from the house, we liked to drive to school together every morning. The little ones liked it because we always sang, and always the same song—"Caminito de la escuela" or "The Little Road to School." We liked it because we could start our day as a family. This particular morning, there was a controversy because one of the dogs had just had puppies, and the kids wanted to take one to school. They always went nuts whenever there were newborns on the ranch—puppies, baby rabbits. But Irish wolfhound pups are extremely delicate—out of a litter of fifteen, you're lucky if five or six survive—so I had to put my foot down.

As he did many mornings, Fernando, our oldest, got tired of waiting on us and drove the motorized four-wheeler on ahead. His class was going on a field trip, and he couldn't wait to get started. Eduardo was still in his bathrobe and sweatpants, since he rarely got out of the car, and I just threw on some old clothes and flip-flops. As we traversed the narrow two-way road that led onto the school grounds, we noticed an off-white Yukon parked in the turnout by a neighbor's driveway, partially blocking oncoming traffic; we had to maneuver our Jeep around it on the shoulder. It would have been about 8:25 A.M., June 13, 2007, a Wednesday. It was a beautiful summer morning, but then, it was always beautiful.

At the far left side of the school parking lot, I noticed a blond man whom I didn't recognize wearing a khaki fishing hat and glasses. He was parked in a light blue metallic Ford KA, a small egg-shaped compact that is common throughout Mexico. Its license plates were from Queretaro, the next state over. But this was right at the end of the school year, and parents were enrolling their children for the next semester, so he didn't seem that out of place. I walked the kids to their classrooms and then stopped off to speak with one of our school administrators for a few minutes, and I happened to mention the man in the fishing hat. She had noticed him too and wondered who he was.

"Maybe he's waiting for someone," she offered.

As I walked back to the Jeep, I looked at him again, and this time he made eye contact with me and smiled. I smiled back. He was fair-skinned and obviously white—American or European—with a pleasant, unassuming air. He didn't seem tentative, like he needed any help, so I got in the Jeep. Eduardo was enrapt in an alternative health program on the radio out of nearby Celaya, so he wordlessly pulled back onto the makeshift cobblestone road. The man in the KA pulled out after us.

By now, the road to school was deserted, the few parents whose kids didn't take the bus having come and gone, but as we approached the point where it converged with the public access road, we noticed a blue pickup truck immediately to our left, on the public road, matching us in speed. The man in the cab stared at us intensely—the look he gave us was chilling—and then he sped up ahead of us and made a U-turn onto our road.

"Look at this asshole," Eduardo said in Spanish. "What the hell is he doing?"

We both thought the same thing at the same time—that we should turn around and go back to the school and call someone. But as he was headed straight at us, and we would pass him in another five seconds, I said, "Let's go to the house and call the cops." He flew by us in a flash, and we made the turn onto the public road, but now the Ford KA that had been following us kept going straight into our alfalfa field, now separated from us by a barbed-wire fence. As we watched him through the breaks in the mesquite trees and waist-high grass, Eduardo with half a mind to follow him and tell him he was on private property, we noticed there were two cars ahead of us moving slower than we were. This allowed the KA to speed up and cut in front of both of them at the next break in the fence line.

He'd been waiting in the parking lot, and now he couldn't wait to get around us? In fact, there shouldn't have been any cars at all on the road at that time of day, yet here we were caught in traffic behind three of them, with a fourth somewhere behind us. But before this could really even register, the Yukon that was parked in our neighbor's turnout suddenly came to life and swerved in front of us, then almost immediately began to slow down.

Just up ahead of us, at the halfway point between our house and the school, the road narrows, flanked by a dense copse of mesquite trees on one side and *órgano* cactus (named for its similarity to a pipe organ) on the other that squeeze the narrow passage like the fingers of a hand. It was here that the Yukon suddenly slammed on its brakes, so that Eduardo just barely missed smashing into it. A second later, a different pickup truck appeared out of nowhere and rammed us from behind, pushing us almost flush up against the Yukon. We both turned to see what had happened, and in the one second it took us to turn back around, two men were out of the Yukon and at our windows. The one on Eduardo's side had a handgun and a hammer, and with a single blow from the gun butt he shattered the driver's-side window. I could hear Eduardo screaming as they dragged him from the Jeep and struck him in the head once with the hammer. There was blood everywhere.

The man on my side had a gun and a club, but my door wasn't locked so he simply opened it. He pointed his gun at me and tried to force me from the car with his free hand, but I grabbed onto the barbed-wire fence and refused to let go. I kicked at him with my flip-flops until he finally wrestled me to the ground, ripping my hands from the fence and opening up my left index finger like a ripe banana. He put the barrel of the gun against my forehead—a silver nine-millimeter pistol with a gold stripe down the barrel—and told me to get up. I stopped fighting, and he took me by the arm and put me in the middle seat of the Yukon. I heard myself say, "Don't kill me, I have children."

The second I hit the seat, someone from behind pulled a thick cotton pillowcase over my head and drew an elastic drawstring tightly around my neck. I was afraid I was going to hyperventilate, and I told them I couldn't breathe. They finally pulled the edge up over my nose, which gave me a limited view of my surroundings. I instinctively reached to my left for Eduardo's arm and could see that he had been handcuffed. His whole arm was sticky with blood, and I started to worry he would go into shock. I told him, "You have to calm down; you have to use your mind." The man driving yelled, *"Cállate!"*—"Shut up!"—in a deep guttural voice that sounded like he was intentionally disguising it. But there were two things that were odd about it: One was that he was extremely calm. The second was that his accent didn't come from any one place. It was just generically Mexican. In Mexico, that's a rarity.

"God is great," I said to Eduardo. *"Dios es muy grande."* I also wanted to remind the kidnappers of God. We were in a Catholic country and I assumed that the kidnappers were Catholic. At a moment like this, I thought reminding them of God may save our lives. I felt a finger encased in a tight leather glove tap lightly against my lips, an action repeated every time I tried to whisper something to Eduardo. It's a gesture you would make to a small child—one meant to convey seriousness but also to comfort. At the time, I interpreted it as an act of kindness, and I instinctively reached out for his hand. I had read a book on miracles and remembered that many people who had been victims of violent crimes or come face-to-face with serial killers had survived because they established empathy with their assailant. I asked him if he had children. Instead, he folded my hands on my stomach and gently patted my belly. When I told him I needed medical attention for my finger, he pulled the pillowcase back down over my face so I couldn't see.

I tried to remember every bump and curve in the road, a Braille map of their getaway that I could produce later, like long sequences of numbers I had memorized. They pushed our heads down in the seat every time we passed another car. I felt us turn left onto the highway, toward the center of town, which made no sense. The drive itself was quiet, almost eerie—well within the speed limit and without any talking—just Eduardo babbling somewhat incoherently and the occasional angry shout of *"Cállate, cabron!"*

Then the man behind me reached under my arms and hauled me over the backseat. I had a sudden vision that I was about to be raped. He laid me on my back and quickly frisked me head to toe, and then I heard the rip of duct tape and he bound my wrists and ankles. Through the bottom of the pillowcase, I could make out his rough outline, as well as the loose skin flapping on my finger. I began chanting to myself, maybe unconsciously trying to ward off the waves of pain I feared were coming. After a brief blast of static from a walkie-talkie, obviously some kind of signal, we abruptly pulled off on the shoulder and stopped. By this point, the fear was overwhelming, and it magnified every sound, smell, and motion—a river of data flowing into my senses, the desperate pragmatism of my body trying to keep me alive.

I heard them put the SUV in park, and then all at once there was a lot of commotion. I heard Eduardo screaming "No!" as his voice got smaller, and then a second vehicle pulling in alongside us, doors slamming, the screams muffled, the engine rev, and then silence. By this time I had sensed that I was alone in the SUV. Using my core muscles like I'd learned in Pilates, I lifted my upper body just enough to peek over the seat. Being that my wrists were bound in front of my body, this enabled me to lift the pillowcase up and see perfectly—and just in time to see an older-model Ford Explorer or Chevy Blazer go up the dirt road toward the highway. The back window of the Yukon was tinted, and I couldn't make out the color—either dark green or black— but miraculously, I got the license plate number and was able to remember it—UPC 5152. Once again, Queretaro plates. This time, they turned onto the highway, away from San Miguel and toward the town of Dolores Hidalgo.

As soon as they were out of sight, I threw myself over the seat and onto the floorboard. I managed to kick the door open with my feet and began hopping toward the highway. Once when I was seven, I won first place in a Fourth of July sack-hop race against a field of forty other kids. Never in my wildest dreams did I imagine this was a skill that one day might save my life. This was not the last time this was to happen.

As I approached the two-lane highway, I could see an old man of at least sixty riding a beat-up bicycle. He was wearing a straw cowboy hat and had a huge machete in his belt. I screamed at him for a cell phone, and the sight of me seemed to paralyze him. I screamed again, and he snapped out of it. He offered to cut the duct tape with his machete, but I didn't want to take the time. My only thought was that if I could reach the police, there was still a chance we could catch them—I had the license plate number and the make and model of the car, and I knew the direction they were heading. Every second counted right now.

Five or six cars accelerated past me as I desperately tried to flag them down without the use of my hands or feet. The fact that I was covered in blood, both my own and Eduardo's, an old man with a machete standing directly behind me, probably didn't help. Burly Mexicans in pickup trucks, American women in small compacts—it didn't seem to make any difference. The old man pointed with his machete, and I could see a city bus fifty feet up the road just pulling back onto the highway. He hadn't picked up that much speed yet, so I hopped into the middle of the highway and stared down the driver, holding my bound hands out in front of me in a supplicant position. I could see him debating whether he had room to veer around, but luckily he stopped.

I hopped up onto the steps and told him I needed the radio, but his radio was broken. No one made a move to help me. I screamed that I needed a cell phone, and finally a man gave me one, but the battery was dead. I sat down on the steps, feeling the chance to catch these criminals draining out of me, as a bus full of Mexicans tried to imagine what this crazy gringa had done to bring this predicament upon herself.

A mile ahead of us was El IMSS, the government maternity hospital, where a lone taxi was waiting beside the bus stop. The driver stopped and let me off the bus. As soon as the taxi driver saw a madwoman hopping toward him, he started to pull away. This time I threw myself against the hood of the car so he had to stop. He opened the passenger door and I told him my husband had been kidnapped. He got on the radio and told the dispatcher, who in turn called the 911 operator, who called the police. Now every detail of where we were and what just happened had to go from me to the taxi driver to the dispatcher to the operator to the police, a rickety five-jointed enterprise that was doomed to failure. After three or four tries they finally got our location, but by that time the kidnappers were long gone.

The point where Eduardo was taken away was on a strip of highway directly across from a strip club where the prostitutes gather at night. A cop in an unmarked car and another one on a dirt bike were the first to arrive. Stopping all traffic in both directions, they acted quickly. The officer in the unmarked car opened my door and asked if I was all right. I tried to impress on him the need to hurry, but my resolve was crumbling and I started to cry. He picked me up and carried me to his car, and I felt myself go limp in his arms.

"Do you feel well enough to take me to the spot where the Yukon is, or do you need to go to the hospital?" he asked me.

"No, I'm okay," I told him. "Let's go."

We sped to the scene in his small, nondescript compact, the officer on the dirt bike trailing us. In the two minutes it took us to make the drive, word had gone out and now the place was teeming with cops of every description. The motorcycle cop peeled the duct tape from my wrists and ankles and it fell loose to the ground. He approached the Yukon slowly, careful not to touch anything. He shined a flashlight into the interior.

"Is this your husband's blood?" he asked in Spanish. I told him yes.

"Is that his watch?"

On the floor of the backseat was a Wenger Swiss Army brand watch and a set of handcuff keys. Neither one belonged to Eduardo. We later discovered that they had also left in our Jeep the hammer they used, along with the butt of the gun, to break the window.

The officer walked around to the front of the Yukon.

"Esta andando," he said quietly. "It's running."

In my hurry to get out of the Yukon, I had completely overlooked the fact that they had left the keys in the ignition and the motor running. I suddenly felt the crushing weight of immense guilt. How could I have been so stupid? I could have followed them, caught up with them, run them off the road. I could have rammed them from behind. Eduardo would be here with me now! I locked eyes with the officer, filled equally with anger and remorse, physically shaking. He must have sensed what I was thinking. He slowly shook his head no. In a moment, once the pain had subsided, I knew that he was right. If I had caught up with them on the highway, Eduardo and I both would be dead right now.

The officer looked down at the ground by the back door of the Yukon, still open where I'd left it. "Is this yours?" he asked.

In the grass, still wet with the morning dew, was a small white envelope. They had tucked it into my clothing when I was tied up and in their custody. On the front was handwritten in black ink *Sra. Jayne*. My heart stopped.

"Señora Jayne." For as long as I had lived in this country, it had been a struggle for people to get my name right. *J*s are pronounced like *h*s, *y*s are pronounced like *e*s, *e*s are pronounced like ehs. If you phonetically sounded out my name the way it's spelled, you would pronounce it "high-neh." If people could see it, they couldn't say it. If they could say it, they couldn't spell it. It was so routine that I barely noticed it anymore. And here a gang of criminals had gotten it right on the first try.

That meant they'd been watching us—probably for months. Or they had informants within our immediate circle who kept them apprised of our routine. This wasn't a random crime. These people knew what they were doing, and they were going to see it through, one way or another. I lunged for the envelope, but he stopped me.

"No," he said. "It's evidence."

TWO

Glowing Energy

BACKGROUND AND COURTSHIP

I was born in 1966 in Silver Spring, Maryland, a suburb of Washington, D.C. My mother's family was one of the first to settle in the colony of Virginia—we have a copy of a land grant from 1780, signed by Thomas Jefferson when he was governor of Virginia, for land the family still owns today. She can trace her bloodline directly back to Daniel Boone's mother, and she says I inherited that pioneer spirit. I always saw it as a gypsy soul.

My father grew up the son of a coal miner in the small town of Brownsville, Pennsylvania. There were two ways out of Brownsville—a football scholarship or join the military—and my father did both. He was so poor that he turned down the scholarship out of embarrassment because he couldn't afford new clothes, a decision he said he always regretted. Instead, he joined the air force, then air force intelligence, and finally was recruited by the CIA. That all ended in 1960, when pilot Francis Gary Powers, flying a U-2 aerial reconnaissance spy plane, was shot down over Russia with my father's contact information in his pocket. The incident occurred at the height of the cold war, and the United States was forced to publicly admit it had been spying on the Soviet Union—and worse, lying about it. Needless to say, as Powers's CIA handler, and with Powers all over the newspapers, my father didn't have much of a future in covert intelligence.

He took a job with Washington Gas Company, a local utility, and founded a subsidiary company as he worked his way up to vice president. My friends always asked me if this was just a front organization for the CIA. I doubt it, but if it was, he never told the rest of us. But then, my father was very good at keeping secrets.

While growing up, I remember that my father had a very keen, analytical bent of mind. He was able to watch a story on the news and see through it right away, explaining to my younger brother and me what was really going on. I either inherited that from him or else I learned it by watching him. If I ever wanted something growing up—a new dress, a skateboard—he would always challenge me to convince him why: "Sell it to me. What's so good about it? Why do you need it so badly?" It taught me to identify value and to recognize its reflection in others. Those two character traits together made me a natural salesperson.

The other thing that influenced me profoundly as a child was that I had a sister who was born when I was two and a half years old, and she never came home from the hospital. She had a severe case of spina bifida—she was blind and paralyzed from the waist down—and she didn't make it. I got to sneak into the hospital once and hold her and feed her with a bottle. But it was really something that impacted my childhood tremendously. I was three and a half when she died, and it was an enormous loss for the whole family. It impacted us financially; the co-pays from having a child in the hospital her entire life were enormous, and my father was holding down two and often three jobs just trying to make ends meet.

Then my brother was born just a few months after her death, and he was a very colicky baby—he cried constantly. I think the sadness, devastation, and sheer exhaustion of having just lost a child after trying so hard not to all came to a head with my brother. My parents were overprotective with him. It made me grow up really fast; I felt like I was the one who was holding the family together. I remember once when I was four, probably three o'clock in the morning, and my mother had been up all night walking with my brother, trying to get him to go to sleep. The crying woke me up, as it often did, and I marched into the living room and said, "Give me that baby!" and sat with him in my little rocking chair until he fell asleep. It seemed like some kind of curse had descended upon us just after I came along, and that I was the only one it had missed.

My mother was very beautiful—she had won beauty pageants and did some modeling when she was younger. She also appeared in lots of TV commercials and was an extra in a handful of movies shot in the D.C. area—*The Exorcist, . . . And Justice for All, All the President's Men.* (My dad was also in the last one—as a security guard who points to the Declaration of Independence—and did some stunt driving.) My mother quit acting to raise her family. But old habits die hard, and when I was six months old she saw a Screen Actors Guild notice looking for six-month-old babies in the D.C. area for a series of American Red Cross commercials. She took me to the audition, and when she handed me to the director, I looked up at him and said, "Da-Da." To the surprise of virtually no one, I booked the gig.

From that point until I was twenty-three, I worked constantly as an actress, in commercials, modeling, local theater, supporting roles on soap operas, and eventually speaking parts in movies. It never stopped. I was a C student without ever cracking a book (but failed Spanish because I didn't care anything about it). I grew up faster than my peers and took on more responsibility much earlier. I didn't have a lot of boyfriends, didn't really date a lot, and didn't do many extracurricular activities in high school because I was always working. I'd be trying out for the cheerleading squad, and I'd see my mom pull up with a makeup bag in one hand and a curling iron in the other, and I'd think, *Oh, I guess I'm not going to be a cheerleader.* There was always another audition, another callback, another job.

About three-quarters of the way through my first year at Montgomery College in Rockville, Maryland, I got offered a part on a soap opera, and work started really flowing for me out of New York. (My mom had sent out some head shots and résumés without my knowledge.) When the offers started pouring in, she said to me, "You're studying theater in college, and meanwhile you have all these work offers pouring in. Why don't you put school on hold and go to New York for a year and see what comes of it? College will be waiting for you when you come back." So she helped me find an apartment on Roosevelt Island, in the middle of the East River, and at eighteen I moved to New York City. My agent lived across the street from me, my mother stayed there with me a lot of the time, and then on weekends I'd take the train home. I lived there three years and in Los Angeles for three years, and I was pretty successful. All those years most people experiment with lifestyle choices—sex, drugs, music, politics, making the friends they'll keep for life—I was working, paying my own bills, and developing a career.

I studied with Janet Alhanti and Sonia Moore, a disciple of Stanislavsky, in New York. After I moved to Los Angeles, I took classes with Sanford Meisner—founding member of the Group Theatre in the 1930s, a first-generation teacher at the Actors Studio in the late '40s, head of the Neighborhood Playhouse until his death. Meisner was the inventor of the influential Meisner Technique, which emphasized finding the truth of the moment (i.e., the scene) over investing it with the emotional memory of one's past experience. He personally trained many famous actors, including Steve McQueen, Gregory Peck, Robert Duvall, Peter Falk, Diane Keaton—too many to mention really. Jeff Goldblum still sat in on our classes a lot.

Working with Meisner, I learned the acting technique that sustained me, but I also learned much about life. I got really good at picking up the subtleties of human behavior, all those nearly imperceptible clues in a scene that tell you what to do and that you learn to react to. I became very good at reading people, and I've used it in virtually everything I've ever done. By the time I knew him, Meisner was in poor health; he had had cancer, he'd been hit by a car, and he was an old man. But he had the most irresistible life force. He used to laugh at me whenever we did improv exercises, because I always had these incredibly complex situations I'd come up with. He told me I wrote a soap opera every time I got up to perform.

Every summer, he chose eight men and eight women to travel to his home on the island of Bequia in the West Indies for several months of intensive study. As a rule, he didn't take anyone younger than twenty-five, but with me he made an exception, even though I was only twenty-one. Theresa Saldana (*Raging Bull*, *The Commish*) was my roommate, and Cary Elwes flew back early for the release of *The Princess Bride*, his first starring role. By this time, my career had started to take off. I got a whole series of national commercials, most memorably for McDonald's, where I was a fresh-faced counterperson and girl-next-door type. From there, I was cast in a small speaking role in the 1990 film *Stella*, a remake of *Stella Dallas* starring Bette Midler in the title role. My scenes were set at a tropical resort—we filmed in Boca Raton, and I appeared on-screen in a bathing suit—and one of the actors whom I played opposite, Todd

Louiso, went on to play Chad the Nanny in *Jerry Maguire* and one of the record store clerks in *High Fidelity*. Bette Midler introduced herself to everyone, was very nice, and worked harder than anybody.

After that, my agent started to field offers for other films. But I could already tell I was losing enthusiasm for acting professionally. I cherish the experiences I had, but I feared they were at the expense of those experiences everyone else has—the ones that ground us in communal life. Plus I wanted a job that had more to do with my mind and less to do with my looks. My agent wasn't happy when I told her I wanted to leave the business, but I still think I made the right choice.

Somewhere in there, I fell madly in love with a guy whose mother was from Spain—my first serious boyfriend— and we spent a lot of time in Barcelona. I was twenty-two and he was twenty-five. I picked up the language very quickly; one day someone told a joke at dinner and every-one laughed but me. At that point in the evening, he had gotten tired of translating, so after dinner I told him it was fine, he wouldn't have to translate for me anymore. Within two months, one of his friends told him that my Spanish accent was better than my boyfriend's. As with most things, once I got it in my head I was going to accomplish this, everything else took a backseat. It looked like we would get married; although we were never formally engaged, we did pick out a church. But the more time we spent together, I came to realize that this wasn't a forever relationship. He was tall and beautiful, but I just couldn't imagine us grow-ing old together in our rocking chairs. So I walked away from it, and after living outside Barcelona in a little town called Caldetas for three months, I reluctantly left the coun-try. But in time, I came to see that one of the things I missed most was Spain itself—the language, the culture, the weather, the food, and most of all, the people and their exciting zest for life, how they take time to enjoy every moment of the day. I think that's where the siesta comes from; you rest for two hours in the late afternoon and then the day is alive all over again, just in time for it to turn into night. You eat late—often 9:30 P.M.—you stay out late, there's music and nightlife. It's always a celebration. It was exotic to me, a port of call for my gypsy wanderlust, plus the men were beautiful. I had fallen for the country and the culture, and I was very sad to leave my adopted home.

But at twenty-three, I went back to the Washington area and got a job with a real estate developer. It was the fall of 1988 and I started as a receptionist, but my boss liked to spend time on his boat in Annapolis, so he taught me how to write the contracts so he could take off weekends. I already had the people skills, and when sales actually improved over time, he graciously hired me to do his job and transferred to the mortgage department. I also enrolled in night courses at the University of Maryland, majoring in journalism. I liked writing and investigating things intensely, building stories out of observed details, which is what I did with acting. I thought maybe I could become a broadcast anchorperson, since I was already comfortable on camera.

Then one day in March 1992 I went to get my hair done. I told my hairdresser all about my experience in Spain, and she said to me, in a nutshell, "I think you need to open yourself up to the idea of finding someone new. Just flip a switch in your mind and be open to the possibility." This was really not what I wanted to hear, but she was a wise person—as hairdressers often are—and her advice had always been prescient, so I decided I would try and keep it in the back of my mind.

On my way home that evening, driving down Old Georgetown Road, I remembered I needed to make some phone calls. I didn't have a cell phone, since they weren't quite as common in those days, so I stopped at a gas station, but the pay phone was out of order. It was dark by now, and I was trying to be careful, when I remembered that the Sutton Place Gourmet was nearby—a gourmet supermarket where you could get high-end chocolates and really yummy cheeses from all over the world. I pulled into the parking lot and was rushing to the pay phone, which was just inside an alcove, when a man and his teenage son came out. It was closing time, and the manager was just locking the door behind them. He said, "I'm sorry, they're not going to let you in. They just locked the door."

I told him, "Thank you, I'm just going to use the pay phone," but there was something odd going on. My heart was racing, and I had butterflies in my stomach. He had Spanish features and an accent, something I was able to pinpoint from my recent travels, plus there was a natural friendliness to him; he was dignified but also unguarded, a combination you find abroad but rarely in American men. He was very good looking—sparkling eyes, dimples, a breathtaking smile—but so were lots of people I didn't give the time of day to. Was this me being newly attentive to what the universe had to offer me? I had no idea. But I definitely felt an electric charge as we passed. I was almost through with my phone call when I heard a car approaching, so I decided I'd take one last look. I turned around with a practiced nonchalance, just as he was driving by, and right as he turned to look at me, and our eyes suddenly locked. I stood there watching him drive away, and then instead of going straight at the light, he hesitated ever so slightly and turned left back into the parking lot.

Now this was interesting. So instead of hanging up, I dialed the weather service and stood there listening to the recording, killing time. After what seemed like minutes, I gave up and started walking to my car. And just as I was putting the key in the car, this red sports car pulled up on my right, and the man leaned out the window and said, "What kind of car is that? It's a really nice car."

"It's a 1990 Nissan, thanks." He was driving an Acura

NSX, this fancy red sports car that might as well have been a Lamborghini. It was just so preposterous. So I kind of laughed. But at the same time, it was charming. I realized this wasn't the kind of guy who did this every day.

We started making small talk. I asked where he was from. When he said Mexico, the conversation switched to Spanish. We talked about things that didn't matter, just to talk. He asked me how I learned to speak Spanish so well, and I told him I loved to travel. He told me I should visit Mexico. I'd been to Acapulco and didn't like it, but he assured me that the Mexican interior was a different country. He told me he knew all the best places in San Miguel de Allende—in turn one of the most delightful places in Mexico—and that he'd be happy to advise me if I ever wanted to go there. So I took his number and gave him my card, ostensibly for travel tips. It was all very pleasant, but I drove home in a daze. Ever since I was a little girl, I've had recurring dreams that eventually come true, sometimes years later. One of them was that I would meet my future husband, and he would appear to me in silhouette. That's what this felt like.

Back home, my mom was doing the dishes, waiting up for me. I had an enormous smile on my face, and when she asked me why, I told her, "I think I just met the man I'm going to marry." She asked who he was, and I told her he was a Mexican man I met in a parking lot, and he drove a gorgeous red sports car.

"Forget him," she said. "He's a drug dealer."

I laughed at her as she turned and went upstairs to sleep. But I couldn't stop thinking about him. It was crazy. I had never felt like this before. Something about him was pulling me toward him like a magnet. When I got to work the next day, I told all of the girls in my office that if an Eduardo called, they were to come get me wherever I was. When it was almost five o'clock and he still hadn't called, I did something I'd never done before: I called him. I planned to ask him a few questions about my "upcoming trip to Mexico." His soon-to-be ex-wife answered the phone. She was very friendly and took a message. (She thought I was the woman from the bank.)

As it turned out, Eduardo was also at a turning point in his life. The son of a wealthy newspaper publisher, Jose Garcia Valseca, a beloved figure and hero of the Mexican Revolution known colloquially in his native land as the Colonel, Eduardo had been forced to leave Mexico sometime after his father's death in 1981. Family friends confided to him that his father's enemies were lying in wait for him, and that his life might be in danger. Tired of being forced to raise a family with armed bodyguards around them, or carrying a machine gun in his car, he finally resettled in Potomac, Maryland, where his sister lived. When I met him, he had investments in various restaurants and nightclubs and was dealing art, traveling back and forth to Mexico City as inconspicuously as he could. He was scheduled to leave again in two days for several months.

Moreover, his marriage of twenty-two years was crumbling in the wake of the recent revelation that his wife had fallen in love with another woman. He and his American wife, Lynda, were still going through the motions for the sake of the children—Eduardo Jr., known as Cielo, was about to graduate from high school, and Aurora, his daughter, was still in college—but unbeknownst to the kids, they were in fact weeks away from finalizing their divorce.

The day we met, Cielo—who was then sixteen and is an artist and a naturally intuitive person—had come home from school and announced to Eduardo, "I'm tired of seeing you every day with this long face, looking like you just lost your best friend. Get a life—get drunk, get laid, whatever it takes. But you need to make yourself happy. This is not right."

Now that's an odd thing for a son to say to his father—especially with his mother in the next room—so it kind of hung over the whole afternoon. It was almost Easter, so Eduardo suggested they drive to Sutton Place Gourmet in nearby Bethesda, right next door to Potomac, to buy truffles and chocolates for the family. All the way to the market, Cielo was really laying into him; he wouldn't let it go. Like me, the last thing Eduardo wanted to do was to enter the dating pool. He had grown kids, for heaven's sake. And if he did, the last thing he wanted to do was marry another American— especially one just four years older than his daughter. One of the only pieces of advice Eduardo's father ever gave him was not to marry an American: "America is where you find flowers without scent, fruit without flavor, men without honor and women without *pudor* [a sense of modesty or shame], and the national drink is Coca-Cola," he said.

At least at the moment, it was looking more and more like his father was right.

Inside the store, Cielo spilled jelly beans from the bulk bin and had to pick them all up, while the shopkeeper was anxious to close for the holiday. At the checkout counter, Cielo kept fussing with Eduardo's hair and collar, and the cashier gave them a knowing look, which to Eduardo, at least, indicated she thought they were a gay couple. To a macho Mexican whose wife had just left him for a lesbian, this was not helping. Outside the store, after Eduardo spoke to me and they'd gotten in their car, his son started yelling at him—swearing, even.

"Go and talk to her, you coward! You're letting her get away! Just look at her—turn and look at her, and I'll leave you alone." And so as they drove by, Eduardo turned to look at me, and our eyes met. Now he felt it too. He had to drive all the way around this big rectangular parking lot just to work up the nerve to talk to me, worried that I would think he was some kind of stalker, with his son getting more and more upset with him, yelling at him now, egging him on.

"When things are supposed to happen, they just happen," he told Cielo.

The next day, when he got home from work, Eduardo's wife, Lynda, told him, "Jayne called. Here's her number." He was really nervous; the divorce was almost final and had gone smoothly. He didn't want to upset the apple cart and rub it in her face, and he still didn't know what to tell the kids. So he went upstairs and asked Cielo, "What do I do?" And Cielo said, "What do you mean? You ask her out."

It so happened that an old friend from Monterey had invited them to dinner and his wife couldn't go, so he called the next day and asked me to join them. He told me to meet them at the Marriott in Georgetown. This way, the pressure would be off him because his friend would be there, and it would be off me because I could drive my own car. My friends already thought I was nuts: "You met this guy in a parking lot? What are you—crazy?"

So from the Marriott, we set out for the nicest Italian restaurant in the city—they in Eduardo's red sports car, I in my Nissan. At one point, as we got near M Street, these two twenty-year-old girls saw them and leaned in either window, and I almost turned around and went home. These guys were players; they must do this all the time. But something inside me had taken over as my north star, so I decided I'd just see what happened. As we were walking to the restaurant, we saw a line coming out of an alley that ran all the way around the block. This was Blues Alley, a world-famous jazz club. He asked me if I wanted to go, and I said yeah. The show had apparently been sold out for weeks, and of course we didn't have reservations, but Eduardo being Eduardo went to the front of the line and told the maître d' that we had come all the way from Mexico City, and couldn't anything be done? She said she was sorry, but she ducked back inside for a minute and then ushered us all to the best table in the house. It was just like that scene in *GoodFellas*—everyone turned to see who we were. It turns out the performer was an internationally renowned flamenco guitarist, and he was fantastic.

At one point, during a break, I asked Eduardo point-blank, "What's your story—are you married? Divorced? Separated?"

Without hesitating, he said, "I'm actually in the process of getting divorced." We didn't talk about it anymore, but something shifted inside him. In a minute or two, he reached over and took my hand. Oh—and the two twenty-year-old girls who acted so familiar? That was Eduardo's daughter, Aurora, and her friend.

We had a lovely time, were the last table to leave, and he walked me to my car afterward. I could sense him stalling, but then he leaned over to kiss me, and sparks seemed to fly off of us. We said good night, and just as I was coming up out of the parking garage, he was standing there with a dozen red roses. He reached through the window and set them on the passenger seat. He didn't even say anything. I just smiled and drove away.

Everything between us in those first few years was like that. It was as if things between us had been scripted, but we didn't know it. Every moment was perfect; every scenario unfolded in perfect order, in perfect time.

The next day was Sunday and I had to work, but he was leaving on Monday and insisted I meet him in Potomac and we go for a drive. While we were out, he told me, "I really want you to come to Mexico. Let's go to the airport and I'll buy you a ticket."

I said, "Wait a minute—I can't move that fast. You're still married, for one thing." So he explained to me the whole saga of his marriage. We went and had dinner, and there were no tables, but everyone at the restaurant knew him, and he told them he had a special woman with him and wanted everything to be perfect. They set up a special table just for us. The owner brought us over a bottle of wine on the house, and the chef prepared an exotic shellfish dish of his own creation right there at the table.

We continued the courtship over the phone from Mexico for the next month and a half, and we fell in love long-distance (and spent a small fortune on phone bills). He would write me the most deeply romantic poetry in Spanish and fax it to me at work, and it really reeled me in. Perhaps at the urging of his teenage son, he sent me mix tapes of his favorite Spanish music. When I finally did visit him in Mexico over spring break 1992, I flew to Mexico City alone and he met me at the airport. We ate breakfast together and then flew to Ixtapa, a beautiful beach resort on the Pacific Coast, where a limo met us and drove us to a hotel overlooking the ocean where Eduardo had rented a suite with adjacent bedrooms. We held hands the entire way. The whole suite was white, the furniture was white, and the last day of the trip, he went to the jewelry store in the hotel and bought me this beautiful ring. It was silver and gold, two interlocking bands in the symbol of eternity. He put it on my finger—I asked him to—and from that day forward, we felt married on a spiritual level.

At one point, we were in the hotel pool and he was holding me as I floated on my back, and he said, "Look." Every single person in the pool had stopped and was staring at us. That was technically our third date, and we both cried when we said good-bye.

"We had glowing energy," Eduardo says today.

When I went to Greece with my mom on a long-planned vacation, he tracked me down all over the country and then flew from Mexico City to Dulles airport to meet me when I got back. From that point on, I just never went home, and by July I had moved to Mexico. Within a month we bought a house, and after I became pregnant with Fernando two years later, we got married. And we were never apart again. At least, not until someone dragged us apart at gunpoint.

THREE

Puddles

SAN MIGUEL

San Miguel de Allende sits on the high plains of central Mexico, about three hours northwest of Mexico City. It was founded by Juan de San Miguel, a Franciscan monk, in 1542, and the center of the city is dominated by Spanish colonial architecture. It is one of three equidistant towns (along with Queretaro and Dolores Hidalgo) in the central state of Guanajuato that in the early years of the nineteenth century contributed much of the discourse, tumult, and political fervor for what would become the Mexican War of Independence from Spain (1810–21), a homegrown revolution of propertied intellectuals that paralleled the American Revolution of thirty-five years before. (The city of San Miguel was later renamed in honor of General Ignacio Allende, one of the founding fathers of the revolution, as was the nearby city of Dolores for Miguel Hidalgo y Costilla, whose manifesto Grito de Dolores guided the decadelong struggle.)

Yet a century later, despite its colorful history, San Miguel was little more than a ghost town. This all changed after World War II when U.S. servicemen, looking for a cheap place to study on the GI Bill, discovered that this postcard-perfect town had a number of U.S.-accredited art colleges, including the Instituto Allende. When *Life* magazine dedicated a short pictorial spread to this postwar phenomenon in 1948, it catapulted San Miguel de Allende into a bona fide arts mecca and self-fulfilling prophecy. The perfect weather and naturally occurring thermal springs that dotted the countryside probably didn't hurt.

It is said that San Miguel is a city full of artists who like to drink, or maybe it's drunks who like to paint. By the 1960s, the city had emerged as one of the stations of the counterculture diaspora, and there are now some twelve thousand English-speaking expatriates at any one time, out of a city of 140,000. There are rich Americans and Europeans with second and third homes elsewhere, widows with apartments in New York who come there for the winter, and lots of people in their sixties and seventies who have retired to warmer climes. Now that the Internet allows many people to work from anywhere in the world, there are also a growing number of young people and families who migrate to San Miguel. It is no longer just a place for older people who come there to retire. That bohemian spirit is still very much a part of the city's character; it's full of people who arrived with a round-trip ticket and never boarded the return flight home.

The expat community drinks at Harry's Bar, sister saloon to the famed Venice bistro favored by Ernest Hemingway, the patron saint of American expatriates, and they dine at El Pegaso, which is owned by the minister who married Eduardo and me. Neal Cassady, whose fictional portrayal as Dean Moriarty in Jack Kerouac's *On the Road* did as much as any single role model to send a generation off in search of alternative lifestyles, was a periodic fixture at the local Cucaracha bar, and the owner can often be spotted midafternoon regaling impressionable literary types with long-polished anecdotes. Cassady also famously died there in February 1968, after drunkenly stumbling into a wedding party of strangers, then suddenly leaving in the rain-swept late evening hours, claiming he wanted to count the number of ties on the railroad tracks to Celaya, forty miles away. He was discovered comatose the next morning a mile and a half outside of town by two farmers, and his body was taken to a local hospital, where he died just shy of his forty-second birthday—possibly of alcohol poisoning, Seconal overdose, years of protracted amphetamine abuse, and no doubt literary conceit, the proverbial candle burning twice as bright and half as long. In a quasi-fictional memoir published later in *Esquire* called "The Day after Superman Died," writer Ken Kesey, whose Merry Prankster bus Cassady famously drove in the years preceding his death, reports that when he was discovered just south of town, a delirious Cassady whispered "64,928"—presumably the number of railroad ties he had counted.

Those same railroad tracks run along one edge of our property, albeit on the other side of town, toward Dolores Hidalgo to the north. When I first came to Mexico to live, Eduardo told me, "Wear something casual, I have a railroad car." I wasn't sure what he meant exactly—a boxcar?—but he picked me up at the airport in Mexico City in this funky old Chevy and drove us to the train station, where they took our luggage and escorted us to the very last track, and there awaiting us was an antique Pullman car, complete with its own balcony and a Mexican flag. A waiter, dressed all in white with white gloves, escorted us to the dining room where a table had been set with fine china, crystal goblets, and silverware made of real silver. The interior of the car was decorated with oil paintings, velvet drapes, and wing-back chairs. As I admired it all, Eduardo said, "I told you, I have a train car." It had belonged to his father, and we lived in it for the first three months, traveling wherever we pleased at the drop of a hat.

Traveling in your own private train car is extraordinary. It's like traveling in time back to another century. The Mexican countryside is so beautiful once you get out of Mexico City. There are mountains and cacti and big blue skies with giant Michelangelo clouds. Everything about it is epic. When we would pull into the different stations, the kids would all come running to see the railcar, and they'd stand and wave when we left. There were two employees on the car at all times: One was the caretaker, who had held that same position under the Colonel when this was his principal means of transportation. His nickname was "El Negro Bernal," which means "Blackie Bernal." This wasn't racist, but rather an endearment because he was very dark-skinned. The other employee was the waiter, who was deaf and could read lips. We would have a fantastic meal and then sit outside on the terrace until the smell of diesel oil overwhelmed us. I loved to look at all of the photographs and paintings on the walls. There was a charcoal portrait of the Colonel in his favorite spot, looking out the window, that I really liked. Whenever we made stops, Eduardo would get off and stretch his legs. Then when the train started to pull away, he loved to come running and hop on the terrace while the train was moving. He scared me the first few times—it was very much like a scene in a movie—before I realized this is something he had practiced his whole life. At every station in every town, he seemed to know the conductors and porters and spoke their private language. It was where I first observed him as a man of the people— someone without airs, who could get along with anyone. When we came around the last bend approaching San Miguel, I told him, "This is where I want to live." He said, "But we're only at the train station!" I didn't care. It was something I just felt. San Miguel's magnetism was pulling me toward it.

At the last town the train stopped at before we arrived in San Miguel, a little man boarded the car. He had a basket full of bunches of grapes that he was selling, and he would help you with your bags for a tip. He looked like a little brown-skinned elf—in Spanish, *un duende*. His name was Arturo and he was born deaf, but a female American doctor had performed surgery on him a few years back, which allowed him to hear. His speech was still poor—although he was my age, he seemed mentally at the level of a twelve-year-old—but he was always eager to help, and he took a special liking to me. From that point on, he occupied a special place in my life. He was always appearing at the oddest moments with these pearls of profound wisdom. He attended our wedding and had an uncanny knack for showing up when something major was going on in our lives, good or bad. I came to think of him as a talisman or good-luck charm who would be there when I needed him.

About three years before I met Eduardo, I had a really intense dream where my mom and I were on vacation in Mexico. We were house shopping and found a fabulous place with an atrium, overlooking a colonial town with a breathtaking view. It was striking enough that I told my mother about it when I woke up. Then when I was living in L.A., my mom and I decided to drive to Mexico for a weekend. We drove down through Tijuana and on to Rosarito Beach. Tijuana was scary for two blond American women traveling alone by car. When we got to Rosarito Beach, it was dirty and disheveled, with stray dogs and drunks, so we had the lobster dinner, admired the view, and left. Later, I went with a group of friends for a long weekend in Acapulco. It was dirty and had too many neon lights for me. Once you left the hotel, it was just another overbuilt beach town with children begging and rats in the streets. So by default, I had decided that Mexico wasn't for me. It wasn't until a good friend who had just spent a month there told me about San Miguel de Allende that the idea sparked some interest. This was only a month before I met Eduardo.

While we were still living on the train, my mom came down to help me look for houses while Eduardo was going back and forth to Mexico City on business. After too many false starts and dead ends, we drove one afternoon to a part of the city called Los Balcones—the Balconies—for its view overlooking the historic center of town. Like a lot of houses in San Miguel, this one looked small from the entrance, but once through the antique mesquite doorway, I felt like Alice in Wonderland passing through a portal into a different dimension. Down a long corridor of handmade terra-cotta tiles with dark green accents, I followed a shaft of light onto a terrace that revealed a giant atrium, with stairs leading down to the lower level. It was the house of my dreams—literally, the house I had dreamed about back in Maryland all those years ago. I looked at my mom and we both got chills. I showed Eduardo, and we made an offer on the spot.

In fixing up the house, adding a pool and an outdoor Mexican-style kitchen made of polished cement and hand-painted tiles with a handmade grill, Eduardo and I discovered we had a flair for this—he in the financing and construction, I with the decorating and design. It was something we liked doing, and so slowly over time, we started doing it professionally. People assumed Eduardo was wealthy because of his family name—apparently some still do—but that wasn't the case. There had been a number of heirs, and most of the fortune had been depleted in maintaining his empire by the time of the Colonel's death. Starting with the money from Eduardo's house in Mexico City, we were able to launch this as a business, and we were quite successful. We specialized in homes in the historic district, which we would take all the way down to their original state from a few hundred years ago, restoring what could be salvaged and then building them back up to their long-lost grandeur. Over time we managed to build up a respectable nest egg.

We were married July 9, 1994, in a small ceremony with fifty of our closest friends and family. With our first child on the way, it was time to bring this peripatetic life of wanderlust and working out of a suitcase to its next stage of evolution, and in Eduardo I finally felt like I had met my soul mate: We were intellectual equals; we were both in touch with our spiritual sides. Well into his forties, he was still a creature of youthful exuberance, while in my late twenties, I felt like an old soul. We were the first couple to be married at the five-star Sierra Nevada Hotel in the center of town. It was a beautiful ceremony out by the pool, with mariachis and Spanish music. Later, a friend told us the rumor in town was that we had filled the pool with Dom Perignon.

Despite the presence of great wealth within San Miguel, it is a very humble, simple place. You still see peddlers with their burros on the street and Indians in the marketplace. Practically everywhere else in Mexico, people are very judgmental; it's a very Catholic country and, as a consequence, very repressive. Everyone goes to mass on Sunday, and women have to buy their clothes at the approved stores. But in San Miguel, it's just the opposite. Maybe it's the counterculture influence of so many 1960s-era veterans, or the port-of-call, Casablanca character that comes from having so many foreign nationals in residence, but even in the nicest restaurants, where you can order Maine lobster or Beluga caviar, there are people in blue jeans and sandals. You find yourself interacting with people across the entire spectrum of possibilities. I had friends who were much younger than me, and much older—one of my best friends was in her sixties, and we took a belly-dancing class together. Even when there were celebrities in our midst, they managed to blend in with the resident parade of eccentrics. Melanie Griffith and Antonio Banderas, who came down to shoot *Once Upon a Time in Mexico* and then *And Starring Pancho Villa as Himself*, are rumored to have a house there. Doc Severinsen, Johnny Carson's bandleader, retired there and still plays locally. Jane Fonda used to spend a lot of time there, as did Lady Bird Johnson, the widow of the former president.

We were friends with both the expats, many of whom only socialized with other expats and never even bothered to learn the language, and the Mexican community of long standing, some of whose families had been prominent in politics and public life for several generations. We met people at cocktail parties who were a who's who of Houston and Dallas society or royalty from Milan or Rome; on one of our walks in town, we met the former curator of the Palace of Versailles. And yet much of our socializing was done with other parents at the Waldorf school. We were also caught up in the lives of our employees, some of whom had been with Eduardo's family for decades and whose families in turn we saw grow up alongside ours.

It is customary to have domestic help in Mexico. Even some of our employees had people who cooked or cleaned for them a couple of times a week. Labor is cheap, and everyone needs a job, so it is not uncommon to have a driver and gardener as well. Even a stay-at-home mom has help. This also makes it a much more formal culture: Lunch is always served with a tablecloth, and the table is nicely set. Food is brought to you on a tray; glasses are filled from a pitcher. Often, I would unintentionally make our employees feel bad when I tried to help them too much around the house. They considered these things their job and found it embarrassing that I would intervene, as if I were second-guessing their judgment. It was another sign of the deep class divisions in a country of one hundred million citizens with a tiny middle class, although we didn't look at it that way. Eduardo would often pay our employees' outstanding medical bills when they became prohibitive, and it was not unusual for us to celebrate holidays together, or birthdays and anniversaries. Any excuse for a fiesta.

Hand in hand with this exemption from the class rigidity you see everywhere else in Mexico, the pace of life in San Miguel is also very relaxing. There are no traffic lights and everything is within walking distance. It's like living in second gear instead of fifth or sixth. My friend who rents houses to all the Americans when they first arrive in San Miguel says it takes at least ten days for them to start to appreciate the virtues of where they are. They're still wound up from where they come from. Even the police are casual. If you were illegally parked, they would take your license plate and you'd have to pay a fine to get it back. But if you caught them halfway through, you could always say, "Hey, don't do that—let me buy you a Coke." Give them fifteen pesos—then, about a buck and a quarter, hardly a bribe— and they would put it back on for you. Crime was almost unheard of when we first moved there. When I arrived in San Miguel, I recall hearing about one murder, which had taken place ten years earlier. There was a serial rapist who preyed on elderly American women and who was finally caught two years ago. A friend's son who graduated from our school was allegedly dealing marijuana and a woman stabbed him dozens of times and left him for dead in a vacant lot, and he almost bled to death. But for the most part, the drug murders and *narcotraficante* atrocities that are commonplace throughout the rest of Mexico seem to have missed our little Old World idyll. Celaya, which is just forty minutes away, with its long history of organized crime, is considered in the mid-range on the dangerous cities thermometer. But for the longest time, perhaps foolishly, we believed we were exempt from the dangers of the big cities.

Early in my first pregnancy, two years after I first arrived in Mexico, Eduardo and I heard about a ranch several miles outside of town that was in foreclosure. With the vision of a family taking shape, I wanted a place where I could have an organic garden, where the kids could play, and where we could literally build a life for ourselves from the ground up. The ranch, named Rancho los Charcos, or "the Puddles," after the momentary lakes and canals that filled the alfalfa fields every time it rained (the name appeared on maps that were two centuries old), had been abandoned and taken over by squatters. The one standing structure on the property was little more than a tin roof, some stone columns, low-hanging wires that ran from a rusted-out generator, and a pile of rocks. There were dirt roads, boarded-up wells, and no infrastructure to speak of, but we were young and in love—young in years or young at heart—and that automatically gives you a rose-tinted prism through which the rest of life is refracted, or why else would anyone ever bring kids into this world in the first place? We saw nothing but potential.

The property went up for auction on New Year's Day 1996, and since no one else showed up we got it for a song. It took two years for all the inspections and everything, and then it was all ours. After we took possession legally, every cent we had went to the ranch. For a while it seemed like a black hole for our money. We didn't travel for a couple of years, we stopped eating out, and I started to buy Fernando's clothes at the Tuesday Market, an open-air once-a-week bazaar on the outskirts of town with hundreds of vendors who sold secondhand clothes from the States, along with farm-fresh produce, automotive tools, CDs, kitchen supplies, and practically anything else you could think of. The first thing we did was put up a fence around the entire property. Then, Eduardo's daughter Aurora, who was living in San Miguel and was a new mother (Sebastian, her son, is six months younger than Fernando), needed a place for her growing family, so hers was the first house we built.

Eventually, Eduardo's son Cielo moved in with his wife, Leti; their daughter, Vera, was born; and Los Charcos was transformed into a family compound.

Now that they were about to be grandparents, my parents wanted to spend as much time there as possible, so they bought a tract of land alongside ours and began to build their own vacation home, a mother-in-law apartment inflated to regal proportions through the caliber and prevalence of indigenous artisans—the woodworkers, bricklayers, stonemasons, and the rest whose rarefied skills can be traced back hundreds of years. Those first few years, we worked on the ranch while we were still living in Los Balcones, making several trips there a day, until we were finally able to move full-time in October 2000, when I was pregnant with Nayah. The ranch was on a hill overlooking the town, and from the beginning, we would take long walks in the afternoon that always culminated in watching the incredible sunsets. It became a ritual with us; whatever we were doing, Eduardo would say, "It's sunset," and off we would go.

There were mineral hot springs on the property and a small railroad siding where we could house our Pullman car. At night, the moonrise illuminated the valley with silver light, ricocheting off the eighty thousand nopal cacti to cast ghostly shadows across the rocky terrain, a spirit army standing sentinel. We fell asleep to the sounds of owls, crickets, the occasional coyote, and the wind through the mesquite and *huizache* trees, and we awoke to chirping birds and a glorious sunrise. Nearby, there were the ruins of a pyramid built on the onetime ceremonial grounds of the Chichimeca Indians. Once Fernando was born, even before there was a house on the land, we used to go out there every Sunday and make a big bonfire and have a picnic, hunt for arrowheads and broken pottery shards, roast potatoes, and then fall asleep under the mesquite trees. One day we were collecting firewood and we got very close to the pyramid, and this eerie silence descended on us. Suddenly a dust devil dropped out of the sky—a kind of mini-tornado. It enveloped us, and then just as suddenly it hopped away across the open field. It was like the Indian spirits were warning us to be respectful of this place, and from that point on we always were.

We quickly became part of the local community: There were extraordinary parties to go to, the mariachi music cascading across the arroyos on most nights from one house or another. There were picnics under the *palapas* we built for shade in our favorite spots, Easter egg hunts at Milou's house next door, horse shows on weekends, or private parties to evaluate and qualify bulls for the bullfights. We all supported each other in different ways; it felt like a neighborhood, and our kids all grew up together.

Nando was born on January 23, 1995, with his dimples showing. He's been a charmer and a little diplomat from day one. He's always been genuinely concerned about the well-being of others, and he kind of rides herd on the rest of us—maybe like I did when I was his age. When Nando was two years old, we got him two piglets and a donkey for his birthday—the first of what would eventually become a menagerie. Emiliano, or Emi, who is five years younger, feels everything so intensely. It all gets processed through the heart. For the first eight hours of his life, I literally had to lay him on my chest so that he could hear my heartbeat, or else he would have a meltdown. Soon enough, eight hours stretched into eight years; he wanted to be attached to me all the time, and one of the earliest ways I went native was to tie one of those shawls around me so that it formed a sling for the baby. Emi's an artist, heavily into soccer, dedicated to whatever currently strikes his fancy, and very much a romantic. I think he's the most like Eduardo. And then Nayah came along, and she's Little Miss Independence. She was talking in complete sentences before she was a year old, and her first complete sentence was "I'll do it myself." She's part tank and part tornado—she routinely used to make her brothers cry. She's also a planner; if she has a playdate, she schedules it out the day before and then sticks to the itinerary.

When I first became pregnant with Fernando, I went about it like I go about everything—I did research. I subscribed to every baby catalog I could find, and in one I spotted a book titled *You Are Your Child's First Teacher*. I liked the title, so I bought it on a whim. It turned out to be a layman's primer on the teaching and child-rearing theories of Rudolf Steiner, the founder of the Waldorf schools. Steiner was an Austrian writer and literary critic in the late nineteenth and early twentieth century who founded a spiritual branch of philosophy called anthroposophy, a kind of European cousin of the transcendentalism of Thoreau and Emerson. He was also active in psychology, the arts, architecture, agriculture, medicine, and various esoteric disciplines.

The Waldorf schools came about after Steiner delivered a lecture at the Waldorf-Astoria cigarette factory in 1919 on the role of imagination in preschool and primary school education. Afterward, the owner asked him if he would be interested in starting a school based on these principles for the factory workers, and he agreed. The first school became operational in 1928, and there are roughly a thousand sanctioned Waldorf schools in existence today. Instead of focusing exclusively on an intellectual education, particularly rote memorization, the Waldorf system integrates intellectual learning with development of the child's will, creativity, artistic ability, and physical exercise. For instance, musical training increases the brain's capacity for mathematics. Physical stimulation in the form of exercise can increase the child's capacity for retaining information. Steiner also recognized that children learn in different ways at different stages of their development: In the beginning, they experience the world through their senses, so learning should be grounded in practical activities. In the elementary school years, learning should be creative in order to engage the imagination. And in adolescence, to accommodate the child's moral framework and growing capacity for abstract thought, education should challenge them intellectually and feature an ethical or social dimension.

When I got to the chapter about kindergarten and pre-school education, I told Eduardo that as much as I loved it in San Miguel, when our son reached school age, we'd have to move somewhere that he could receive a Waldorf education. And Eduardo promised that when it came time, he would bring the school to us. The more we talked about it with other parents, the more it made sense. We found out there was a Waldorf teacher visiting in town, and so we invited her to our house for breakfast. About twenty minutes into the meeting, I asked her, "What would it take for you to move down here?" Her eyes got really big. But in the end, she took the job. She went home and packed up her house, and Eduardo agreed to pay her salary and expenses for the first year. We originally rented another ranch on the other side of town to house the school. But another school opened at the same time as ours, and enrollment the first year was not what we had hoped for. The rent was a thousand dollars a month, plus Eduardo was subsidizing the salaries for the teacher and staff, and we had to suspend work on the ranch to keep the whole thing afloat. We eventually built a schoolhouse right on the property—converting planned stables into classrooms and the caretaker's house into a teacher's cottage—and we rented a bus.

We started with kindergarten and a couple of grades, which turned out to be ambitious. It was really tough the first couple of years, not the least part of which involved bringing a whole new educational system into a conservative country like Mexico, where alternative education didn't really exist. In Mexico, there are generally two educational

options: public education, which like everything else controlled by the government is starved for funding, and private, which usually means Catholic school. In the larger
cities, you may have a third option such as a Montessori
school or a French or American school, which many of the
foreign kids attend. There was one private nonsecular
school that opened in San Miguel in the 1980s, but it had
no real creative component, and the bilingual aspect left
much to be desired. Waldorf schools offer a holistic
approach—they're spiritual without being religious—and a
lot of people don't get it at first or feel it clashes with their
traditional beliefs. When you found a Waldorf school, ide-
ally you start with a study group. Once they fully understand the concept and embrace it, the school grows out of
the community. This is no small task.

The gossip on the street was that we were a hippie
school, that we were doing black magic, every weird label
in the world. It turned out Eduardo and I were completely
unqualified for such a task. Neither of us had a background
in education, and I had just had my first child. It was only
the complete unwillingness to fail that made it happen. We
formed a parents' group and met once a week. If you get a
school up and running, you're allowed to call it Waldorf-
inspired, and then they keep pretty close tabs on you. We
made a decision early on to offer full scholarships to kids
who couldn't pay in order to fill the classrooms, and when
the girls from a nearby orphanage asked if they could attend, Eduardo and I, along with some of the other parents, found sponsorship for that—mostly from people in the
United States, Canada, and Europe. Within a couple of semester cycles, teachers at the middle schools were noting
the difference: Although they didn't excel at standardized
tests, which they had little experience with, our graduates
uniformly had a broad vision, a natural curiosity, and a
genuine desire to learn. And you could tell just by the way
they would clamber off the school bus in the morning to

get to class that we were doing something right. We started the school in September 1997, and it's grown steadily ever since. Suddenly we went from being just another couple you'd see at cocktail parties to the couple with the private school. It wasn't just how we spent our time and where we focused our energies. It became a source of pride and a part of our identity.

As the school year wound down in May 2007, the kids were looking forward to a trip we had planned back to the States. Fernando was twelve and just finishing up the seventh grade; Emiliano was seven going on eight and in the second grade, while Nayah, one year younger, had just finished first grade. We wanted the kids to grow up bilingual and bicultural, so we often traveled extensively in the States over the summer. We were planning to stay with my mother in the Washington area, then to see some friends in Virginia and drive to Massachusetts. We had a whole little tour of the northeastern United States planned, much of which we were going to spend camping, and the kids were excited. I was finishing up my school administrative work: We were expanding to include junior high grades, and I had hired a teacher from Minnesota, so his classroom and living quarters needed to be ready. I had placed an ad on a website called "Waldorf World," and he answered; he came very highly recommended by the Association of Waldorf Schools of North America. I was doing the interior decorating for our friend Luis Alberto Villarreal Garcia, a senator from the state of Guanajuato. He was getting married and moving into a new house, and he always loved how our house was decorated, so I offered to help him with colors, fabrics, and tiles in exchange for the many favors he had done us as a lawyer in the past. I was also going to undergo reconstructive surgery on my breast, scheduled for July 11, since I was now two years past starting chemo and effectively cancer-free for fifteen months. I'd been seeing a psychologist locally, Dr. Beverly Nelson—Dr. Bev to her patients—

who was helping me with the emotional aspects of cancer, and I was really ready to put that entire subject behind me.

And then there was this land deal.

Several months before, a real estate developer from Austin, Texas, named Cal Wimberley (not his real name) had contacted us about a golf course and luxury resort he wished to build in the area. After some negotiation, he had agreed to purchase two hundred acres, a little over half of our property, for a significant amount of money. This would include my parents' house, our natural hot-springs pool, and the land surrounding the school, which he had agreed to support with a yearly fifty-thousand-dollar grant, and for which he would build a new library—all of which was stipulated in the contract. We had bought the ranch partially as an investment, and we had always invested in real estate ventures over the course of our marriage but never anything on this order of magnitude. The deal was large enough that we actively encouraged the rumor that we had entered into a business partnership, and any money would come to us over time and not as a lump sum. We also executed the contracts in such a way that not even a secretary at the real estate broker's office saw copies, nor did we tell my mother or Eduardo's adult children. We also were very discreet around our friends.

Eduardo had seen firsthand the folly of ostentatious living. He had grown up in a home where the outward signs of wealth were an armor designed to protect you on the battlefield of corporate combat, and all it did was make you less safe in the world of haves and have-nots. We never wanted to have bodyguards around us. We only built a wall around parts of our property to keep out the dust from the road. And although the possibility of violence seemed remote—kidnapping was a phenomenon confined to Mexico City and urban centers, and anyway, there were far better high-value targets than us—discretion seemed the better part of valor.

In addition, I had worked in real estate and knew how mercurial these big land deals could be. Wimberley hadn't solidified his financing yet, so the terms were all conditional, and we had only received a relatively small amount of money so far.

There was also the matter of our neighbor across the highway, Oscar Gutierrez del Bosque, who had been involved in a multimillion-dollar resort venture of his own. When I was pregnant with Nayah, we sold one-third of the ranch to Richard Leet, an American businessman, who became a great friend and neighbor. We also sold ninety hectares, or about 225 acres, to Oscar and his wife, Norma. Although the tract of land was technically bigger than what we sold to Cal Wimberley, it was at a time when land values were much less, and the transaction involved fewer buildings, phone lines, and thermal wells and less infrastructure and electrical wiring, so the purchase price was dramatically less. (Later, Oscar had his own extensive business dealings with Leet, which went dramatically off the rails and resulted in suits and countersuits for millions. We were fortunate not to get caught up in that whole imbroglio.) Although, now, for reasons that remained largely unfathomable, we were involved in a property dispute with Oscar and Norma over, of all things, the Pullman train car that had belonged to Eduardo's father and that was resting on a railroad siding on a corner of our land. Although the two deals were completely unrelated, who knows how it would look to Oscar and others in the community? Best just to play our cards close to the vest.

That night that we went out with our friends Sandy and Derek—the night we strolled through the plaza and Eduardo sang with the mariachis, and just a few days before the kidnapping—was the first time we had let ourselves celebrate, even a little bit. Something about success seemed elusive—a cruel joke at our expense, perhaps, or a red cape waved in our faces to inflame us. Every time something good happened, it seemed like something bad was right around the corner. We felt like we were being tested, and the only way to appear worthy was not to appear too willing. The universe was sending us mixed signals. All we had to do was decode them, and everything would be fine.

FOUR

Signs

DAYS BEFORE THE KIDNAPPING

In early June 2007, I was reading a book called *Ask and It Is Given: Learning to Manifest Your Desires: The Teachings of Abraham* by Esther and Jerry Hicks. Esther claims to receive wisdom from a cluster of spirits whom she refers to under the umbrella name of Abraham. The ideal that Abraham puts forth is that your goals can be obtained by creating a clear pathway to them in your mind—a concept not entirely different from the law of attraction, manifestation, or "visualization" in self-help literature. I practiced visualization when I was first diagnosed with cancer. I don't know if I buy into the "nebulous mist" and cloudlike entity of Abraham, but the book contained an introduction by Wayne Dyer, an author for whom Eduardo and I shared an affinity.

I'm drawn to books like these. It's not that I accept every point in these books at face value, exactly, but I sift through them for things that I can use or that strike a note of recognition within me. I was raised Methodist and went to church every Sunday, until one day my father finally got fed up with the preacher asking for money and we didn't go back. By my early twenties, I had decided that organized religion wasn't for me, but I still felt a spiritual longing, which I've pursued ever since. It was refreshing when I first met my husband, who hailed from such a conservative Catholic country yet took an avid interest in things like Deepak Chopra and meditation. Like me, he believed that the search for truth is an ongoing exploration, just the opposite of some fixed orthodoxy, and that this search is part of what keeps one alive and vital. Having lived through them now, I find that traumatic events like kidnapping or cancer tend to focus the spiritual parts of you. Material things no longer have any importance; you survive each day, you eat, you feed your kids, and you focus on the things that matter—namely, your family and the distant signposts of a higher, spiritual plain.

At least in part, my interest in exploring the boundary between the spiritual and the mystical stems from various experiences I've had—things I couldn't explain afterward. I've always considered myself an intuitive person. I'm sensitive to my environment, other people—all those things I tapped into as an actor—and there's a place where that hyperawareness borders on something else. I'm very logical and rational in how I go about most things, especially when tackling a problem. But there are instincts and affinities that often go into rational decisions that come from somewhere else altogether.

My sister died when I was three and a half, and as I said, it had a profound effect on me. Her name was Marsha. Years after that, from the time I was seven or eight until I was fifteen, a couple of times a year, I would have vivid dreams of her. It's something that I had no control over. She was always the age she would have been had she lived, a couple of years younger than me. And she always looked healthy. Here's how it would happen: I would wake up in the middle of the night to go to the bathroom or just roll over in bed, and as I was falling asleep again, somewhere in that state between wakefulness and dreaming, she would appear before me. It felt like a dream, except that in the dream, I knew I wasn't fully asleep. She would tell me that she loved me, that she was okay and not to worry about her. Once, showing me a beautiful new dress she had, she twirled around in my bedroom. Another time, she was on a swing in the backyard. It was always comforting to me, because I'd had a lingering empty spot in my life where I felt like she belonged, and it always made me sad I never got to have a sister. I used to rub my mom's belly when she was pregnant and imagine what it would be like.

But once when I was fifteen, I realized that I wasn't totally asleep when it happened. This wasn't a revelation in the dream; now it was my conscious self intruding, and it started to freak me out. I never mentioned my sister to my parents, because my mom would start crying and my dad would walk out of the room. But this time I went to my mother and I told her about the latest dream, and that this had been happening to me my whole life. She started crying, and she asked me to describe this latest dream. When I was halfway through it, she stopped me and continued describing it in her own words: "There were out-of-focus people around the kitchen table, and there was a huge pink and white, heart-shaped birthday cake, and everyone was singing 'Happy birthday, dear Marsha.'" My mother recalled a dream that was exactly the same as mine. We checked the calendar, and this would have been Marsha's thirteenth birthday. Once we began comparing notes, we figured out this had been happening to both of us at roughly the same time for the last seven years.

I told my mom, "We've never done this before, but I think we should go to her grave—you and I together—and we should take some flowers." So we did. After that, the dreams stopped.

I then learned from my mom that she'd had other similar experiences. She had a brother, Robert, who was killed in a motorcycle accident when he was twenty-three. The night it happened, before anyone knew about it, she had a dream that another brother, Ted, had been killed. Two weeks later, she dreamed Robert was standing at the foot of her bed, and when she reached out to touch him, he disappeared. Again, she felt like she wasn't entirely asleep.

I have had similar experiences as an adult. When I was pregnant with Nayah, in my sixth or seventh month, I was visited in the middle of the night, only this time it was by Eduardo's dead father, the Colonel, whom I never met. As with previous experiences, this happened after I got up to use the bathroom and as I was drifting back to sleep. As I lay in bed, I entered what I can only describe as some kind of an altered state of consciousness and could suddenly feel exactly what it was like to be the Colonel: I could connect with the Colonel's thoughts, his memories, his feelings about his life and relationships. I was suddenly transported to his office, which I had never been in or even seen pictures of, in a house that I also never entered. All I knew of the Colonel's home was that it was in Mexico City and it now housed an extension of the Chinese embassy. In this dream-like state I could look down and see my hand signing a huge check, with this great florid signature: *Colonel Jose Garcia Valseca.* I looked around the office and noticed the doors, the windows that were louvered and opened with a hand crank, and the rosebushes that stood outside, with an open window across the way. The next morning, it so unnerved me that I soaked in a hot bath to steady myself—I couldn't stop crying. When I told Eduardo about it afterward, he quizzed me on the layout of the office. I could still see it in three dimensions and described it down to the smallest detail. Eduardo was shocked at how every one of my details matched the real office.

I can also see something akin to this in my children—that they too have this sensitivity.

Once, when Emiliano was three and a half, we were due to go to the States to spend Christmas with my folks. I called my dad just before Thanksgiving to ask him for a recipe, and Emi heard me on the phone and came over and pulled on my pants leg, wanting to speak to him. Dad was running late for a dental appointment, so I didn't put him on with Emi, and after I hung up, Emi had a major meltdown. He was hysterical, hyperventilating, unlike anything I'd ever seen before—enough so that I had to call my father back.

Emi got on the phone with him and said, "Poppop, you don't understand—you have to stop smoking. I've been telling you this for so long, and you're not listening to me. You're going to die!"

We were both flabbergasted—not just by what he said, but because he'd never done anything like this before. I got back on the phone and said, "Dad, I'm so sorry." He asked me, "Did you put him up to this?" I assured him I didn't. Less than a week later, my father dropped dead of a heart attack.

What am I to make of this? Were these simply coincidences or educated guesses—finely calibrated hypotheses built from near invisible clues hidden in plain sight? Is it the brain's capacity to extrapolate detail from secondary sources or to secrete such empathy that we can experience false memories as if they were truly lived in? Are they signs, sent to us from beyond, up ahead, by the cosmos, a higher intelligence, ourselves? I have no idea. But I have learned to trust my instincts—often the hard way.

In the days and weeks leading up to the kidnapping, I had the sense that something was wrong. It's the same feeling I had the week I was first diagnosed with cancer, like some life-changing force was about to impact me and my family. There was something in the air—I could see it both in physical acts I could interpret and in the unspoken vibrations I should have heeded. But we had been through so much, and it finally seemed like things were turning around. I wanted to believe things would get better, and I let this inner voice be drowned out by my rational mind.

Approximately two months before the kidnapping, several broken-down trucks appeared in various locations on the dirt road that leads to the highway. The city has since paved it, but back then the road was far less traveled and rough enough that we would often see trash trucks en route to the dump on the side of the road with a broken axle. That's the reason we had a Jeep with four-wheel drive. So it wasn't unusual to see cars broken down on that road, but not three or four over a period of two months, and not always in front of our gate. We joked about it; it was like an epidemic. The last time was the entire week before the kidnapping, and we considered having it towed. But then one day, it suddenly disappeared, so it became a nonissue.

About six weeks earlier, some men had made an appointment to come see my mother's house, the one next to the school. This was right before the Cal Wimberley deal, and we had quietly put part of our property on the market. A potential buyer had contacted Gustavo, one of our most trusted longtime employees. After their visit, my mother called and said, "You know, these people were not like any buyers I've ever seen. They didn't ask the typical buyer questions. As a matter of fact, every question was about you and Eduardo. They wanted to know how much of the land was his, how many hectares he had, how much I thought the ranch was worth. One of them said to me, 'Oh, he comes from a really rich family, doesn't he?'"

My mom went back to D.C., and then the day of the kidnapping, I called her and she flew back the next day. But thinking back on it later, I asked her what the men had been wearing. She said, "You know, it's funny now that you mention it. One of the guys was probably in his forties. The other guy was older—late fifties to early sixties. But they never took off their hats or sunglasses." It was the exact same description as the kidnappers. When I asked Gustavo how he had come across them, he said an intermediary who swore he had done business with them before had connected them. Gustavo said he turned all of this information over to the police.

I remember about a week before the kidnapping, our friends Sandy and Derek—the ones who strolled through the plaza with us the night Eduardo sang with the mariachis— were supposed to come to our house for lunch. I was preparing the food in the kitchen, and I saw them drive up in their Honda Element, but they didn't get out of the car. Instead, they sat there for a good ten minutes without moving. I finally went out to see if they were all right, and they laughed it off with some joke. But after the kidnapping, they told me they felt like they were being watched. They're both artists, and sensitive to things like I am. It was such an intense feeling that they almost turned around and went home.

Then several days before Eduardo was abducted, I was walking the kids over to the school in the afternoon, where they liked to play on the jungle gyms and swings. We had the dogs with us—two Neapolitan mastiffs, three Irish wolfhounds, three rat terriers, a Saint Bernard, and two Akitas—and at one point about halfway between the pool and the school, roughly where the kidnapping took place but inside the property line, all the dogs went ballistic. They were always on high alert, life on a ranch being full of small things that dart quickly, but someone or something had set off a trip wire inside their central nervous systems. The mesquite trees and brush were very dense, so all we could see was that they were digging furiously. I assumed they'd found a rabbit hole, except they wouldn't let up. We were almost to the school and I had to call them to catch up with us. Slowly, one by one, they straggled back. We took a different route home to avoid the diversion. Later on, the police told me they found a mound of cigarette butts on that exact spot, all the same brand.

Summer had always been our favorite time of year in San Miguel. Spring is very dry, since it generally hasn't rained much since September or October, so by May it's very dusty. Brush fires are a constant threat, and Eduardo always opened fire lanes around the ranch to contain any runaway blazes, which are easily whipped by the constant winds. Sometimes they still jumped these firebreaks; one damaged the kids' treehouse once. Shopkeepers often shut down for the month and go on vacation rather than face the constant gray swirl in the air. But as soon as it starts to rain, everything turns green again and the skies turn bright blue with white fluffy clouds. It turns into a Garden of Eden: The fields of nopales cactus suddenly bloom with yellow orange flowers and sprout hundreds of new rackets, the paddle-shaped branches you can sauté and eat. The mesquite trees produce a long purplish podlike fruit similar to sugarcane that is delicious to chew on; the kids would eat them all day long. There are wildflowers everywhere. And what used to be a desert turns into an oasis. It is exquisite. Typically the day is perfect in every way—mostly in the mideighties—and then in the evening it gets cool. Often the clouds roll in and it rains while you sleep, many times with thunder and lightning. I put up chandeliers in the kitchen that held real candles because many times we lost power and it would take a day or more to get it back. In the morning, it was always so beautiful after the rains came through. On nights that it didn't look like rain, sometimes we would pitch tents in the front yard by the fountain and camp out under the stars. It was like going on an adventure without leaving the ranch. We built bonfires, roasted marshmallows and hot dogs, and sang under the stars. The coyotes howled at night. We'd fill the pool with water from the hot springs and all go for a swim.

On our long evening walks around the perimeter of the ranch to watch the Mexican sunsets, Eduardo and I would talk about all kinds of things—often our fears and concerns about whatever was going on in our lives. We'd hold hands. Sometimes we'd stop to kiss. Eduardo would always pee on his favorite cactus, declaring, "Now *this* is real luxury!"—a universal manly pleasure that escapes me. We talked about the whole Cal Wimberley deal before we went into that— every detail of the terms, the benefits versus the cost, whether this was something we really wanted to do. He had come to us with an offer after buying up some of the sur- rounding property from the neighbors. We had always talked about the possibility of selling off part of our land, and it had increased dramatically in value since we had bought it. We also discussed the need for secrecy, how our safety might depend on it, and even whether we should con- sider getting security or a night watchman. We weren't wor- ried, but we did want to be prudent. Ironically, it was on these walks that anyone with long-range surveillance equip- ment could easily have learned of our plans or figured out the easiest way to get at us. Why didn't they just grab us then?

Two days before the kidnapping, I was feeling anxious about our impending return to the States and about my re- constructive surgery. Like he always did, Eduardo tried to be supportive, saying, "No, you're fine—you're going to be okay." This was the day I noticed that the broken-down pickup truck in front of our gate was gone. I got a really strange feeling about it. Then on our way back to the house, Fernando overtook us on the four-wheeler and told us, "I just feel like something really bad is about to happen to us as a family." Fernando is an excellent judge of character— he often sees through people way ahead of the rest of us— and he has frequently made predictions that come true the next day. But Eduardo told him, "You've got to snap out of it. We all have those feelings sometimes, but if you dwell on them, you allow bad things to happen to you. Just think positively and you'll be fine." And since he'd just said essentially the same thing to me, I felt like I should offer a positive example.

The next morning, Nando left on a field trip and was gone all day. Tuesday was the day Eduardo taped his weekly public affairs talk show *Contrastes* (or *Contrasts*), so he was in town all afternoon doing some work. I had a rehearsal for a dance performance coming up that weekend—a belly-dancing troupe, called Belibeya, done tribal-style, all in a group. We actually got professional gigs and were scheduled to start regular Friday and Saturday night shows in a few more days, which I was forced to drop out of. Afterward, I went with another dancer to see our seamstress, Juanita Otero—Gustavo's mother—for a last-minute costume fitting. Coming home by myself in the Jeep at sunset, a dark-colored older-model Ford Explorer was broken down on the dirt road to our ranch, blocking the road. As I got closer, I could see there was one man in the driver's seat and another two bent over under the hood. There was no way a normal car could get around them, and I'd heard plenty of stories of makeshift roadblocks that turn into ambushes. My heart was racing. Since I was in the Jeep, I decided I had just enough room to squeeze by on the left if I drove up on the rocks. I didn't even slow down, and if somebody had stepped out in front of me, I was prepared to run them over. As I passed by them, I got a good look at one of them in the rearview mirror: a thin man in a baseball cap and sunglasses, fifty or fifty-five, with olive skin, dark curly hair, a long mustache, and wrinkles around his mouth that made him look like a smoker. He looked scary and threatening. All three men had mustaches, hats, and sunglasses, and none of them looked like they were working on the car. It smelled like a setup.

These were the same guys that grabbed us the next day.

I'm pretty sure the dark SUV was the car they spirited Eduardo away in.

When I got to the gate, I hurried and unlocked it, then called Eduardo and told him what had just happened. Again, he was reassuring: "Honey, it's nothing. Cars break down all the time. If I call the cops, they'll think I'm crazy." But later on that night, when he was leaving the TV station, he told me he had the definite sensation he was being watched.

He'd had the same feeling for months.

FIVE

The Snail

AFI ARRIVES

High-neh.

That's how it sounds phonetically when native Spanish speakers try to pronounce my name. I answer to Jenny because it's easier than trying to explain what a *y* is doing in the middle of "Jane." Staring at the careful lettering on the front of the envelope, nestled in the early morning dew where it had slid off of me in my blind panic, it seemed fragile, almost dainty—a party invitation, or was it a note of consolation for my loss? The officer standing over it seemed prepared to restrain me if I suddenly lunged for it.

"We have to wait for the experts to dust it for fingerprints," he told me in Spanish.

Soon the state police were swarming over the crime scene, trailing back and forth to their vehicles with bits of equipment or evidence like the leaf-cutter ants that would strip the laurel trees in our garden, carrying their bounty hundreds of feet back to their vast colonies along teeming trails, conveying whispered crumbs of information to each new figure they passed. When the press began to arrive moments later, they hid me behind a clump of trees so there wouldn't be any photos of me released to the public. Kidnappers often threatened to kill their victims if the police were called, so a media blackout was standard protocol, and victims' names were rarely mentioned in the newspaper.

From the time we are little in the United States, we learn to dial 911 if there's an emergency. As an American—a white, middle-class American, at any rate—I instinctively trusted the police. But the police in Mexico are a different animal. Most public employees are so dramatically underpaid by the government that it's generally accepted they will subsidize their income in creative ways. There's a saying in Spanish that translates as "You can't dive in the water without splashing me." Every intermediary in the chain of commerce expects to get a little taste of the profits, and public officials are no exception. It's like a life tax you inadvertently add on to the cost of doing business. With the police, this obviously opens the door to more serious problems. Our local law enforcement had a pretty good reputation, as far as sleepy little Mexican villages go. But every crisis is someone else's opportunity, so you think twice when it's you in the crosshairs.

The police asked me over and over again to explain exactly what had happened. No sooner had I gone through the whole thing than another detective would arrive and ask me to run through it again. It was like they were trying to trip me up, to see if any part of my story contradicted any other. This didn't surprise me: There are many cases in Mexico in which a spouse's murder is set up to look like a kidnapping. As the wife of a man who was rumored to have inherited great wealth and who was left behind, I was a logical suspect. But it still felt a little unnerving.

An ambulance had arrived by now, along with many other police cars. As I was being interviewed, the paramedics unobtrusively took my vitals and looked at my finger, perhaps preferring to keep my attention focused elsewhere. One of them said to me softly, "You need to go to the hospital." I refused to go anywhere until I'd read the contents of the letter, which they were still examining for clues.

The cop on the dirt bike brought me a muffin and a bottle of water as I sat in the open bay of the ambulance. "You've been through something very shocking," he said. "Your blood sugar could drop. Eat this and you'll feel better." I tried to drink some water, but it almost made me gag.

The question I get asked the most about everything that has happened to me—including by the police right after it happened—is what made me react the way I did? Why did I fight back? Why did I try to establish empathy with the most sympathetic of the kidnappers? How did I have the presence of mind to memorize the license plate number, or hop into the path of an oncoming bus, or aim to throw myself over the hood of a taxi to get him to stop? I can't tell you. Maybe it's my natural Virgo fastidiousness. Or maybe I've been trained to live in the moment and to respond to a situation free from my natural inhibitions. I guess the short answer is that if you focus on the problem at hand, the one right in front of you, then you don't have to worry about the really scary stuff: Why am I not paralyzed by this crushing fear? How will I live if my loved ones are taken from me? What if I fail? What if I do my very, very best, and it's not good enough?

I asked the police to call the mayor, who was a friend of ours. He was out of town, so his assistant agreed to come instead. We had been there no more than fifteen minutes when our former employee Gustavo Otero showed up and somehow bluffed his way past the police line. Gustavo and his brother Oscar, our driver, whom we called Coco, were the sons of Juanita Otero, the seamstress Eduardo and I had met in the town square right after we bought the house in

Los Balcones; I had seen her only a day earlier for my costume fitting. Juanita made all of our curtains and bedclothes by hand, all beautifully embroidered with colonial Mexican designs. Gustavo had managed the ranch for us for years until he gained so much knowledge about the construction trade that, with Eduardo's help and our recommendations, he went into business for himself and did very well. Juanita and Gustavo were guests at our wedding, and Juanita's daughter was an overnight babysitter when we had to travel without the children.

Our ties to the Otero family had been close for years. When they and other families of a neighborhood called El Nigromante were victimized by a government housing scam, Juanita approached Eduardo as the son of a former newspaper publisher. Many residents of the neighborhood had bought their houses through a federal program that enabled the poor to afford their own homes. They made their down payments, got keys, and moved in, but they never received their property deeds. Soon after, they received official notices that the down payments had not been made and were threatened with eviction. Many families paid twice out of fear of losing their homes. Eduardo exposed the program in the national newspapers, in conjunction with First Lady Cecilia Ocelli de Salinas, and hundreds of families were allowed to keep their homes. He was always doing things like this, and it made him controversial in certain quarters.

Gustavo looked visibly shaken when he arrived at the scene. He said that he'd received a call from the ranch and happened to be driving by, and when he saw the police cars, he assumed it was me and talked his way in. I gave him a hug and broke down crying. He was shaking. I borrowed his cell phone to call the ranch—I needed to know where my children were and that they were all right. I talked to Cielo's wife, Leti—my stepdaughter-in-law—and they already knew what had happened. People from the school had seen the Jeep abandoned and called her, so she had picked up the two younger kids and had them at her house. She hadn't told them anything yet. (Fernando was still on a field trip.) I told Tina, our cook, to have Coco bring me my cell phone and both of our address books. I needed to mobilize a support network quickly. And right now, more than anything, I needed information. A few minutes later, Coco showed up with my phone and phone books. He told me he had to go to the police station, where they were interviewing all of the employees.

Once I had my phone, my first call was to Eduardo's sister Lupe. I remembered a conversation from a few months before when she told me about a friend whose son had been kidnapped, and it had all ended well. They were friends of former president Vicente Fox, and he had recommended a private consulting company that negotiated the release. In the end, the family paid a fraction of the asking price, and their son was returned home quickly and safely. I was only interested in cases that had been resolved successfully. Whatever those families did to ensure a positive outcome were the steps I wanted to consider. Lupe had already heard from someone at the ranch, and Cielo and Alonso—Guero ("Blondie") and Oncho (short for Alonso), cousins and close friends since childhood—were on their way to me.

The next call I made was to my mom. She was visiting friends in Virginia and responded in her usual bright, enthusiastic way. "Oh, hi honey," she said.

"Mom," I told her, "I have something to tell you, and it's not good. First of all, I'm okay. The kids are okay. Eduardo has been kidnapped. I don't have time to explain. I need you to come immediately."

"I'm driving straight to the airport," she said. "I'll let you know what time I'll be there."

I then called one of Eduardo's close friends, a businessman in Mexico City who had a friend who had been kidnapped. Especially in Mexico City, kidnapping had reached such epidemic proportions that no one was more than two degrees of separation away from someone who had experienced it firsthand. In San Miguel, we imagined we were exempt from that kind of thing; kidnapping was one more unnecessary burden of life in the big city. Besides, there were some really wealthy people in San Miguel, and none of them took any added precautions. If I were to make a list of the top fifty prospects to be kidnapped in our little town, I doubt we would even be on it.

My mind wandered back to a conversation I'd had a few months before with Rafael Loret de Mola, well-known writer, father of one of the most popular television news anchors in Mexico, and son of Carlos Loret de Mola, one of the Colonel's star journalists (later the governor of Yucatán) and Eduardo's mentor. He and his wife, Claudia, were moving to Madrid and we were saying our farewells at our favorite Italian restaurant, la Trattoria da Andrea, on the outskirts of town. They are both writers and warned us that organized crime was taking over and that the government was doing too little too late. Claudia said that Mexico would soon experience a bloodbath and that they were leaving. They saw it all coming. We had already heard from many of our friends that we were sitting ducks out in the country with virtually no security. But I'll never forget, Rafael said to Eduardo, "The danger for you and your family living in such an exposed way is that you have a last name that most people associate with a great wealth. You no longer have that kind of a fortune. If they ever kidnap you or a family member, that detail makes it especially dangerous for you. You will not be able to meet their expectations and you could be killed or, worse, lose a child." He warned us to get out of Mexico while we still could. When I spoke to him later he didn't even want to be reminded of the conversation. It was as if he were a prophet or something. The whole thing made him very uncomfortable.

Eduardo's businessman friend gave me the name of a different private negotiator from the one Lupe had told me about, but the outcome was similar: All the parties had approached it like a business negotiation, professional mediators formally conducted the transaction, and the deal was consummated efficiently and in a timely fashion. I hung up and began leaving messages with every kidnapping consultant, expert, previous victim, or person of influence I could find a contact for. As I made call after call, I watched the police work the crime site—dusting for fingerprints, collecting evidence in plastic bags—all the forensic, *CSI*-style business that's the stuff of American TV drama.

Finally, two policemen came over to me with a digital camera and showed me a photo of the letter from the kidnappers.

Sra. Jayne:

Eduardo is with us. Go to your house. Open an e-mail account with this address . . .

It gave a Yahoo! address that combined Eduardo's name with San Miguel.

Password:
"Cafeteria"
We will be in contact.

I felt a bizarre sense of relief to think of this as a kidnapping. If that's what it was, then I could look at it as an equation, where each side had an agenda and a clear path to its goal. It meant Eduardo was still alive—his life had value in the equation. Hopefully, we would be able to meet their price, and that would be that.

With some semblance of resolution, I finally agreed to get in the police car and go to the hospital. The officer who had carried me from the taxi drove me, and Gustavo came along for support. At the hospital, the doctor assigned to me seemed far too interested in gossiping about what had happened to me, so I asked for an old family friend who was in residence there. When he saw me, his eyes got wide. I told him I needed his discretion and that I was in a big hurry, so he stitched me up without the novocaine even having taken effect. There was so much blood that he put a trash can with a plastic garbage bag in it under my hand. He kept stopping and staring into my eyes to make sure I wasn't going into shock.

We got back into the unmarked police car for the drive to the Ministério Público to file papers and press charges. It lies just outside of town on a winding road people call El Caracol, or the Snail, because it coils like a snail's shell around the town at the foot of the Sierra Madre, and because traffic there invariably moves at a snail's pace—not unlike the proverbial wheels of justice. This time was no exception. My initial flurry of phone calls was starting to produce results, so I was fielding calls on my cell phone while Gustavo scavenged scraps of paper for me to take notes on. I gave his cell number as a backup so people could reach me; I had turned the back of the police SUV into my private office. The dispatcher radioed from police headquarters that the station was crawling with reporters and we should pull over and wait on the side of the road for further instructions. During this brief hiatus, I heard back from the two negotiators, who each confirmed they routinely charged $2,500 a day, plus expenses. Between professional negotiators, household surveillance, private bodyguards, bulletproof limos, and specialized insurance policies, K&R—kidnapping and ransom—was becoming one of Mexico's growth industries. As these burgeoning professions expanded to meet a need, kidnapping itself was forced to seek new markets beyond the metropolitan centers—for which the idyllic enclave of San Miguel de Allende represented a golden opportunity. Those who couldn't afford the going rates were forced to choose between the state and federal police.

Something else peculiar happened when I spoke to both of the negotiators. I recited my story almost verbatim, having now told it two dozen times or more. In both cases, they asked me if the criminals had left anything besides a note. When I mentioned the hammer left on the front seat, their tone and demeanor changed. It was as if suddenly their enthusiasm for my case had changed. The first guy, whose name I got through Lupe, told me that I should speak with a friend of his who was with the AFI—the Agencia Federal de Investigación, or federal police, Mexico's equivalent of the FBI. The other consultant wanted to collect more information from his associates and said he would call me back. When I asked them what it meant, they were vague or seemed unwilling to speculate. They put more stock overtly in how many cars they used, what they looked like, how they acted, what kind of guns they used, and whether or not they said anything.

The call came from the police dispatcher to proceed to the parking lot of El Pollo Feliz—the Happy Chicken—a fast-food restaurant on the highway to the ranch that the kids liked because they had play tubes and a ball pit, kind of like McDonald's. We had just been there on Sunday. There we rendezvoused with the state police from Guanajuato, and I was transferred to their big white SUV. I was amazed to see that they already had a laptop set up and were monitoring the e-mail address from the kidnappers. It was decided we would return to the ranch, where I could fill out the necessary paperwork in privacy.

As we turned in at the front gate of the ranch, the state police identified themselves and waved us through. There were more police cars than I had ever seen. Everything was in lockdown. Parents from the school lined the road, since no one was allowed past the police barricade. Every teacher, neighbor, and employee was being interviewed. It reminded me of a funeral cortege or some national tragedy, shock and sorrow etched into the faces of all these people I knew, standing outside their cars, while I was whisked past them, unable to comfort any of them.

As we approached the house, I remembered that many of Eduardo's guns, part of his father's antique gun collection, were out on open racks in the dining room. I wouldn't be able to let the police in the house with guns out. I whispered to one of the ranch hands, who was beside me, to help me hide them once we got inside. I invited the state police to sit on the patio and offered them some cool lemonade to drink, which they gratefully accepted. Tina, our cook, appeared pale and ghostlike in the entryway, her eyes swollen from crying. I asked her to please look after our guests and excused myself. Once the guns were under lock and key, the ranch hand confided to me, "I'm glad you thought about that, Jayne." I felt an eerie calm coupled with a surge of adrenaline, the likes of which I'd never felt before. My mind was racing at light speed.

I no sooner got the arms safely stowed away than Cielo and Alonso came through the door, both slightly out of breath and buzzing with nervous energy. They had made it here in record time from Mexico City, where Alonso lived full-time and Cielo was studying cinematography. Both of them were in expert physical shape, handy with a gun and ready to go the distance if it came down to it. I was only seven years older than Cielo, but we had made our peace with each other and had a deep respect and love for each other that had developed over the years. On occasion, I could see in his impulsive behavior the young man Eduardo must certainly have been, and it fascinated and exasperated me in equal measure. And at other times, I didn't know what I would ever do without him. Now was one of those times.

While the policemen waited politely on the patio sipping their lemonade, I called another longtime friend of Eduardo's, a member of a prominent, wealthy family. He had always been a bit of an eccentric but had kept a low profile since his daughter had been kidnapped a few years before. She was returned after less than two weeks, and she suffered only slight damage to one eye after being tightly blindfolded for so many days. He had enlisted the AFI to negotiate her release, and he strongly recommended letting them handle my situation as well. He had been very impressed with their efficiency and professionalism.

"Jayne, if you need *anything*, I'm here for you, okay?" he told me. "If you need advice, someone to guide you, if you need money, whatever—just give me a call."

I hoped he meant it. In Mexico, they have a saying: *Las palabras se las lleva el viento.* Words are taken away with the wind.

Collecting myself, I went back out on the patio where the police were waiting.

"We need to know if you will sign the proper paperwork," they told me. "If you will sign these forms on the dotted line, we will be in charge of the case and we'll start investigating immediately. Someone will come up from Guanajuato and live in your house twenty-four hours a day, seven days a week, until this is resolved and your husband has returned safely."

"How much experience do you have in the state of Guanajuato?" I asked. "I wasn't aware that this was a big kidnapping hub."

"Yes, there have been several kidnappings," they told me. "We do this on a regular basis."

"Then what's your track record?" I asked. "How often have these cases been resolved successfully?"

"One hundred percent of the time," they assured me.

"Does that mean that you've successfully negotiated the safe return of one hundred percent of the victims or that you've arrested one hundred percent of the bad guys?" I asked.

"Both."

After a suitable amount of time, I excused myself again to talk it over with my family. Once out of their presence, I was almost beside myself. I knew firsthand that the Guanajuato police hadn't solved 100 percent of the parking violations, much less violent crimes. Their confidence seemed preposterous. Alonso said, "Well, these guys seem nice enough, and they're already here. Why don't we just go with them?" But I didn't feel good about it. Cielo agreed.

"One hundred percent of the time?" Cielo said. "Sounds like a crock of shit."

While we were weighing the decision, I called the consultant whom Eduardo's friend had recommended, Jorge Septien, the one Cielo had spoken with while I was with the state police. He said that based on the amount of preparation, number of cars used, and the other details given to him, this was something the AFI should handle. He advised Cielo to get a relative in Mexico City to fill out the appropriate paperwork, then politely dismiss the state police in my courtyard without telling them we had made up our minds. He encouraged me to contact Benito Roa Lara, the head of the Department of Kidnapping and Ransom at the federal level, who was well respected in the business as well as internationally. Outside of Control Risks, the gold standard in the industry, he said I couldn't be in better hands. This tipped the scale, and Cielo and I agreed to go with the AFI. So while Alonso patrolled the perimeter with binoculars on Nando's four-wheeler to look for anything suspicious, Cielo called Luis, the son of Eduardo's other sister, Mini (short for Guillermina), in Mexico City to file the appropriate paperwork. I thanked the state police, took all their cards, and told them I would call them once I'd had time to consider the matter more fully. The AFI called us back almost immediately and told us to dismiss all police from the property—both state and local, lock the doors, and wait by the phone. Someone would be on his way to us shortly.

That decision made, the whirlwind momentarily subsided, and I was able to let my guard down momentarily. Tina had made vegetable soup and her famous chipotle chicken, and Leti tried to get me to eat, as I hadn't eaten anything since the previous evening. But I couldn't even stand to smell the food, and the only thing I could drink was water. How could I eat and drink, sit at this beautiful table with people catering to me, when I didn't know where Eduardo was, if he was being treated well, or if he was even alive. I was overcome with guilt that it was me who was free and not him—the father of my children, my partner and provider, the love of my life. These kinds of thoughts gushed into my brain and threatened to overwhelm me. Much better to stay busy and keep my mind occupied. Guilt and self-pity are a luxury in the best of times, and in my present circumstances, they could prove fatal.

While Cielo checked and loaded the firearms, making sure they were all in working order, I made phone calls I had neglected in the day's flurry of activity.

I called the vet to come take our new puppies to his house, where their needs wouldn't go overlooked. I had to call the doctor who was to perform my reconstructive surgery in July and cancel the appointment. I didn't know how long this was going to stretch out to, so for the time being, the future was effectively off the table. I called our banker and informed him of the situation and asked for his cooperation.

"If Eduardo or anyone else calls you, you are to contact

me before doing *anything*," I told the banker. "This could be very dangerous for all of us. I will be the only one making decisions here, okay?"

"Of course, Jayne," he said. "I hate to remind you at a moment like this, but you know that I cannot give you anything without his signature, right?"

"Yes, I know that," I said.

Eduardo was born into a wealthy family with a famous last name: In Mexico, Garcia Valseca was like saying Hearst or Rockefeller in the United States. When we got married, we decided as a couple that it was best to put everything in his name. It got complicated when we tried to put both names on deeds or bank accounts because I was still an American citizen—there as a resident only. I felt that he was sensitive about these things based on the divorce and his past experiences with women, so I didn't push it. I loved him. I didn't care who controlled our finances, so that's the way it was. Now it turned out to be a complication I didn't know how I'd get around. Most people who have been kidnapped are reluctant to talk about how much they've paid, since it's an advertisement for how much you're willing to pay, and there are many repeat victims. The highest ransom I had heard of anyone paying in San Miguel was $400,000 in a kidnapping that had happened decades before, and that was just a rumor. Of course, I had heard of multimillion-dollar ransoms being paid in Mexico City and throughout the country, but this was still at the point when people in San Miguel felt isolated from what was going on in the rest of the country. I suppose we changed all that. If you were lucky, kidnappers settled for 10 to 15 percent of the original asking price, and I expected the final demand to come in at around $250,000. Between our checking account and a CD, and some money borrowed from family and friends, I thought that would cover it. If I needed more, I was already making a mental list of what I could sell. But if I was not able to liquidate assets, then that was going to make everything more complicated.

"I'll call my boss and find out if there is any possible way I can help you with this," he promised.

In retrospect, it's a wonder I had the presence of mind to call all the people I did. I was on adrenaline in a big way and sharper than ever. I'm sure it was also in an effort to feel like I was doing something and keeping my panic at bay, but it was very clear to me that whatever confusion and hysteria I was feeling at the time, this precipice of chaos I could feel myself being drawn to, the same would be true of everyone this incident touched. Unless I could override this automatic entropy and seize the levers of control, starting with anything to do with finances, I was quickly going to lose whatever little power I had in this situation.

I had decided not to tell my two youngest children the truth about the kidnapping quite yet. I hoped that I would be able to resolve this whole thing quickly, and by the weekend it would be over. I spoke with Dr. Bev, and she told me she would come over Sunday and help me break the news to them. But Fernando was almost a teenager, and he would figure it out if I tried to keep anything from him, plus I was going to need his help in the days ahead. He was on a school field trip in Dolores Hidalgo, learning about the reproduction cycle of cactus. Between watching his bus driver and teacher field calls on their cell phones and the color drain from their faces; being stopped at a police barricade when the field trip was unexpectedly cut short; and having Alonso meet him at the bus and walk him to school to get his homework—and seeing broken glass, pieces of the Jeep, and what looked like red paint on one of the white fence posts—he was pretty certain something was very wrong. He thought we'd been in an accident.

It turns out his school bus had come upon the crime scene within moments of the kidnapping. A ROAD CLOSED sign blocked their access, which was highly unusual, and the bus was forced to use our private road through the alfalfa fields—the one where the Ford KA drove parallel to us. At the second gate back onto the main road, they could see the Jeep abandoned behind them and traffic cones blocking access from the other direction. When Fernando first walked in the door, he was as white as a corpse, and my heart dropped. I pulled him into the bathroom, along with Cielo, where no one could overhear us. He asked me, "Mom, what's going on? Is everyone okay?"

I said, "Honey, I don't know how to tell you this, but let me start by saying that everything is going to be okay. Something really bad has happened, but let me tell you right now that I am going to do everything possible to remedy the situation. If it takes my last breath, I'll give everything we have. Your father has been kidnapped." His eyes got big and he fell backward, like I'd struck him in the chest.

After a second, he said, "So what happened?" I told him what I knew, and he asked, "Is he going to be okay? Are they going to hurt him? Are they going to kill him?"

"I just don't know," I said. "All I know is that we are doing everything we can possibly do, and Cielo is here, and I'm here, and we're going to dedicate ourselves to getting him back. I will do whatever it takes." This was very hard for him to hear, and it was nearly as hard for me to say without breaking down. Without telling anyone, Fernando took his bike up to a rocky point on the hill where you can see the whole ranch below and where he could be alone. There he broke down and cried. The AFI later told us the kidnappers probably used this exact point to conduct surveillance on our movements in the weeks before the attack.

Leti brought the little ones back after the media circus had finally settled down, and I made a point of trying not to show them I was upset. Things were fine until dinner, when Emi asked, "Where's my daddy?" I told him that Eduardo had to go away on a business trip, and that he would be back soon. This seemed to hold them for the time being, but I knew that wouldn't last for long. He told me later that same day he was worried about me, since I seemed so sad, I was constantly at the computer wearing a horrible face, and I didn't want to play with him when he asked. When it was time to go to bed, Fernando pushed his bed up against Emi's and closed and locked all the windows. When Emi asked him why, Fernando told him, "Well, I mean, just because I love you." He also put his baseball bat between the bed and the nightstand and slept with the pocketknife my father gave him under his pillow.

In the evening, we received a call from an AFI agent named Raul. He told us he was in Mexico City getting ready to board a bus for San Miguel. He asked for instructions on how to get to the ranch. He would be arriving in the middle of the night, and he would call us when he was here. Afterward, Cielo and I wondered if we'd made a huge mistake. He's coming by bus? Why not a bulletproof Suburban with GPS tracking and machine-gun mounts?

That first night, Alonso slept in the master bedroom with a loaded handgun by his side. Leti and Cielo slept in the living area of my loft bedroom, and Cielo kept a loaded revolver and a shotgun by his side. I had the Colonel's old snub-nosed .38 from the 1960s in bed with me, loaded with hollow-point bullets that exploded on contact. It was like the Alamo. If they were going to get to me, they were going to have to make it through some serious firepower first.

The second I lay down to try and sleep, the waves of emotion washed over me again. My embroidered sheets and fluffy down pillows conjured images of Eduardo lying on a cold concrete floor somewhere, dazed and blinded from an untended head wound. The stillness and quiet were a canvas on which were etched his screams. Every blind alley of thought ended in tragedy and despair. I spent most of the night looking at the clock.

The phone rang several times during the night. Cielo answered it each time—it was always Raul, asking directions on how to find the ranch in the dark. About the fifth time, Cielo said, "Forget it, man, I'll come get you at the bus station." It was after 3 A.M. when they finally got back to the house. I hurried downstairs to meet them, just in time to see Cielo come through the front door with a look of disappointment on his face. Behind him was a tiny, dark-skinned boy of no more than twenty wearing a baseball cap, glasses, a backpack, and a cheap leather jacket that seemed to swallow him whole. He looked like a college student on summer vacation. I said a polite hello, showed him where the bathroom was, and offered him a glass of water, then pulled Cielo into my office and closed the door.

This is who the AFI was sending us? Was he even armed? Was he old enough to shave? I could see Cielo thinking the same thing. We had argued for letting the AFI handle the case, and now they had delivered us an Eagle Scout. We quickly agreed we would all get a few hours of sleep and then send him back on the first bus in the morning. We ambushed him in the dining room and let him have it as diplomatically as we could.

"Look, we really need someone much more experienced," Cielo said. "This is very serious; Eduardo's life is at stake here and we can't play around. No offense, but I think we have made a mistake." He stopped us dead in our tracks in a very calm, certain, confident sort of way, telling us that he got this reaction all the time.

"Listen, it's very late, you're all still in shock and trying your best to make the correct decisions—I understand," Raul said. "But you need to get some sleep, as do I, and you need to give me a chance. I've been doing this for several years now, and I'm not as young as I look. I'm dressed like a schoolkid for a reason. I arrived on the bus unarmed for a reason. I could make a more dramatic entrance—an unmarked SUV, federal plates, lights flashing, siren wailing—

and it might make you feel better about me, but it also might cost your husband his life. There is a way this all works, and I will explain it to you in the morning, but kidnappers sleep too, so for now, you should too, and we will start afresh tomorrow."

And with that, he said good night.

SIX

The Train Car

OSCAR AND NORMA

Despite just a few hours' sleep, we were all up early, Raul included. On his advice, I decided to keep the kids home from school for the rest of the week. I think I told them something vague—there was a problem at the school, class had been canceled. Cielo and Leti kept Vera home as well, so it wouldn't seem unnatural. I got good at giving short answers and then distracting them with something fun they could do with one of the housekeepers while I did what I had to do. Once my mom arrived, they were thrilled to see her and it was a huge distraction.

There was no word yet from the kidnappers. As the employees arrived, I was reminded that all of them had been taken in for questioning. They were normally very chatty in the mornings and joked and gossiped while they worked, but today there was silence, broken only by an occasional whisper. Raul joined us all at the breakfast table. I introduced him as someone who was helping me for a few days. The children each greeted him in turn, as is the custom in

Mexico: Fernando shook his hand, as did Emiliano, followed by a big hug, and Nayah gave him a big hug followed by a kiss on the cheek. This is expected of children toward invited guests in the home, which Raul was, as far as they could tell. Mexico is funny, in that it's full of friendliness and customs to reinforce it, superficial hugs and kisses, and yet it's hard to find someone you can really trust. Nayah also had a lot of questions for him: Who was he? Where did he come from? What was he doing there? He told her they would have plenty of time to talk later, but right now he needed to talk to Mommy. He seemed from the start to take a protective interest in the kids. Later, I saw him speaking confidentially with Fernando, trying to explain as much as he could, in language that a twelve-year-old could understand.

Raul asked me where he could set up a command station—a place where employees could not see his computer screen. Perhaps it was my father's intelligence training, but he was very particular about where he sat in a restaurant or other public space, with his back to the wall and a clear line of sight to the entrance and exit. Eduardo's father was the same way, and we instinctively practiced that as a family. When I showed Raul to a chair at the end of the dining room table with a bird's-eye view of the foyer and all our comings and goings, his look to me indicated we were on the same wavelength. We made a makeshift situation room out of the planned master bedroom suite we hadn't finished building yet—detached from the main house across a courtyard that served as an outdoor hallway, one of the luxuries of Mexico's year-round perfect weather—and that we could seal up tight like a Cone of Silence. We had it custom built, and I never even used it outside of as a situation room during those few months. Most of the time, I slept in Nayah's room.

Raul impressed upon me the need to decide on my "inner circle"—my trusted allies who would be involved in making decisions. From now on, we would only discuss sensitive matters inside that room, and no information could leave the circle. Kidnappers often got their intelligence from informants on the inside, usually a trusted employee. Any breach of security could put Eduardo in danger. I quickly designated Cielo and his wife, Leti; Alonso; Eduardo's sister Lupe; and my mom as members of my brain trust. They weren't the only people I trusted, but they were the only ones I would share certain things with—namely, the details of my negotiations with whoever was behind this and any decision that resulted from them. As a matter of expediency, I kept my mother out of most of the decisions because I wanted her to be upbeat for the kids' sake. If she had known the details of what was going on, it would have drained her. Lupe and Alonso couldn't be around all the time, so I shielded them from the bulk of it after a couple of days. Over time the circle got smaller, until eventually it was just a circle of one.

I told Raul that I was very concerned about our finances, as Eduardo's signature was required to access our money; without that, I would be able to come up with very little. He told me these negotiations were always based on the victim's ability to pay—that's why it was a negotiation and not a demand. As far as I was concerned, they could have it all—cars, jewelry, watches. Whatever they wanted. I considered us "ranch poor"—what money we had was largely tied up in real estate investments. But you can't put a building or a piece of land in a duffel bag and send it down a dark alley, especially when it's not in your name. Whatever I could put my hands on, they were welcome to it. As Raul was preparing to address the members of the inner circle, my mom arrived. I was so incredibly relieved to see her. As we hugged, she cried, I cried, and then I pulled myself together. I immediately put her to work and asked her to stay with the children while we listened to what Raul had to say.

Raul's presentation was very professional and very thorough. He walked all of us—Cielo, Leti, Alonso, Lupe, and myself—through the many types of kidnappings, a kind of Kidnapping 101. There were countless kidnapping rings in Mexico, some more feared than others. There were drug gangs who had expanded into the kidnapping racket as a natural offshoot of rival warfare and strategic assassination. There were express kidnappings, where prompt payment guaranteed you expedited service. Some gangs were organized, some not so much. Some were professional; some were unbelievably amateur. There were kidnapping rings that routinely cut off fingers and ears, and there were rings that collected the ransom and then killed their victims anyway. Some started out planning to return their victim until their appearance or identity was accidentally compromised, and then they killed their abductee just to be on the safe side. This last category was becoming more and more common.

But at the top of the food chain was something commonly referred to within law-enforcement circles as *secuestros de alto impacto,* or high-impact kidnappings. These were sometimes politically motivated and almost always involved millions of dollars. They were performed by highly professional groups with complex infrastructures built of discrete cells and many moving parts. Their planning and resources meant they could hold their victims for a longer period of time without fear of getting caught. The good news, if that's what we were dealing with, was that they typically treated their victims better. They were professionals, and their behavior was designed to produce an optimal outcome for all parties. The bad news was that they rarely settled for smaller amounts of money (i.e., less than $1 million) and they held their victims for extended periods of time, usually months or even years. If you paid quickly, they merely upped their ransom demands. The fact that there had been numerous vehicles involved, a half dozen men, expensive guns, precision timing, a detailed plan, props, signs, nice clothes, and expensive cologne—all pointed to a well-oiled criminal enterprise with plenty of experience. One such ring that Raul highlighted as operating here in Mexico was similar to the FARC in Colombia: It was politically motivated and raised money for its progressive causes by kidnapping wealthy businessmen. It all sounded pretty far-fetched to me.

Raul also said that on occasion what might at first appear to be kidnappings were really acts of revenge, where the victims were later found dead or "in pretty bad shape," or else never found at all. For this reason, we needed to check all of the newspapers on a daily basis and call the local hospitals and morgue for any John Does who may have come in. Kidnappers also used the daily newspaper to communicate with the families through classified ads or to publish "proof of life" photos, guaranteeing that loved ones were still alive. Coco stopped off and bought all the papers every morning and I went through them carefully, and I called all the hospitals and the morgue. I was like a sponge, soaking up every bit of wisdom Raul imparted and brainstorming how to put it into practice.

He explained to us how the negotiation process would work. He attached a small recording device to the phone and asked Tina to answer the phone each time, to give us time to start taping if it were the kidnappers. He asked me to buy a whiteboard and markers and a new cell phone, which was something the kidnappers typically required. He explained that all negotiations would take place directly between the kidnappers and myself; he couldn't act on my behalf, even if the kidnappers would allow it. In Mexico, that is specifically prohibited by law—it opens authorities to all sorts of liabilities if negotiations are unsuccessful and, in an environment like Mexico, would only breed more corruption. He promised he would coach and support me every step of the way, based on his considerable experience in these situations. But all decisions ultimately would be mine.

Then he asked us questions: Did Eduardo have any enemies? What were his politics like? Could I think of anyone who might have anything against him?

Eduardo has a strong moral compass and is not shy about standing up for what he thinks is right, regardless of the consequences. For instance, he is genuinely not class conscious, in a country where the classes don't really mix—even in San Miguel, which is more casual than almost anywhere else in the country. He would occasionally be taken aside by some weekend neighbor out managing his expensive horses who claimed to have Eduardo's best interests in mind, who warned him against having a beer with the stable hands or something—how it wouldn't look right in polite society or how he could jeopardize his standing in the community. It was ridiculous. And he wasn't afraid to challenge those who crossed him or behaved inappropriately, in a way that many people of his background would find appalling. I remember one time some drunks mistakenly drove onto our property and backed over some construction materials trying to turn around. They were really too drunk to drive, and Eduardo ran out there with his shotgun and physically pulled them out of their car, demanding they come back when they had sobered up. That time, our night watchman quit, because he was convinced they were going to come back with guns to get even. Eduardo isn't confrontational necessarily—it's more like he's unfiltered—but he does have a strong sense of right and wrong, and occasionally he takes matters into his own hands.

This boldness carried over into his politics. Although he wasn't active in any political party, Eduardo often supported candidates he liked, many of whom were our friends. He had recently endorsed the mayor in his successful election bid, and he actively campaigned for our good friend Luis Alberto Villarreal Garcia, now a senator from Guanajuato (and Emiliano's godfather). But he ruffled a lot of feathers by taking the side of those without a voice. He even managed to anger the former president of Mexico, Luis Echeverria, a political rival of his father, by blowing the whistle on some of his wrongdoings, including secretly investing in the news service UPI, which made international headlines and cost him a lot of money.

And then his TV show, *Contrastes*, was like a local *60 Minutes* every week, and it made him enemies too numerous to count. A live weekly talk show that lasted between sixty and ninety minutes, it was cohosted by Eduardo and Lucy Nuñez de Zavala, the niece of Manuel Avila Camacho, the former president of Mexico and now the mayor of San Miguel de Allende. People could call in and ask questions or comment, and they talked about whatever was the topic of concern in town at the moment. They picked on the previous mayor, Jesus Correa, quite a bit, as well as anyone who superficially appeared corrupt—and the aggrieved parties often showed up at the station to defend themselves, making for compelling television. One time they exposed the local slaughterhouse for letting blood-contaminated water drain next to government housing, collecting in large stagnant pools. Another time, he and I took on the local director of ecology in a live debate over the municipal trash dump that was burning out of control, making people sick. Eventually, the dump was upgraded and the governor of Guanajuato came to inaugurate it. In his speech, he formally acknowledged Eduardo's efforts on behalf of the community. The show was enormously popular; people loved him and stopped him on the street to thank him.

Eduardo never took a salary for the show, and he wasn't interested in a career in politics. He just finds it impossible not to stick up for the underdog—especially if it's the government or powerful special interests they're up against. He routinely called bureaucrats "thieves with licenses." In a place like Mexico, as you can imagine, this keeps him busy.

In the months leading up to the kidnapping, the local station had been featuring his name prominently in radio and TV commercials, and I thought it was focusing unnecessary attention on him. At one point, he even mentioned the name of our ranch on the air. I loved for him to try and help people of limited means, but not by putting our family at risk by exposing where we lived. (When I brought it up with him, he told me I was being paranoid and that nothing was going to happen to us, although he was careful not to do it again.)

But really, the only person I could think of who hated us enough to want to see us punished was Oscar, whom we were in a property dispute with. I kept thinking back to something a friend of ours had said, a wealthy businessman with his ear to the ground. We were having lunch one day, and Eduardo was recounting the latest in his struggle with Oscar over the train car.

"You need to really watch it," our friend said. "You do not want to rub him the wrong way. He's capable of anything. He's very dangerous."

Oscar Carlos Gutierrez del Bosque—who was usually just called Oscar Carlos—and his wife, Norma Izquierdo del Bosque, hail from Torreón, a city in the north central state of Coahuila about 250 miles south of the Texas border. Oscar was a real estate developer and powerful figure. I think Oscar's wife was the brains of the operation. She is a trained lawyer with an impressive understanding of the Mexican legal system. She even has two brothers who were onetime AFI agents—a coincidence the AFI assured me they would investigate thoroughly.

Oscar showed up in San Miguel de Allende in 2004 with plans to build a multimillion-dollar golf resort and gated community on land adjacent to our ranch. At one point, he even brought golf legend Jack Nicklaus here in a helicopter to promote the deal—and presumably impress potential investors. He was thick, broad-shouldered, flashy, with an ostentatious Rolex watch and icy blue eyes, and I distrusted him from the first time I laid eyes on him. Norma had an intense, almost savage gaze. They gave me the willies. We first met them through Aldo Perez, a local who parlayed an Ivy League education into a sizable fortune selling software to the U.S. government. He became partners with Oscar on a previous development in Torreón, one that predictably ended in recriminations and lawsuits much later. But at that stage, no one seemed to know too much about either of them. On occasion, Oscar billed himself as a yoga instructor and his wife as a kindergarten teacher.

They would do things like set up a meeting, which their assistants would call to confirm—"They'll be arriving by helicopter"—and then they'd fail to show up. They seemed extremely sketchy, and they tried way too hard to impress us. Eduardo and I even argued about it several times. I didn't want to sell to them, even though we needed the money; frankly, I didn't want them as neighbors. But Eduardo's position was, we've just got to be careful when we're dealing with them. We went to the grand opening of Los Azulejos, the resort they'd built in Torreón, and it was impressive.

Then that deal fell through, and they disappeared. Eighteen months later, they showed up back in San Miguel de Allende with new partners and a new plan for a high-end golf resort. By now, we had sold the land they'd had their eye on to Richard Leet, an American businessman from Detroit with an electronics fortune; he had retired to San Miguel and was a good friend of ours. He built an actual castle, called Los Huizaches, named after a tough indigenous tree similar to the mesquite, that was visible from the roof of my mother's house, and he had a private plane that he kept at the airport in Queretaro. They said they would buy the remainder of the land they had originally wanted— a field of cactus, basically—and asked if we would connect them with Richard Leet. We did. We also warned Leet at that time that any deal had to be handled with care. Then we made sure our banker was present at the closing, and we structured the deal so that the deed would only be transferred once the funds had cleared. Because we saw them coming, we got our money. Others were not so lucky.

Soon enough, Oscar and Richard Leet became best of friends; Leet was going to invest in the golf resort, Oscar was going to buy his castle, and Leet was going to build a second castle called Los Pirules—named for an indigenous Mexican pepper tree much like a weeping willow—which he quickly broke ground on. During a party to celebrate their good fortune—the theme was "Adios, Los Huizaches"—with spirits flowing and no doubt mariachis playing, Leet signed a good-faith agreement without benefit of due diligence, which it's doubtful he understood, as it was in Spanish. There was even videotape of Leet handing over the keys to the castle—which Oscar relied on heavily at his trial after Leet sued him.

Within a matter of days, a dozen of Oscar's bodyguards showed up in pickups and seized control of the land, literally removing Leet from the property by force. He had to leave behind his personal items, furniture, millions of dollars of artwork—everything. Neighbors later saw everything being hauled away on flatbed trucks.

Leet filed suit employing as his lawyers our friends and lawyers Iñaki Garcia Gioricelaya and his partner and nephew Ricardo Villarreal, Luis's little brother, who appeared regularly on Eduardo's TV show as a conservative commentator. Iñaki was equally well connected—his father had been a Supreme Court Justice. Oscar's ability to prevail in the courts at last failed him, and he was sentenced to six months in prison. Norma was arrested as well but was released after several days. Since there was a check made out from Oscar to us, we were forced to testify in court, which cleared us of any wrongdoing, and were almost subject to undergo a federal audit, which all together created unnecessary tension in the months leading up to Eduardo's medical problems and subsequent depression. Later, drinking with Eduardo, Oscar's brother observed, "Here's my brother, buying a Rolls-Royce"—referring to the luxury resort—"and he can't even afford to put gas in it." Richard Leet lost Los Pirules to creditors and left the country.

The property that Oscar took possession of abutted our land across the highway. This was where we housed the railroad car, which Oscar subsequently offered to buy from us. Eduardo refused, calling it a family heirloom. In response, Oscar posted armed guards and refused to let us back on the property. When Eduardo went to confront him about it, Oscar claimed that Leet had defrauded him and all would be resolved in the upcoming trial; he asked us to be patient. His reasoning came bundled in an implicit threat. "Look, you should be happy that I have control [over the railcar] with my bodyguards," he told Eduardo, "because there are undesirables in the area, and they could easily break into the train and destroy its contents."

This standoff played out over the next two years, coinciding with my cancer diagnosis and subsequent treatment in the States, and so Eduardo was forced to pick his battles and table this one for the time being. I knew from my experience in real estate that possession is often ninetenths of the law and felt that Oscar was merely running out the clock on any statute of limitations. Eventually, after giving them ample warning, Eduardo filed a lawsuit against Oscar.

Eduardo even went to see him in jail at one point. In clear, measured tones, he assured Oscar that he bore him no animosity, that he only wished to be compensated for the damage to the train car and our legal fees, and that if those terms were met, he would personally do what he could to expedite Oscar's release. He said that Oscar seemed very low and depressed, and so he intentionally framed all his arguments in a positive light: Why would anyone—especially a father—wish to spend another day in jail, especially over something so silly? He continually emphasized that this could all be over with tomorrow. Of course, once their jailhouse face-off entered the rumor mill, it became common knowledge that Eduardo had gone and taunted this proud and powerless man, pushed him past the breaking point, leading inexorably to this tragedy that had befallen us.

As if to seal the connection in the public's mind, even as he sought to mine it for sympathy, Oscar released a mass e-mail mere hours after the kidnapping, a wild tirade accusing us, Richard Leet, and others of conspiring to unlawfully imprison him. The subject line was "Secuestrado en Guanajuato" ("Kidnapped in Guanajuato"). Only Oscar cast himself in the role of the beleaguered everyman whose life was unjustly stolen from him. Addressed to Richard Leet, the message read in part:

> RICHARD BERNARD LEET, search for your own inner peace and tranquillity, and don't ask EDUARDO GARCIA VALSECA and his wife to support you with their lies, by claiming that on July 4, 2004, you celebrated U.S. independence at the Pullman train car. Richard, do not place Eduardo Valseca and his wife in jeopardy, nor take from them their own peace and tranquillity. Do not live in dread by failing God; don't lie, don't slander, don't hurt innocent children. You cannot keep acting as if possessed by Satan . . . The government is corrupt and rotten. [THIS JUDGE], bought by your lawyers with your dirty money, will keep harming and kidnapping innocent people unless you go to San Miguel de Allende and admit your mistakes, or at least withdraw your accusations, and Eduardo Garcia Valseca and his wife do the same. Don't follow Satan's plan, because God is bigger than us all.

The e-mail was addressed to a broad cross-section of local Americans and Europeans, as if he just took the local foreigner's telephone guide, called *Juarde* ("Who are they?"—get it?), and bulk-copied the addresses, in an effort to blanket the expatriate community. I saw it on Thursday and passed it on to Raul as soon as I read it, and he dutifully copied it up the chain. People forwarded it to us for the next six months. Iñaki told us he had seen Oscar being interviewed on television the Monday before the kidnapping using identical language: *secuestrado en la cárcel de San Miguel*. I tracked down the videotape, but it's now in the possession of the AFI.

Sitting in prison, watching others move ahead with their own resort development on the same stretch of highway he had identified first—perhaps even catching wind of our Cal Wimberley deal, Oscar's intended empire slowly seeping into our pockets—it's easy to imagine how Oscar might have twisted his mind into a spring-loaded trap bent on revenge. Even if he didn't finance and orchestrate an elaborate military-style campaign against us costing hundreds of thousands of dollars, he conceivably could have tapped one of his putative connections to the underworld to single out Eduardo as a prospective victim. You don't have to be Othello to exact revenge; you just have to be Iago.

Although Raul listened carefully and intensely when I presented my Oscar and Norma theory, I could tell he didn't think that they had anything to do with it. But he remained professionally neutral.

"We will look at all possibilities," he said. "We will leave no stone unturned."

SEVEN

The Message

FIRST CONTACT

After everyone had gotten over the initial shock, people
started showing up at the ranch to see me—most offering to
help, but others who just came out of the woodwork. Some
brought flowers, platters of food, or treats for the kids. A lot
of people didn't want to tie up the phone, in case the kidnappers were trying to call. Some had tidbits of information
they were convinced could aid the authorities, and much of
this had been inflamed by their imaginations running wild.
One gentleman saw the same cars we did, having happened
along right after the kidnapping, and was convinced the license plates were all from the state of Coahuila. Several of
these vehicles had been abandoned and left behind, and I
knew for a fact that they weren't, but that was no match for
the zealousness of those who were determined to help. Virtually everyone had a theory: It was Oscar; somebody said
he'd used men from Durango. Others were certain it was
one of the targets of Eduardo's TV show. Our architect
friend Alan Wilkerson's brother Tony was sure that Eduardo

had been spirited away in a plane. (He later said he saw a private plane take off from the local airstrip hours after the kidnapping but admitted it could have been anyone—including anyone with a private plane who was freaked out by the first local high-impact kidnapping.) I followed up on every lead.

The teachers from the school came by and offered their support in any way. Milou, our next-door neighbor, brought over roses. Eduardo's daughter Aurora and her boyfriend came from Veracruz. (She had moved away in 2000 after her divorce.) The whole Villarreal family came by one at a time—Luis was on vacation in Spain, but he sent his relatives instead. Tom the Texan, a genuine Texas cowboy who had given me riding lessons, told me, "Back home, we just go in and git 'em." Martin Peña came by and told me it was probably the same people who had kidnapped his sister years ago in León, then proceeded to tell me the whole very long story, which in the end wasn't really a kidnapping at all. (It ended up being some sort of revenge scenario in Guadalajara combined with extortion where the victim ultimately escaped owing to the ineptitude of the assailants and had nothing to do with our situation.) There was even a woman to whom Eduardo had promised to help sell her antique terra-cotta roof tiles to someone he knew in construction. She actually came into the house and started to march up to my bedroom when Cielo stopped her and kicked her out. During all of this Los Charcos was still a fully operating ranch with employees coming in and out. There was no way to effectively monitor who was coming and going. She called me relentlessly to see if I could help her sell her stupid tiles. I know she was desperate, but it was too much.

The phone rang nonstop. Our banker called and said he'd come by to see me as soon as he could. We heard from my mother's good friends, Mary Jordan and Kevin Sullivan, Pulitzer Prize–winning ex-bureau chiefs of the *Washington Post* in Mexico City, now living in London, who had contacted then U.S. ambassador to Mexico Tony Garza and Arturo Sarukhán, now the Mexican ambassador to the United States. In quick succession I heard from Noah Seltzer (not his real name), the FBI's legal attaché at the embassy; the U.S. consul; and high-level officials in the Mexican government. Seltzer basically told me there was nothing they could do if the AFI didn't formally solicit their help, as Eduardo was a Mexican citizen and Mexico was out of their jurisdiction. I reminded him that I was an American citizen and had also been kidnapped, albeit for fifteen minutes. I was currently being extorted, and my extortionists were using a U.S.-based Yahoo! e-mail account. At one point, I even put him on the phone with Raul, who was obviously very uncomfortable with this breach of protocol. Afterward, Raul told me that if the FBI were needed, his superiors would surely contact them. He also stressed, as diplomatically as he could, that at any time I could change my mind and go with a private company, at which point they would immediately retire from the case. I had the sense it was a matter of unspoken national pride.

(I would come to hear many times that there is a lot of gray area in these matters, and the AFI makes that kind of decision on a case-by-case basis, yet every time I would penetrate the FBI chain of command thanks to some random contact I generated, I was told I had to go through Noah Seltzer in the U.S. embassy. From the first time I heard his name I started to call him on a regular basis, and eventually it was almost as if he was doing me a favor by taking the call. He told me, "We're keeping tabs, and we're occasionally calling the AFI people, and they seem to be doing what they're supposed to be doing, and there's nothing we can do about it." That got really frustrating. Meanwhile, I'd tell the AFI that I wanted the FBI on board—I was an American citizen, and the FBI had a proven track record—but they'd just say, "We don't need them right now. The technology they have we can't use here because we don't have the infrastructure." They even told me they were tracing the e-mails, but that it would take twenty minutes, by which time the sender would be long gone. This is patently wrong: According to international security consultants I've spoken with since in the United States, they could have determined the point of origin instantaneously. It's doubtful whoever sent the messages knew their content or where Eduardo was being held, but that's true of almost any criminal enterprise: You start with the people at the bottom you can get to and leverage them for others up the chain. Even I know that, just from watching television.)

My brother, John, a webmaster for large communications companies, also managed to reach several high-level FBI officials, which at least served to put me on their radar. He offered to cash in his retirement account if it would help me. He even found a consultant online who just happened to be in San Miguel de Allende on vacation. The man said he was ex-FBI and an expert in kidnap negotiation. John saw it as an omen and told him where the ranch was, and he actually showed up at our gate. I didn't answer, but later he sent me an e-mail saying that he would be glad to help me for free as long as I paid for his meals and hotel bill while he was in San Miguel.

Some journalist friends had also contacted a man they knew at Control Risks, a London-based independent security agency primarily used by corporations. He called and said his starting rate was thirty-five hundred dollars a day plus expenses and travel. Even so, he was very generous with his time and knowledge over the phone and told me he would be available when I needed advice, as time permitted. He gave me the details of a similar case in Mexico in which Control Risks was unable to achieve closure, which was subsequently handed over to Benito Roa, the AFI's director of its kidnapping division, and ended with the successful release of the victim. With the nature of the crime and given my circumstances, he assured me I could not be in more capable hands. (I had heard the same thing after the fact from a cousin who worked for Crucible, a division of Kroll Associates, the other industry leader.) That made me feel good about the choices we had made.

Arturo, my patron saint—the man who sold us grapes on the train car—called every day until I got back to him. Sometimes he would show up at the front gate unannounced and ring the bell—he was afraid of the dogs. He always had simple, practical advice for me: "You should send the kids to the U.S. and leave them with your mother; it's unsafe here." "Don't leave the house, Jayne—there are very bad people, they could be watching you. Be very careful." His eyes welled up with tears when he would impart this wisdom; I'd never seen him this way before. He told me that his mother and he prayed nightly to St. Anthony—"San Antonio," the finder of lost things—for Eduardo to come home safely. They had absolute faith this would work, and their confidence never wavered.

Our lawyer friend Iñaki called midmorning and said he needed to come to the ranch to see me, because the phones were not safe to use. (Raul had already told me the AFI had bugged the phones and all my conversations were being monitored.) He arrived an hour later in a car that wasn't his, looking disheveled and slightly frantic. Iñaki usually resembled a Ken doll; his hair and clothing were always immaculate, and he traded on his thousand-dollar Colgate smile. Today, he was pale and visibly shaken. He asked to talk to Cielo, Raul, and me privately, and we sequestered ourselves in the situation room.

Iñaki was in touch regularly with Aldo Perez, Oscar and Norma's former business partner. Like Leet and the others, Aldo was finding it impossible to bring Oscar to justice, even after Oscar was sent to jail and even with Aldo's huge fortune to pay lawyers. Through the course of hiring private detectives, Aldo had discovered that Oscar had a cell phone inside the San Miguel jail with three separate SIM cards. Then on June 10, the Sunday before the kidnapping, Iñaki's uncle's apartment was broken into. The apartment is located right next to Iñaki's law offices, and Telmex, the Mexican phone company, had accidentally installed the phone in Iñaki's name. Someone broke in, looked through closets and cabinets, and then left without taking anything. Iñaki saw the two incidents as related and interpreted it as a direct threat. He sent his wife and two children to stay in the States where they would be safe; he was driving a borrowed car and he no longer went to his house. His partner, Ricardo Villarreal, had also stopped driving his own car, so as not to be so easily recognized. Everyone was panicking, thinking they would be next.

Lucy and her husband, Javier, also stopped by. She told us that a woman had called the TV station recently, preferring to talk with her rather than the local police, whom she felt couldn't be trusted. She lived in El Nigromante, and for weeks she had been watching a house where the inhabitants were all men; there were never any women and lots of SUVs, all with Queretaro or Mexico City plates. Lucy had been trying to decide what to do with this information when Eduardo was kidnapped, and she hoped it might help. Raul sent it in as a *tarjeta*, his term for information he sent over the wire to his superiors in Mexico City. There would be lots of these before we were through.

Lucy told me that a cameraman at the station who worked during the day as a prison guard had observed Oscar becoming progressively more and more agitated. Guards had to pull him off of one of his own lawyers after he physically attacked him. She also confirmed that Oscar was caught with an illegal cell phone, which seems to have been the worst-kept secret in San Miguel. Raul promised to follow up, and we made a note to look into that further. She also reported that a group of Tibetan monks affiliated with the Dalai Lama were visiting San Miguel and, after hearing about our plight, had offered to come pray with the family. Prayer of any kind sounded good right now, and I asked her to accept on our behalf.

In the days ahead, I would call several psychics, one of whom I had seen on the Discovery Channel. I found meditation impossible, with this river of thoughts coursing through my mind, but my friend Judith sent over a shaman and healer named Greywolf who offered me a prayer of enlightenment—intended for the kidnappers. I made an altar to Eduardo where I could light incense, stare at his picture, and recite the prayer when it all got to be too much. It had a lovely Spanish colonial cross, an old rosary, some beads I got from the Lacandon Indians in Chiapas, some candles, the Virgin of Guadalupe, a small Buddha and some incense, along with pictures of Eduardo. (The boys later made their own tiny altars and would talk to Eduardo every night before they went to sleep.) Another friend named Celena came and did an "angel healing," which amounted to a long spoken prayer. I was open to it all—shamans, mystics, psychics, angels. At this point, I was ruling nothing out.

Later on, while I was sitting at my altar, frustrated that I couldn't meditate, I exhaled sharply and it came out as a growl. It made me feel much better, and there was no one else around, so I kept doing it. I felt like a wolf. During my chemotherapy, I had visualized myself as a fairy with a magic wand, and I would go into my body and wipe away the cancer, little by little, until it was all gone. Now I became a female wolf, stalking the grounds to protect my family. Then I imagined my whole family as my wolf pack, and we were hunting the men who had Eduardo. We surrounded them, growled, bared our teeth—it was exhilarating. I even put a picture of a wolf on the altar as my private totem. When the kids saw it, they wanted to know what it was all about, and once I explained it, they wanted their

own pictures of wolves. We even added wolf photos for
Cielo, Leti, and Vera. They loved to visualize alongside me;
it was like a role-playing game where we got to turn the
tables on our aggressors.

In the afternoon of the second day, Raul asked me to
take him to the scene of the crime. He wanted me to retrace
my footsteps and walk him through it all, step by step, from
the time we left the house until I was abandoned on the side
of the road. It felt so terrifying to me to even get back in a
car. I asked Raul if he knew how to use a gun. He did. I
asked him if I could furnish him with one, and he accepted.
He also wanted to know if we had any guns for ourselves. I
wasn't entirely honest. I could tell he was uncomfortable with the idea of us having loaded guns in the house.
Too bad.

We went through the whole reenactment, frame by frame.
It was very hard for me; my mind was full of clashing images, too many to recount, like reflections in a broken mirror. There was dried blood on the ground where I had cut
my hand and more blood where Eduardo was pulled from
the Jeep and struck with a gun butt. There was lots of broken glass scattered on the cobblestones and swept onto the
shoulder by passing traffic. He showed me where they had
set out orange cones and detour signs to divert any other
cars. They used seven vehicles in total, all of which were
left behind except for the one they drove off in—all of them
purchased secondhand with cash in an untraceable manner.
The action was carried out with military-style precision,
with every angle covered beforehand. He said it was very
likely they had staked us out for months.

The drive back from the school had taken no more than
a minute, and then another minute to trundle us into the car.
It was another ten minutes to where they abandoned me, and
everyone I saw during that time prior to having the pillowcase put over my head—the man in the Ford KA, the one in
the blue pickup, the three in the Yukon, and the one in the

truck behind us—had worn baseball caps or fishing hats, hunting vests, and glasses or sunglasses; they were all light-skinned, clean-shaven, well dressed, perfectly manicured, and smelled of good cologne. Their alikeness served as a uniform; it was designed to make them interchangeable, so that it was difficult to identify any one of them.

The entire weekend following the kidnapping, I checked the e-mail every fifteen minutes, but there was nothing. Sunday was Father's Day, which brought with it a whole new set of problems. The kids had made Eduardo cards at school, so I had to explain that Daddy would be home as soon as I could make that happen, and I would hold on to them in a special place so we could give them to him when he got back. And not only the younger kids—having Eduardo away for Father's Day was very hard on Cielo as well. In the afternoon, Dr. Bev stopped by to try and help me explain to the younger ones why our life was in disarray. She basically just held my hand while I explained that their daddy was away but not on the kind of trip they might imagine.

I explained the concept of people taking things that don't belong to them because they didn't come from a loving family like ours and they didn't understand about love. I told them that there were actually people, really mean people, who stole other people for money. This was called kidnapping, and it's what had happened to Daddy. I told them that I was going to get him back, and that was why Raul was staying with us. Of course, this was very difficult for them to grasp. Dr. Bev helped me formulate my arguments beforehand and gently edged me toward an explanation that the kids would be able to understand. More than anything, she provided me with moral support, which in the end was no small thing. She worked at her office with Fernando, who was holding on to a lot of guilt because he felt he could have somehow stopped it all from happening. She also found me a wonderful therapist who used art and games to defuse trauma and who came by the house every Saturday morning to work with Nayah and Emiliano while Eduardo was in captivity.

As the days, weeks, and eventually months went by, the children's questions would change. At first, it was the obvious: When is he coming back? Why did they take my daddy? Who would have done this to him? Why are they so mean? Father's Day was the first signpost they had by which to compare this with their previous experience, and so it inspired a new round of questions: Who is he spending Father's Day with? Why can't we be with him? All of the other children have their daddies on Father's Day; why can't we have ours? Over time, as the days settled back down into a routine, the routine itself was made new by his absence: Are they feeding him? Do they give him foods he likes or yucky food? Can he use the bathroom? Where does he sleep? Does he have clean clothes? Where does he bathe? Who does he talk to? Birthdays and holidays were the worst, because they could see him in their memories going through the motions. That always brought the pain back into sharper focus: Are they mean to him? Are they hurting him? Why are they so mean? What did we do to make them do this? They started to have bad dreams. It was extraordinarily difficult for them to understand how anyone could put a family through this. They could not understand this kind of cruelty. At one point, obviously having overheard us talking, Emiliano gave me his piggy bank and told me to immediately give it all to whoever was holding Eduardo.

I wanted to say something to comfort them, so I usually followed up with, "I'm sure these people aren't very nice, but Daddy is a very smart, very strong man and he's good at making friends, so maybe he's talking a lot to them. I also know that what they want is money, so I imagine they are going to take care of Daddy or else they won't get any money from Mommy. And Mommy and everyone else is working very hard to get Daddy back as soon as we can." I also explained to them that in the ads we were running to communicate with the kidnappers, I was asking them to take good care of him please, which was true. I never shared anything more with them. I knew that if and when Eduardo made it home, we would have a chance to talk about everything that happened. He would be home, so no matter how horrible it was, it would already be part of the past.

On Monday, the kids went back to school for the first time since this whole thing began. Raul said they'd be all right, since the last place in the world the kidnappers were going to come was here. Just in case, I asked the mayor's office to provide police protection at the school, which it was happy to do—less for us than for the school and the other kids. Raul asked if he could tag along with Cielo and me. He acted like he was really excited, but I think he was really just there to protect us. Whenever he was out in public with us, Raul made every effort to blend in, and he acted like he was our driver. If anyone ever asked who he was, I was to say that he was a friend of the family, in from Mexico City to stay with me until the kidnapping was over. No one ever pushed it, but they had to know that he was probably a bodyguard. That was our fallback. When I was asked if I was being supported in any way, I said that I had a good support system and that I was negotiating as best as I could. In that way, he was free to move among us as he needed.

That Monday, the kids were in a school play, followed by an afternoon concert—Emiliano was performing in *The Golden Goose*, a singing part. I took a video camera so I could hide behind it and wouldn't have to talk to anyone. I was done with being a public spectacle. Everyone kept staring at the bandage on my hand. After the play was over, we went out onto the playground while we waited for the concert to begin. While we were talking, Leti reached Cielo on his cell phone. An e-mail had arrived from the kidnappers—

it came in a zip file with a password that only I would know. We rushed home, just in time to find the Internet completely out—a common occurrence in Mexico but one whose timing could not have been worse. In desperation, we raced to Cielo's apartment in town, which he had only visited once to pick up some clothes since he and his family had moved into our house a week before, following the kidnapping. As I sat in front of the computer, I was shaking so much I thought I'd pass out. (Although these service blackouts were a frequent occurrence, I eventually got the cell phone number of the owner of the local Internet provider, called Unisono, and used to call him at all hours. He would come out to the house himself at times to repair my Internet connection or loan me special equipment.)

The message opened on a riddle, the password to the encryption:

> In what geographic location did Jayne and Eduardo meet (state)?

I felt violated. The day and place that we met had always seemed so special to us. We didn't celebrate our wedding anniversary the way most married couples do; we celebrated the anniversary of the day we met. Now it would have a sinister connotation as well.

"Maryland."

The message inside read as follows:

> We hope you got home okay.
>
> For Eduardo's liberation we demand $8 million U.S.
>
> All communications will take place in the following way: We will write you by e-mail, and you will respond by placing ads in the newspapers that we designate.
>
> Every message will have a password. If there is no password, the message will not be from us. Don't respond to this e-mail; we will not receive it.

ALL AMOUNTS must be in dollars.

Confirm by publishing the following ad in the want-ads section of El Universal newspaper on June 20, 21, and 22, in the Animals and Pets section:

Buy chow chow dog, Austin, vaccinated, with complete pedigree. 8,000 pesos. Tel. XXX-XX-XX.

Raul explained that eight thousand pesos meant eight million dollars.

I wanted to cry, but I couldn't. I've never felt so helpless. Eight million dollars! How was I going to come up with eight million dollars?

I asked Raul what we were going to do. I didn't have that kind of money; what I even had access to was nowhere near that range.

"Jayne, calm down," Raul said. "This is why I'm here. This is a negotiation. Whatever your economic reality, we will communicate that to the kidnappers. They have to know that you won't be paying eight million dollars. That's what they hope to get. But they know we'll negotiate." He called his superiors in Mexico City and forwarded the message to them. We headed back to the ranch, where our local Internet provider had one of their employees up on a ladder trying to improve our service. They would make dozens of visits to the ranch over the next few months. Having a decent Internet connection had now become a matter of life or death.

But that wasn't the last surprise of the day. According to Raul, AFI director Benito Roa himself would be paying us a visit at the ranch tomorrow.

EIGHT

The Hammer

EPR

The morning felt like an eternity. Even Raul looked nervous, which was setting the rest of us on edge. Benito Roa Lara, the AFI's celebrated director of the kidnapping division, finally called from his SUV. He was at the entrance to the ranch but refused to drive in because there was a truck with two men in it who looked extremely suspicious, recording every car that entered the dirt road that led to our property. At his behest, we called the mayor's office and had them send out local police to ask for identification. The men identified themselves as topographers with the state of Guanajuato doing field research in anticipation of paving our roads. We had been lobbying the government for years to do as much, and it was heartwarming to see that all the recent attention had reminded them. Roa wasn't totally satisfied and turned around in our driveway, aiming his white Ford Excursion in the getaway position.

He exited the car along with his two assistants—one male and one female—dressed in matching navy blue pinstripe suits. Roa himself was dressed casually, the maverick by comparison, and all three were armed and serious. Raul and I escorted them into our makeshift situation room, along with Cielo and Leti. At Roa's request, we closed all the shutters and sent the gardeners away, so that no one might inadvertently hear what he had to say.

He opened his laptop and told us that what he was about to show us was highly confidential; it had not been published in any newspaper, and we would not find it on the Internet. Eduardo had been kidnapped by an organized ring of violent leftist revolutionaries called the EPR, or Ejército Popular Revolucionario (i.e., the Popular Revolutionary Army). No doubt noticing my Castilian-tinged Spanish accent, he compared this group to ETA in Spain, the Basque separatist movement whose bomb-driven terror campaign had been responsible for close to a thousand deaths. Unbeknownst to many of its followers or more sympathetic observers on the left, the EPR finances itself in large part by kidnapping wealthy businessmen who will pay enormous ransoms. It routinely holds its hostages for six months or longer, it's motivated purely by ideology, and it uses its prodigious ransoms to buy explosives and cheap arms along the U.S. border. Although the EPR is dedicated to the overthrow of the Mexican government, its membership is international: ETA operatives fleeing Spanish authorities had found their way into the organization, as had American paramilitary contractors and former Cuban intelligence agents. Many EPR members had received explosives and paramilitary training from the FARC in Colombia, the Marxist-Leninist peasant army opposed to the Colombian ruling elite and U.S. imperialism that has been in existence for over forty years. There were even furtive hints that the group was at least partially funded by Venezuelan president Hugo Chavez, the ideological heir to Fidel Castro, and the emerging bête noire of the U.S. foreign policy establishment in the western hemisphere.

At one point, Roa showed me a computer screen with a list of purported victims' names, none of whom I recognized. Each listing showed the amount of the ransom demanded, the amount eventually paid, details of the kidnapping, and before and after photos—the difference between which was often inconceivable. One victim, Ron Lavender, seventy, a rich Los Angeles native who had lived thirty-five years in Acapulco and ran a successful real estate company catering to expatriate Americans, was kidnapped in 2001 and held in a horse trailer in the jungle in the dead of summer. He was released after three months when his health became precarious. The victim immediately before Eduardo, Nelly Catalina Esper Sulaimán, niece of the former president of the World Boxing Council, was held for twenty months in the state of San Luis Potosi in a small boxlike room lined with black cardboard, allowed to leave only to use the bathroom. Although her family was told that she was raped every day, she was actually treated quite well—her captors even allowed her to watch television. (According to the AFI, like us, she also ran a nonprofit school and de facto charity.) After briefly working with the local police, the family enlisted Control Risks in London to negotiate the initial $25 million ransom. Against the advice of Control Risks, the family reportedly offered to pay nearly the full amount early on, and the ransom was merely raised accordingly. Benito Roa and the AFI took over after a three-month period when negotiations fell off entirely, finally securing her release for approximately $2.5 million in February 2006, after she had been in captivity for a year and eight months.

When the EPR took credit for explosions at some Banamex ATMs in Mexico City six months later, two participants were caught on bank security cameras, identified, and apprehended. They led authorities to a small hut in a rebel stronghold in the mountains of Oaxaca, where an impoverished peasant family stood guard over a package containing bundles of hundred-dollar bills with serial numbers that matched those from Sulaimán's ransom, thus confirming the EPR's involvement. Other victims allegedly had been forced to walk days into the mountains, stopping along the way at designated points to dig up food and other supplies. All of the surveillance photos Roa showed us looked like the guys who grabbed us. I requested a police sketch artist, since I clearly remembered what several of the kidnappers looked like.

The EPR is understandably secretive about this part of its legacy, as it contradicts its public profile as champion of the working class. There are multiple cells of the group known to the AFI operating at the same time, ours being the most vicious. The cell the AFI suspects in our case is selective in its victims, generally targeting one a year—seizing the person in the summer months and releasing him or her sometime around Christmas. One hundred percent of this cell's victims have returned home unharmed, according to the Mexican authorities.

No one seemed to know exactly how large the EPR was or what kind of public support it enjoyed. This was due at least in part to the fact that the AFI had only been in existence for six years. The connection between local police and the criminal element is traditionally seen as porous at best, and those officers discovered to be involved in kidnapping or drug trafficking are merely expelled from the force, leaving them free to join up with their would-be former adversaries. This is why the AFI was designed to control its recruits through every stage of their development, from education to field training to ultimate assignment—shock troops like Raul, just out of the academy, meant to put a public face on the internal war against casual corruption. And so it was only recently that public confidence in a national police force could justify its being called in the event of a kidnapping or other federal crime. Before that, families just negotiated on their own or through pricey consultants.

While this may have gotten their loved ones home intact, it didn't allow the AFI to build up a body of evidence about these groups and their habits.

Roa also confided that the EPR usually leaves a telltale trademark—a pristine hammer, in this case—as a kind of calling card. (There were others, but he wouldn't tell me what.) He emphasized that this was privileged information and a matter of national security and asked me to keep it to myself for now. He assured me that both Genaro Garcia Luna, the nation's top police official, and President Felipe Calderón would be kept apprised of their investigation. He also tried to prepare me for some of what might be in store: The kidnappers would attempt to pressure me with handwritten letters from Eduardo, angry phone calls full of vicious, terrible things, plaintive communiqués telling me or the children good-bye, photos of him naked or beaten, maybe even made up to look like he'd been beaten—anything to push the buttons of his loved ones and expedite the asking price. I had to be prepared for this and to remain strong in the face of it. This could be a very long journey.

We have a saying in Spanish: *Me cayo el veinte* (The coin finally dropped). It refers to the Mexican pay phones, where you have to dial and then drop the coin in the slot to establish a connection. It means "I get it"—I suddenly see what you're saying. Something about this man in my makeshift conference room, coming to my house just to show me his secret spreadsheets and classified photos, the amounts that families like mine had to pay just to remain intact, all displayed matter-of-factly as line-item perversions of some rancid idealism, suddenly impressed on me the seriousness of what I was dealing with. Something I knew in my mind but had been dreading realizing in my heart.

I asked him why this group would have chosen us, when there were so many more attractive targets—that is, far wealthier people—in San Miguel.

"This group has only made one other mistake before," said Roa—citing an Italian man living in Mexico whose fortunes they had overestimated. "This"—meaning Eduardo—"will be their second."

Or perhaps more to the point, why would someone with a progressive, left-wing political agenda, dedicated to the socialist overthrow of the government, target Eduardo, who was a tireless champion of the poor, the powerless, and the disenfranchised and who had such a high-profile position advocating on their behalf? The slightest financial inquiry would have shown that we operated a nonprofit private school, whose enrollment was at least partially funded by scholarships, much of which we had subsidized—either directly or by arranging sponsorship—for students who couldn't afford it otherwise. We were also paying many of the operating expenses and utilities for the school, which would now be severely curtailed by the drastic change in our finances. We weren't Banamex selling out to Citibank, allowing U.S. infiltration of Mexico's financial sector. If there was anybody who practiced a policy of "think globally, act locally," it was us.

In the days that followed, I threw myself into researching this strange new world that had suddenly opened up before me. I spent hours on the Internet—scouring obscure websites, ordering books, corresponding with whoever would entertain my questions. I contacted the name I had at Control Risks, who had encouraged me to follow up with him if he could be of any help. I told him about the first e-mail contact we had received, and about Benito Roa's assurances that we were dealing with a secret rebel army—a conceit that, frankly, I was having a hard time wrapping my brain around. Surprisingly, he found this scenario entirely plausible.

I made a mental checklist of all the people I had known in Mexico who had undergone a similar ordeal. There was the friend of Eduardo's whose daughter had been kidnapped—

he had close friends inside the AFI who confirmed it was an inside job involving an employee and his family. He later hired private investigators to help secure their convictions. Another childhood friend of Eduardo's had been kidnapped and kept for two months in a contained space, and he also seemed fine afterward. Even Eduardo's cousin had been kidnapped when she was fifteen—by an inept band of college amateurs. It's really fairly common.

No one knows exactly how many kidnappings there are in Mexico annually. According to a 2006 study by the Dutch group IKV Pax Christi, Mexico is the number-two country in the world for kidnappings, and the number-two per capita behind Iraq (with no data available for either Lebanon or China). Mexico City's *El Economist* reports that the country's kidnappings doubled between 1994 and 1995—from an estimated one thousand to two thousand. (The *Washington Post* claims that number has now doubled again.) That was the same year that fourteen separate political organizations banded together as the EPR, a sort of reinvigorated umbrella association of leftist guerillas. The group publicly announced its existence on June 28, 1996, at an event in Guerrero State commemorating the one-year anniversary of the Aguas Blancas massacre, in which seventeen farmers were gunned down by police on their way to join a protest march for workers' living conditions and to draw attention to the arrest of a local peasant activist. At the event, masked participants read from a manifesto written by a "Captain Emiliano" calling for armed social revolution. There was public speculation at the time that the group was actually government provocateurs. (Although the EPR has expressed its solidarity with the Zapatista rebels in the state of Chiapas, Subcomandante Marcos of the Zapatistas apparently wants nothing to do with them.)

According to the *New York Times*, the EPR is fewer than one hundred members strong, with a "core leadership" that comes from PROCUP (in English, the Clandestine Revolutionary Workers' Party Union of the People), founded in the 1970s in the state of Oaxaca, which waged a campaign of kidnappings and assassinations—often against fellow leftists—throughout much of the ensuing decade before apparently burning itself out. Although most of the EPR leadership shares PROCUP's Oaxacan roots, new members are recruited from the massive slums surrounding Mexico City. The group is organized in discrete cells and recognizes no formal leader.

Soon after the 1996 airing of its manifesto, the EPR was orchestrating coordinated attacks on police and military garrisons or engaging in dramatic ambushes and firefights with the army. A general amnesty issued by the governor of Oaxaca in 2000 released 135 suspected PROCUP members from prison and may have given the EPR a second wind. During the 2006 presidential campaign, in which the right-wing candidate Calderón narrowly edged out his opponent Andrés Manuel López Obrador in a race that Obrador never conceded, the EPR took responsibility for a series of pipe bombs that exploded at the headquarters of the PRI (the former ruling party) and the election tribunal. It is also suspected in a host of other crimes, including the 2004 lynching and burning of two police officers in the Tláhuac district, the 2006 robbery of a Banamex bank in Tecamach-alco, and several other high-profile kidnappings.

There is also the sense, particularly in the Mexican press—as there was talking to Roa—that somehow, the implicit church-and-state division between populist agrarian political movements like those in Chiapas or Oaxaca, powerful *narcotraficante* gangs, and traditional organized crime no longer apply. Categorical lines have become blurred, as land movements allow safe passage to drug traffickers for a price, drug cartels like La Familia inspire an almost cultlike fervor, and career criminals suddenly find their skill set in demand as a variety of forms of extortion become a new source of fund-raising.

Nowhere did I see this articulated as succinctly as in the movie *Proof of Life*, directed by Taylor Hackford in 2000, based in part on the book *The Long March to Freedom* by Thomas Hargrove. In the film, with a script by Tony Gilroy, Russell Crowe, playing a London-based Kidnapping and Ransom expert, attributes the abduction of Meg Ryan's industrialist husband to the ELT—the Liberation Army of Tecala, the mythical South American country in which the story is set.

"This is a land reform movement," says Alice Bowman (played by Ryan), parroting the popular political consensus. "These people are revolutionaries."

"Initially there was a political agenda," says Terry Thorne (Crowe). "However, what you have to understand is that today's version of the ELT is a completely different animal. Twenty years ago, they were just another struggling Marxist revolutionary group hiding out in the mountains. The end of the Cold War changed everything. The money from Moscow dried up, and the ELT had to find a new way to support itself. So they got into the kidnapping business, which has made them millions. Then they realized that they were sitting on an even bigger gold mine. Behind Colombia, Tecala is the world's biggest supplier of cocaine. And the ELT had the weapons and an endless supply of young, poor, illiterate soldiers. They came in hard, they came in fast, and they took over the drug trade. Whatever political agenda they started with has at this point become completely perverted."

While that description sounded a lot like the people who had Eduardo, it doesn't seem that these people have taken over the drug trade.

When our banker finally came to see me a week later, I wasn't completely prepared for what he had to tell me. He reiterated that he could not release Eduardo's funds to me without his signature. That part I already knew. Then he surprised me by offering me whatever meager savings he had as a loan. This was a man with small children to raise and bills to pay. I didn't know if he meant it or not, but either way, I was touched by the offer. He then said, on the authority of his superiors, that there was one way around this funds embargo: The bank would release Eduardo's money to me—minus the amount of an outstanding loan—on the condition that I contact renowned anti-kidnapping expert Felix Batista to take charge of the negotiations. Batista worked with ASI Global out of Houston—he was Cuban American and a former army major. I would be responsible for paying all of Batista's fees.

I spoke with Batista three days later, and he was very nice—he sounded both wise and experienced, and he reiterated much of what the AFI had told me about the EPR, reaching the same conclusion. But if Batista became involved, Raul and the AFI would immediately withdraw. If this lasted the six months they predicted, Batista's fees could easily eat up our savings, leaving me nothing to negotiate with. I thanked him for his time but declined to engage him at the bankers' behest. I was going to have to find another way through this maze. Batista disappeared more than a year later, in December 2008 in Saltillo, Mexico, where he was giving a lecture. While dining at an upscale restaurant, he received a call on his cell phone from an unknown party. After giving his computer and phone to his dinner companion, along with instructions on who to contact in the event he didn't return, he exited the establishment to a waiting car, where he was greeted by someone he appeared to know. He was never seen again, and his body has never been recovered.

Two days after our meeting with Benito Roa, the recommended text for our first want ad arrived newly vetted from AFI headquarters in Mexico City:

Looking to buy Austin Chow Chow puppies vaccinated with complete pedigree. Ours got lost a few days ago, and we are incredibly worried now that we know he is hurt. It would give us peace of mind to know that he is okay. We will offer a reward based on our realistic economic possibilities.

Although the kidnappers freely communicated with us through e-mail—often with handwritten letters from Eduardo attached as scanned images—they demanded that we place our responses as want ads in the Mexico City dailies—first *El Universal*, and later *Reforma* (the conservative newspaper). Forcing us to use newspaper classified ads to communicate with them made it impossible to pinpoint their location. But by doing it this way, they also made it more difficult for family members to respond at length, since want ads carry a maximum length of one hundred words. They don't want to hear your sob story—all they want to know is how much money you've got for them.

The AFI advised against including a formal offer at this time. Since the kidnappers generally held their hostages for six months minimum, it was in our interest to run out the clock—to use up as much time as we could at every stage of the negotiations, in order to keep the eventual number as low as possible. I found this unnerving. The ad ran June 21, 22, and 23. The next day, June 24, a second e-mail arrived from the kidnappers. It was sent from the address cielolindo22—"Beautiful Cielo"—@marihuana.com. I noticed that they opened a new e-mail address every time.

What do you call the dog Carlotta?

Bran. (The dog's 2nd name.)

Ma'am and Associates:

They were poking fun at me for turning to the authorities. They didn't feel threatened in the least.

We don't see any numbers.
   Our demands are in clear amounts.
   They are within your "realistic economic possibilities."

We were then instructed to place an ad in the Animals and Pets section of *El Universal* reading: "Buy chow chow dog Austin, vaccinated, deloused. 8,000 $." When we suggested—in code—that they talk with Eduardo to better understand our financial situation, their follow-up e-mail urged timely compliance, lest Eduardo "have to remind you in the future under more adverse conditions."

Our response attempted to walk a fine line between being compliant and noncommittal. Taking stock, I could come up with about fifty-three thousand dollars using everything in my checking account and everything I could liquidate quickly, including ten thousand dollars left to me by my grandmother. No one among Eduardo's friends and family had answered my call yet to arrange a loan. His siblings are no longer wealthy, and his extended family of significant means didn't want to get involved—I assumed because they figured if they loaned me money, they'd never see it again. None of the property was in my name, not even the cars. I couldn't get a loan using the building as collateral if the building wasn't mine. I couldn't sell the old tractor and lose the income of the alfalfa crop, but even if I could, I would have gotten very little for it. When I tried to sell the handful of paintings we still had from the Colonel's art collection, Eduardo's friends told me not to sell them because I'd get nothing for them and get taken advantage of. It was then that a trusted friend came forward with a loan. When I offered to send a painting to him as a guarantee, he would hear nothing of it. My mother's assets are structured in a way that didn't allow her to help me. My father had worked hard all of his life and left her with a comfortable amount to take her into old age, but it was not set up to be able to liquidate at the drop of a hat.

In probably our third ad, we finally offered the fifty-thousand dollars as a good-faith gesture. Raul told me that in dealing with the kidnappers, I would have to adopt the role of the submissive housewife—"feeble, weak, *muy desgastada*"—worn down. That is what the kidnappers expected and what they wanted. He even had Cielo and me practice for when we had to portray this role on the phone. I was skeptical, but I became the character they wanted me to. At least playing a role was something I knew how to do.

The first time I left the property for anything social was to a princess birthday party, a mother–daughter affair for girls only. I went with my mom and Nayah. I called in to the AFI agent every thirty minutes until he finally told me to loosen up. Something strange happened when we left the party, though. I was followed by what looked like a police officer on a dirt bike, twisting and turning through the narrow streets of San Miguel. He followed me all the way to the turnoff for the ranch and then appeared to radio someone ahead. On the dirt road that led to the ranch, there was a police pickup truck that came out of nowhere just ahead of me. It was just like the morning of the kidnapping, and I called Raul in a blind panic. He drove out to meet me, but by the time he got there, they were all gone.

At the end of June, several days after Fernando's graduation from the sixth grade, my mom took the boys back home to the East Coast. Nayah was too little and couldn't be away from me for that long—the kids were all traumatized to begin with—so she stayed behind with me for the summer. (In retrospect, I don't know how I would have stayed sane without her.) Several days later, Nayah and I followed so that I could undergo my regular cancer checkup. It was there on the Fourth of July that I received another e-mail from the kidnappers calling my last message "ambiguous" and demanding that I tell them how much I was prepared to pay. I also received my first letter from Eduardo—hand-lettered in a tight block script and attached as an e-mail file. It started out by cutting the asking price almost in half.

Jayne:

The deal I have is $4,450,000 . . . There is no way to negotiate. Please concentrate while I explain this to you, or they're going to kill me. Move urgently. I would pay all of it for you. Don't let anyone advise you differently. Life is cause and effect, and in this very fragile moment, I'm totally in your hands. You can resolve this favorably. Don't think about any other possibility, because there is none. Money is a trap. We are going to find happiness being together again. We will always have enough as long as we're together, you and I. Just focus on getting the money or I will never see you again. I promise this is very serious and delicate; do it urgently, I beg you on my knees. [Cal Wimberley] should help us, Richard Leet—everyone. Offer everything as collateral. I don't have a lot of time left. I beg you for my life. I still want to live. I'm desperate. Help me by raising the full amount, not a cent less, if I'm going to ever be free. We have to be bigger than our problems. Resolve this— we're almost halfway there.

A second letter went into greater detail on whom I could ask for money, and for how much—including my mother, which contained the confidential details of her retirement account and home equity. It made me crazy to think of what they must be doing to him in order to acquire this information.

I don't mind being left with nothing. Money comes and goes. But my life will not come back. The only wish I have is to be with you all, to see you again. This is worth more than money . . . Make sure I'm alive before you give them the money. I adore you with all my soul and my heart. You are everything to me.

Eduardo.

This last part finally sounded like the Eduardo I knew, rather than someone fastidiously dictating his words in what they hoped would resemble a blind panic. Eduardo was always practical, even in the most dire of circumstances. And yet this telltale pragmatism made his words all the more chilling:

Make sure I'm alive before you give them the money.

The next day, three bombs fashioned from fire extinguishers packed with fuel oil and ammonium nitrate destroyed two thirty-six-inch stainless-steel pipelines owned by Pemex, the state oil monopoly, cutting off the supply of natural gas to the states of Guanajuato, Queretaro, and Salamanca and threatening to disrupt the economy. The EPR claimed responsibility for the bombings, in reaction to two of its members being seized by the government who were currently being held against their will in an undisclosed location.

I knew how they felt.

NINE

The Box

EDUARDO IN CAPTIVITY

While I was undergoing all of the above, Eduardo was facing his own dilemma—far greater than mine, by any measure. Some of the details are in the public record, and some of them have been lost to time. Although I wasn't there, this is what I've been able to piece together from a variety of sources.

Still in shock, bleeding severely from the head, his field of vision a gray glow from the morning sunlight strained through the thick cotton pillowcase over his head, Eduardo was suddenly wrenched from the backseat of the white Yukon and thrown into another, dark-colored vehicle. His ears were ringing from the hollow sound of screaming, which he eventually realized was his own. As far as he knew, I was still beside him.

As this second vehicle sped over the bumpy dirt road of the switchback where they released me and turned left back onto the highway, past the entrance to the new golf course and toward the town of Dolores Hidalgo, he could feel the presence of his children being physically pulled out of his chest, the heartstrings snapping like thick roots being rudely unearthed, their heat and weight diminishing into abstraction. He kept asking these men what they wanted, but the man driving told him to shut up—*"Cállate!"*—even while disguising his voice and remaining cool as a cucumber. They pushed Eduardo's head down in the seat every time there was other traffic, aggravating what was probably already a concussion. After what felt like a half hour on what would have been Highway 51 north out of San Miguel toward Dolores Hidalgo, based on the pattern of the curves and speed bumps, the vehicle left the highway and drove for a short while through a residential area, over a grate, and into a garage whose door opened and closed automatically. (At one point, Fernando had one of his dreams that Eduardo was being held in Celaya, but that would have been in the exact opposite direction.)

The car moved into the garage and then someone, quite possibly the driver, lifted Eduardo out of the car. With his vision still obstructed, they passed what felt like a metal detector wand over his face and body to make sure he wasn't carrying one of the GPS tracking devices favored by politicians and CEOs, either inlaid in a tooth as a filling or embedded beneath the skin. Then the person threw Eduardo over his shoulder like a sack of potatoes and carried him up a single flight of stairs, smacking Eduardo's head into an open metal window as he rounded a corner. He carried him into a room that was completely unfurnished, save for a pair of bunk beds and a large box—twenty-seven inches wide, seven and a half feet long, and six feet tall, like a piano box stood on its side. Here they put on ski masks and stripped him of his original clothes and pillowcase, and gave him a white undershirt and jockey shorts to put on. They opened a tiny door at one end of the box and slid him inside like a cadaver on a slab, then triple-bolted it with three heavy padlocks.

Finally able to see, it took a moment for his eyes to adjust inside the box. Built completely of wood, the floor, walls, and ceiling were lined with a dull gray indoor–outdoor carpeting, extremely rough to the touch, so that almost any movement left his arms, knees, elbows, and feet scraped and bleeding. Beneath that were factory-made faux-marble tiles, and the box was pushed into a corner and blocked by concrete walls on two sides. Twenty-seven inches was just wide enough for him to lie down flat on his back with three inches to spare on each side. He could sit up, stretch his arms and legs over his head, and stand with considerable effort if he hunched his shoulders forward.

There was a halogen light recessed in the ceiling that they mostly kept turned off and a second brighter light behind unbreakable plastic—more like a spotlight—which they always left on. From the start, loud music constantly blared through a tinny three-inch speaker, which served the dual purpose of covering up all conversation outside the box and shattering his powers of concentration. They also had motion sensors and a video camera trained on him at all times, which presumably fed a monitor in the other room. Outside the box, there was always someone in the room with him on one of the bunk beds, whom he could intermittently hear moving around, and beyond that (or so he was led to believe) a platoon of men armed with automatic weapons.

For ventilation, there were two small fist-sized holes with hoses attached to a pump—one to pump air in and one to suck the air back out. There were no other openings in the box, save for a small peephole in the door they could look in through. They provided him with a plastic one-liter water bottle, the kind you'd find at any convenience store, which they refilled and never cleaned, as well as a small ice chest or beverage cooler for the elimination of bodily waste. This was constantly doused with Clorox bleach, whose fumes would continually burn his nose and throat in such a confined space. The box was never cleaned, nor had it been before he got there: At one point, he discovered long curly gray hairs embedded in the carpet, presumably from the previous victim. The AFI was dutifully apprised, but we never heard anything back.

There were five or six people at any given time in the compound where Eduardo was held, all but one of them Caucasian. Whenever any of them entered the box, Eduardo was instructed to draw himself up at the far end and look away from the door, then to put on a hood they would toss to him, to protect their identities. And any time he was in their presence without a head covering or blindfold, it was because they themselves were compeltely covered from head to toe (wearing coveralls and ski masks).

But kept in virtual isolation as he was, Eduardo's instincts were soon sharp enough to easily distinguish his captors and even to recognize them before they entered the box. All wore mustaches—either out of some veiled allegiance or else a desire to be rendered indistinguishable—and the one time they shaved him, they left his own mustache intact. (They referred to themselves as blood brothers—*hermanos de sangre*—and Eduardo came to regard their mustaches as a point of pride or virility, like beards to the Taliban.) As much as possible, they interacted with him in writing—passing him notes with instructions on them, and giving him pen and paper when they required a response. On the few occasions they spoke Spanish to him, they were proficient in the language, but their voices were strangely devoid of any regional accent or color. It was as if they had learned Spanish in a vacuum. The mistakes they made in writing were also those of nonnative speakers; they had only a tenuous grasp of slang and often confused or mangled native idioms. Several slang expressions they used were of Colombian or other South American origin.

For this reason, Eduardo believed that at least some of

them were Americans. He also had a strong suspicion that they may have been trained as Special Forces operatives or mercenaries. Everything they did was on a military schedule—bringing food, bringing water, clearing away refuse, emptying the slop bucket—until suddenly it wasn't. Routines were established seemingly just so they could be broken, whether it was sleep patterns, the kidnappers' demeanor, or any other set of expectations that could be interrupted and leveraged. Some of what they did resembled what we've come to learn was standard protocol at places like Guantánamo and Abu Ghraib.

Although the AFI said that a group like the EPR usually compartmentalizes its various functions—surveillance, extracting the victim, managing him in captivity, conducting negotiations—several of these kidnappers were involved for the duration. Primary among these was the driver of the getaway car, the apparent operational manager, who demanded that Eduardo refer to him as El Jefe, or the Chief. Whenever he entered the building, he was accompanied by the strong smell of coffee. But even more strikingly, the energy level surged. El Jefe was in charge of all direct communication with Eduardo, and everything he did seemed calculated to instill fear. In his early forties, he wore military-style uniforms of either all black or all white—coveralls that zipped up the front and, as near as I can tell, were identical to the kind worn by police forensic specialists out in the field, down to the patch over the heart—sometimes with a matching small-brimmed canvas hat. He always wore the same gloves, with a Maltese cross insignia on the back. He was brusquer, meaner, more aggressive—he turned the music up louder and had less patience, mainly with things that were beyond Eduardo's control, like how the negotiations were coming. At one point, he lost his temper and inadvertently began swearing—mouthing the words "goddamn motherfucker" under his breath in English. He was definitely an American. (This was corroborated later by another EPR victim who does not wish to be named, who admitted that they heard their captors speaking fluent English in an East Coast accent.)

The other figure whom Eduardo interacted with on a regular basis was the medic. Younger than the rest—maybe thirty-five—with a full head of curly orange hair, he was tasked with checking on Eduardo's medical condition and basically keeping him alive. He was nicer than the others, softer—at first, Eduardo thought he might be gay—with a cultivated bedside manner befitting someone trained in the medical profession. He examined Eduardo's head wound within the first hour and told him, "You need stitches, but we're going to see if we can fix it another way." He later brought antibiotics that he injected Eduardo with to combat infection. He also brought anti-inflammatory medicine for an old leg injury that the kidnappers had aggravated when they dragged him from our Jeep. Eduardo had broken his leg so severely in a car wreck in his midtwenties that the doctors were convinced they were going to have to amputate it, before Eduardo's father had a specialist flown in who saved the leg. It had now swollen to twice its original size and would restrict Eduardo's movements for weeks to come.

Unlike the others, the medic seemed to take an interest in his well-being and would routinely touch his shoulder or hand to emphasize a point. At one point, he mentioned having worked in a hospital, and another time, after he was absent a few days, he explained that one of his kids was sick. Eduardo once saw his face by accident and remembers it as kind. When Eduardo once observed, "You seem like a nice guy, you have an education, you have kids—why don't you leave the group?" The medic answered, "If you try and leave, they kill you and your entire family."

Within the first hour of Eduardo's incarceration, El Jefe entered the box wearing a black Lycra mask that covered everything but his eyes and lips (revealing his mustache), dark sunglasses, and a hat. He told Eduardo that I was being held in another box down the hall, and that I had already told them everything. He made Eduardo answer a whole series of questions about our finances, ostensibly to compare our answers, in order to decide whether or not they were going to kill him. He had to write everything down: available cash, number of bank accounts, property, assets—down to the value of the last concrete post on the ranch. He was told that if his answers didn't match mine, they would know he was lying. After that, they demanded even more information—things that only Eduardo and I would know, all the e-mail clues, tidbits they could use in their letters to chip away at me and play their psychological games. They sucked as much information out of him as they could. At one point, El Jefe told him, "You haven't gotten up in five days. You look like an idiot. Why can't you be more like your wife? She gets up every morning and exercises." This was my standard routine, which they would have known from their surveillance. Eduardo was so convinced of what they were telling him that at times he could hear me screaming through the walls. (The AFI later told me that the kidnappers would sometimes use tape recordings of people screaming to fool their victims into cooperating.) His only solace was to retreat deep into the recesses of his memory and to reflect back upon the improbable chain of events that had led him to this coffin-shaped world.

Eduardo's father, the Colonel, who died in 1980, was by all reports a beloved figure in his public life and a tyrant in private. He was a diminutive, extremely elegant man, round in the middle, double-chinned, and balding (he often wore a hat, which he would tip to the adoring crowds that seemed to follow him everywhere), who nevertheless exuded enormous magnetism and personal power, according to all those who met him. Part of this was certainly due to his eyes, which raised the pulse whenever they focused on you, and a rich, distinguished voice that he used to maximum effect. There was something formal, almost regal, in even his most mundane actions. He literally came from nothing to become the most successful newspaper publisher in all of Latin America, bringing cheap color newsprint to Mexico's underclass and leveraging the resulting influence it brought him into political prestige and power. Citizen Kane, *the fictionalized biopic based on William Randolph Hearst, is his story as well—from his stint as a child being raised by distant relatives, to his ruthlessness and drive in creating a private empire, to the motivating search for love that eluded him his entire life. Like Kane, he saw the world in black and white and put a premium on loyalty. He was a fantastic poker player, skilled at keeping a secret, pettily vindictive, and he rarely ever smiled.*

The Colonel was born January 7, 1901, in Puebla, and his history mirrored that of Mexico in the twentieth century. With barely a third-grade education, he left school to become an empanada vendor on the streets of Puebla. As did many of the young men his age, whose childhoods were displaced by the violent times, the young Garcia Valseca joined the Mexican Revolution. He took part in a reported seventy-four battles and was shot once and almost killed, for which he was awarded the Cross of Honor forty years later, and advanced to the rank of colonel, an honorific he retained throughout his life. After the army, working door-to-door as a peddler, he realized that in small towns, he himself was often the bearer of news from beyond the region. This led him to the revolutionary idea of printing comic books, called historietas, *on cheap newsprint rather than expensive glossy paper, suddenly making them affordable to the semiliterate masses. This led to his first newspaper in 1941, a sports daily with pinup photos in the centerfold, eventually establishing a chain of thirty-eight. For thirty years, beginning in 1948, the year Eduardo was*

*born, the Colonel sat next to Mexico's president every year
on a national holiday to honor freedom of the press. They
even made a movie in the fifties about the annual bicycle
race he sponsored, called* Legs of Gold, *starring Clavil-
lazo, one of the most famous comics of the day. (There is
also a character based on him in Carlos Fuentes's es-
teemed 1962 novel* The Death of Artemio Cruz.*) One of
Eduardo's earliest memories was attending the race with
his father and hearing the entire crowd chant his last name.*

*The Colonel cultivated an extremely ostentatious life-
style, no doubt as an advertisement for himself and his
company. He always traveled by limousine or in his custom
fleet of six-door Mercedes Pullmans (extremely rare), Ca-
dillacs, Lincoln Continentals, and the like—all chauffeur
driven. He had four private railroad cars, one of which he
housed at Grand Central Station during a two-month trip
to Europe for thirty-five hundred dollars a day. The most
famous story about him is that upon arriving at a private
dinner in his honor, he was informed his Mercedes limousine was not able to negotiate the final turn of the driveway.
Rather than walk the final hundred feet, he had a retaining
wall torn down.*

*When he was a child, Eduardo's family lived in a huge
eighty-thousand-square-foot house in the exclusive colonial
enclave of San Angel in Mexico City. They had their own
swimming pool, private bicycle course, movie theater,
frequent parties with magicians and clowns, forty-two
full-time employees—everything they could ever need inside this compound, so that they would never have to leave
it. The private school they attended was two and a half
blocks away, to which they were delivered by chauffeur-
driven limousine. On the rare occasions when they were
forced to leave the property, they were accompanied by a
motorcade of federal police, earning them the nickname
"the Untouchables," after the U.S. gangster series on TV,
from their fellow students. The Colonel, meanwhile, lived in*

*his penthouse apartment in Mexico City, and Eduardo
rarely saw him and was rarely alone in his presence.*

*Like many great men, Eduardo's father was extremely
selfish. He dominated Eduardo's mother—his second wife,
and one much younger than him—and required that she
minister to his needs around the clock. When she wanted to
spend time with her children instead, he had the children
sent away to boarding schools in Switzerland or, in Eduardo's case, Canada. As in his professional life, if not
more so, the Colonel demanded complete obedience from
his children. He brooked no dissent, and his behavior bor-
dered on emotional cruelty. Their relationship was severed
when at eighteen Eduardo attended a wedding against his
father's wishes. When he returned, he was not allowed back
in the house. His father eventually tracked down his whereabouts and had him arrested and held in solitary confinement for ten days. Soon after, Eduardo left for college in the
United States, where he got married. But it was exactly this
compartmentalized upbringing that may have provided the
skills he needed to withstand the intense psychological
abuse that still lay ahead.*

Initially, Eduardo's captors were nice to him. They ate
well—home-cooked Spanish sausage, elaborate salads—
and they often shared their meals with him. Within a day,
they brought him paper napkins and a ratty, cloth-covered
camping mat to sleep on. At night, they gave him tiny slivers of Valium to help him sleep. After about a week and a
half, El Jefe came to him and said, "We need the money as
soon as possible. Who do you think we should release
first—you or your wife?"

Eduardo said, "Release me, so that I can get you the
money immediately."

As soon as he said that, El Jefe told him, "That was the
wrong decision. You took the long road. You're going to be

here for months. In fact, I don't know if you're ever going to get out of here." That was ten days in. They told him I had been released.

Almost immediately, their treatment of him changed dramatically. This most likely corresponded to our first monetary offer and their realization that they weren't going to get the kind of response they'd been hoping for. They stopped providing him with napkins, pulled the mat out that he slept on, and stripped him naked. Where they had initially knocked before entering, now they just entered at will, were rougher with him, started calling him names. They would bring him a bucket of cold water to wash his face in, then douse him with it instead. They left him naked most of the time now; it was so cold at night that he would wrap toilet paper around him in a futile effort to keep warm.

They routinely flooded the box now with earsplitting heavy music, amplified by the sharp contours of the wooden and concrete box, the high decibels so piercing that he often feared he would lose his hearing. They also took away his nightly dose of Valium so that now he was no longer able to sleep. Having been through extended bouts of insomnia before when his health was at its most precarious, he remembered a specialist in Mexico City telling him that kidnap victims who were subjected to this sort of prolonged stress often went insane. "It's tough on the nervous system," Eduardo remembered him saying. "The body can only take so much without going to sleep, and eventually you die."

Saying that he was "wasting their time with bullshit," they stopped feeding him regularly or even giving him food that could be considered edible, really. For weeks, they would feed him cold chicken broth from the refrigerator, then just the chicken head on a plate, its tiny eyes popping out, or nothing but the bones and feet. He would be forced to survive on banana peels, or eggshells, or half a lemon, which he would devour rind and all. Even in the best of times, his diet mainly consisted of baby food. They refused to change his drinking water for months, until it was filled with bacteria and smelled rancid, and he could see tiny bugs floating in it. Eventually, they fed him so little that he produced only three small bowel movements a month. Or they would torture him by withholding the container in which he urinated so that he had to beg them for it, his bladder close to bursting.

But all of this paled before the physical violence he was routinely and brutally subjected to.

They rarely were triggered by anything that he did, and most probably were in reaction to my responses in the classified ads. The first time, El Jefe sent two of his underlings in after they forced me to make my first dollar offer, which wasn't even in the six figures. But that was more of a warning. The ones to fear were those administered by El Jefe himself—the *golpizas sangrientes*, or bloody beatings—where he would beat Eduardo until he got tired, sometimes twice a day. El Jefe usually acted alone, although sometimes he would bring in someone else to gag Eduardo or hold him down. He always wore gloves and used a thick rubber truncheon, like the batons that military police carry. He had a whole series of them, and they graduated to harder and less flexible models over time. At one point, Eduardo was beaten so badly that he almost lost an eye through infection, and another time, after El Jefe kicked him repeatedly with reinforced steel-toed boots, breaking two ribs, Eduardo couldn't move for a month.

As bad as or worse than the beatings themselves was the uncertainty. El Jefe would say he was coming back in three days to administer the next beating. The anticipation became unbearable. Then he wouldn't appear on the third day, only to turn up unexpectedly on the fourth. No matter what he had been subjected to the night before, Eduardo would always force himself to tell them good morning, just as he always thanked them for his meals, no matter how horrific they seemed at the time.

On Friday nights, the Big Boss arrived—*el Jefe de todos los Jefes*, the one from whom El Jefe took his orders. Eduardo could always tell from the smell of cigarettes and a shift in the energy when the Big Boss was on his way. We think this may have been the man we'll call the Thin Man, whom I saw on the dirt road outside our house the afternoon before the kidnapping. It was always very serious when he arrived—sometimes Eduardo could sense the change in the mood two days ahead of time. Everyone collected indoors during his visits, and it was never a party atmosphere. The first time it happened, El Jefe gave him a pen and paper and told him he had to come up with a list of reasons why they shouldn't kill him. He produced four or five pages. On other occasions, when Eduardo was writing letters to encourage me to pay, he was forced to hurry to make the deadline of the Big Boss's arrival.

To preserve his sanity, Eduardo found mantras that he would repeat over and over again, thousands of times. The first was "Calm your mind down," to ward off the rising tide of panic that always lapped at the top of his mind. The other was "Trust the universe," a surrender to the larger forces and higher powers passing unseen around him. He would visualize the Milky Way, spinning out into other galaxies, and his place in it, imagining an order and design that would incorporate him and so protect him. He pictured his brothers and sisters, the privileged life he was born into—elegant, formal, cosseted, restrictive. He saw his father, a warrior and pillar to those around him, the salt of the earth turned patrician overlord of a handwrought empire, now surrounded by snarling dogs and devils. At one point, my friend Celena appeared to him in the box, which freaked him out; this happened, by the way, at roughly the same time as she and her friend were conducting the angel healing with me. He asked her to leave and she finally did. The medic told him he was hallucinating, except they didn't feel like hallucinations. He would stare at the gray walls and ceiling of his makeshift tomb for days on end, every stain and shape expanding into meaning, talismans of a swirling, dimensional life that had now deposited him here, and which now formed a twisted braid and lifeline back to his past, a tenuous pathway to his salvation.

There's a saying in Mexico that everyone has a tail to step on. The Colonel managed to tread softly through this fraught landscape for three decades, where his empire was matched only by the size of his ego, the Achilles' heel of all self-made men. He bragged to the cousin of an ex-president—Gustavo Diaz Ordaz, his lifelong rival—that he had outlasted the discredited politician, the powers that be turned against him. A ten-million-dollar government loan was called in suddenly, citing implied irregularities, and some angel investors waiting in the wings (Eugenio Garza Sada and Fernando Aranguren Castiello) were separately gunned down—allegedly at the hands of urban guerillas belonging to the 23rd of September Communist League, a revolutionary umbrella group that was the direct forerunner of the EPR.

Soon after, the Colonel's newspaper chain was seized by President Luis Echeverria and placed in the hands of a major campaign donor. Shorn of his holdings, and with them his identity, the Colonel's health went downhill quickly; he began drinking heavily and stopped eating, and his body began slowly shutting down, until he was confined to a wheelchair and had lost the ability to speak. Eduardo worked and cared for his father during this period, until his death in 1980. Carlos Loret de Mola, a star journalist at the Colonel's newspapers and the father of our friend Rafael Loret de Mola, as well as Eduardo's mentor, advised Eduardo to leave the country, saying his father's enemies represented a legitimate threat to him. After Eduardo relo-

cated to the States in 1984, Don Carlos, as he was known, announced plans to write a book about the Colonel and his downfall, to be titled The Colonel: How He Founded and Lost 37 Newspapers, and How Eugenio Garza Sada Tried to Rescue Them and Lost His Life, *that would fully chronicle the extent of government complicity and corruption. As Don Carlos was driving to the beach at Ixtapa on the Pacific Coast to finish the manuscript, his car left the road in a still unexplained single-vehicle accident and was later discovered at the bottom of a cliff. His body, along with that of his twenty-nine-year-old secretary, was found naked, sprawled in the underbrush, allegedly thrown free of the car, which was burned beyond recognition. All of his research materials were with him in the trunk of his car and were destroyed in the fire. Some of the same figures involved in the takeover of the Colonel's newspapers were later part of an attempt to purchase the beleaguered U.S. wire service United Press International, then in bankruptcy, for forty-one million dollars—a venture that ended in disaster.*

By virtue of who he was and where he came from, there were large parts of Eduardo's life that were predetermined—probably before he was born. A part of that was his enemies, many of whom he inherited, often through the simple vantage point from which he viewed their actions. But another part of it was others' perceptions of him. The Colonel lived a public life, his antidote to being an extremely private person. There are no messy entanglements, no daunting emotional lapses or human inadequacies, if you live your life alone in a crowd. He plastered over every surface with the veneer of money, having come of age without it, in the belief that it would seep into the foundation and take root, and that's the enduring public impression of him. It's an impression that persists to this day, long after the money was gone. Eduardo's inheritance was not insubstantial, as was that of his siblings, but it was not the kind of institutional wealth, say,

that would normally attract the attention of highly capital-
ized kidnappers who pride themselves on their financial re-
connaissance. And so there was a disconnect between him
and what he represents.

It was that shortfall, a field of graded shadow, in which
he now found himself—alone, and with little more than his
wits to guide him.

TEN

The Package

JULY/AUGUST: DENIAL/ISOLATION

In the world of cancer—the support and recovery groups surrounding cancer survivors and the people who think and write about how to cope with it—there is something known as the five stages of grief. It comes from Elisabeth Kübler-Ross's 1969 book *On Death and Dying*, written to apply to any traumatic situation such as a terminal illness or the loss of a loved one, of which cancer is emblematic. You can find something akin to it in Esther Hicks's "emotional ladder" concept in *Ask and It Is Given*. In short, the stages are denial (or isolation), anger, bargaining, depression, and acceptance.

Denial: How can this be happening to me? There must be some mistake. Maybe it's all just a bad dream. I will ignore it for as long as I can.

Anger: This isn't fair! What did I do to deserve this? Someone is going to pay.

Bargaining: Okay, I'm calmer now. I understand this has happened to me. But if there is a higher power, if it will just let me [state your conditions, the least you are willing to accept], then I promise that I will [state your concession, the most you are willing to give].

Depression: I can't take it. It's all too much. I can't go on. I give up.

Acceptance: This has happened. What will happen next is beyond my control. I am at peace with this realization.

Not everyone goes through all five stages, nor do they always experience them in the exact same order. But this is a good working template—a road map for the path you'll likely take through an unfamiliar emotional landscape. If you have some idea what to watch for, it might not be so overwhelming once it's upon you.

I managed to make it through my brush with cancer without going through any of them. Unless motivation *is* denial. I refused to accept that this was beyond my ability to affect it or that science knows with any certainty everything that pertains to my condition. So I learned everything I could, took every step that seemed prudent or rife with possibility, and either through these efforts or their exact opposite—the statistical wisdom of the universe and the biomechanics of fate—I dodged a bullet.

But in retrospect, it very much describes how I responded to this tragedy that befell our family. For most of that summer, I was in a daze. After I returned from the States, there were just Cielo and Leti, Vera, Nayah and me. The house was so empty, with both of my boys gone. I hadn't realized how much being a mom and having to put on a happy face for the kids had helped keep me strong and distracted from my reality. I had a nanny—Raquel—but her mother took sick soon after Eduardo was abducted, and this cut back on the time she could spend with us, just when I needed her most. For being the youngest, weakest, and most dependent on me, Nayah was really the strongest one in the whole family—I couldn't have made it without her. She has always been very close to me. She really missed her daddy, but as long as I acted okay, she was okay. Most of the time she seemed to deal with it pretty well. On the one hand, she was very attached to me at this age, while on the other, she loved to climb in my lap, tell me how much she loved me, and shower me with hugs and kisses. She acted like she knew that was what I needed most.

One day, when I'd been in the dining room with Raul talking for a long time, I got up to go to the bathroom and found her in my walk-in closet in a corner, kneeling and praying in a tiny whisper. She didn't notice me, so I was really quiet and just watched and listened. She went on for a long time, praying for God to please bring her daddy back. When she finally noticed me she ran over to me, hugged me, and cried for a long time. When I asked her about it, she told me she couldn't tell me what she was praying for or it wouldn't come true. We spent a lot of time during those months taking long walks, picking wildflowers, having potato-sack races (she apparently inherited my gift for hopping), and playing dolls on the living room floor. She would get into her little play kitchen in the toy room and put pretend ingredients into the pot and then serve it to me on the little plates of her toy china. She loved to go play with the rabbits and always took a basket with her. In the rabbit hutch, which was very big, we usually had lots of babies. She would pick out two or three and put them in a basket with a baby-doll blanket from her room and carry them back to the house. She'd play with them until I made her take them back to their mother. In her make-believe world, she was safe from the hostile forces that threatened our family, and for just a moment every day, I could enter that world and feel safe myself.

I checked my e-mail obsessively while I was away, without incident. Then, as soon as I arrived home, there was another e-mail waiting for me from the kidnappers:

What do Jayne's kids call her breasts?

Toto.

Sirs:

Apparently, it seems that time doesn't matter to you.
    Doesn't matter to us either. It might affect Eduardo, though.
    Eduardo has made a proposal, and every time you respond in a flippant way, we will know how to make him pay for it.
    If he can't convince you, we know how to use other "arguments."

They instructed me to place an ad in *El Universal* with an offer of $4,450,000, now formally adopting Eduardo's overture of half off.
    There was also another handwritten letter from Eduardo included as an attachment:

Our children are going to know that by not paying this pinche *money, you left me to die in the most frightening way. I am living in torment. I already explained that you have to take the million and a half dollars we have, ask your mom for five hundred thousand dollars, and the rest I will borrow from [Cal Wimberley . . . etc.] We have to give them all of it. If you don't do it quickly, I'm not going to last many more days. I swear to you on my life, I'm suffering more than you can imagine: They beat me, tie me up, I don't have clothes, I'm naked, I haven't eaten, I'm in a tiny room with constant light and very loud music. I'm going crazy—I can't handle this torture anymore. It's too much, more than I can take. If I do get to leave healthy, I'll make more money by working hard, I promise you. Give them everything we have—and*

*everything we don't have as well. But if you take your
time and don't pay, then I promise you, I'm going to die
very soon—in a matter of two or three days . . .*

   *If it were you in here, I would have gotten you out
already.*

                                                    —Eduardo

The classified ads I was instructed to place always had
the most random subject matter—Austin chow chows, telephone systems, exotic birds, farm machinery, spa treat-
ments. I kept combing through them for possible clues, as
I did with the riddles with which they always opened their
zip files:

   In what state does Jayne's mother own a home?

   Are they telling me they know where my mother lives
and roughly what her house is worth?

   What is the name of Cielo's daughter?

   Are they threatening Vera?

   In what city did Aurora attend college in the U.S.? . . .
   In what sport did Aurora win medals? . . . What was
   the name Eduardo called Aurora when she was little?

   (Washington, D.C. Swimming. *La Barcarola*, or the
Little Boat.)
   Are they pursuing a second line of negotiation now with
Eduardo's children?
   It all seemed like a calculated psychological campaign
waged against me—to wedge their fingers into my brain
and turn my thoughts against me. Or at least in my dimin-
ished state it did. (The worst was when they got the answer

wrong to their own riddle. My brother finally sent me some software to crack passwords on zip files, which worked within seconds.) When the newspaper published our ad in the wrong section, we'd spent a long night worrying that we'd waited too long to respond and there would be consequences. (Luckily, the kidnappers scoured the entire paper every day in case something like this occurred.) I estimate that I easily spent four thousand to five thousand dollars in classified ads alone. This went back and forth, on and on, even as Eduardo's messages became more plaintive, his mental state desperate, and his attacks on me more vicious.

One thing I noticed is that the e-mails always seemed to arrive either before nine o'clock in the morning, around lunchtime, or between six and seven in the evening, and never on Saturday or Sunday. It's like whoever was sending them (or resending them) was working a day job, and these were the only free times he had. I dutifully informed Raul, who sent one of his *tarjetas* to Mexico City for the AFI higher-ups to look into.

A week later, on July 19, another e-mail arrived:

Given your answer and your evident rejection, the proposal formulated by Eduardo is now null and void. In regard to what you have offered us up to this point, we agree to modify our initial demand. The amount to pay for Eduardo's liberation, unharmed, is 7,900,000USD.

They were canceling the half-price offer but knocking off a hundred grand as a good-faith gesture.

Following our close call when the state police came to the house on the day of the kidnapping, I decided it would be a good idea to register all of our guns and make sure they were legal. At the same time, I joined a gun club and made it a point to become fully proficient with firearms. The fact

Up the stairs is the "Jardín de San Miguel," or the town's main square.
This is a central meeting place where townspeople gather.
From collection of Jayne Garcia Valseca

The main entrance to our house at the ranch.
From collection of Jayne Garcia Valseca

Our kitchen, where I stood to make Eduardo's banana pancakes.
From collection of Jayne Garcia Valseca

The Pullman railroad car that Eduardo inherited from his father. His father used it as a mobile office from which to open new newspapers in small towns where there were no good hotels or highways. Eduardo and I used it to throw dinner parties. It was our first house when we moved to San Miguel. *From collection of Jayne Garcia Valseca*

Eduardo surprised Emiliano with a mariachi serenade, as he has done countless times. They came through the kitchen door and exploded in song with "Las Mananitas," the Mexican birthday song. Pictured are the whole family, the nanny, and our favorite mariachi group. The door in the background is the same one that Eduardo came through in 2008 after his seven and a half months in captivity. *From collection of Jayne Garcia Valseca*

Nayah looking out the window, deep in thought. This is the same window where Eduardo eventually passed by and where my mother spotted him the morning he came home. *From collection of Jayne Garcia Valseca*

Here we posed for our Christmas card photo, taken in October of 2006. My hair was still growing in after having had chemotherapy the year before. This was one of the last family photographs we took before the kidnapping. *Lander Rodriguez*

The road where we were ambushed and kidnapped. *From collection of Jayne Garcia Valseca*

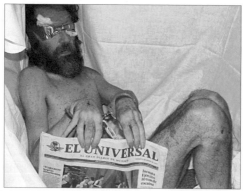

Eduardo in the first "box" where he was held for the majority of his time in captivity. Here he is covered with bruises, abrasions, and dried blood. He is handcuffed and in chains, holding the day's newspaper as proof that he was alive on that day.

This is the final "proof of life" photo that was sent to me just a few days before he was released. It took me about twenty minutes of staring at it to accept that it was him. He had been given a haircut and his beard had been shaven a few weeks prior to this in preparation for his release. He holds the day's paper as proof of life.

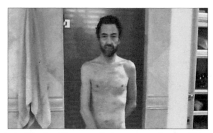

This is a photo I took with my cell phone a week after Eduardo was released. Here he stands in the bathroom at our friend's house in Mexico City. He had already gained ten pounds since being freed.
From collection of Jayne Garcia Valseca

My "after" picture, enjoying a moment of bliss in Maine
in the summer of 2010.
Christine Guinness

Together again.
This photo was taken just before the two year anniversary
of Eduardo's release from captivity.
© 2010 Melissa Ann Pinney

that I was, for all practical purposes, a single mother with three small children; that the AFI, U.S. law enforcement, and the American embassy were not offering me any kind of protection; and that I was miles out in the country, with a revolutionary army keeping tabs on me, hostile neighbors fanning the flames against me, and who knows what kind of enemies waiting in the wings all made it an easier decision. A local artist and gallery owner, Michael French, had two friends—one American, one Canadian—who were ex–army championship shooters, and they offered to help get me up to speed. They came over the Sunday after I got back and we went out to where we had started building our dream house, before the school began to eat up all of our money—basically just a big hole in the ground that was going to be our wine cellar. We set up targets to practice. Cielo and Leti went with us.

I'd always been a good shot: My brother and I would plug our dad's heirloom tomatoes with a BB gun, then giggle when he sliced into one while making a sandwich and started yelling at us. When I was sixteen, I used to go with a boyfriend to turkey shoots on the weekend—where you shoot at a turkey-shaped target with a shotgun—and I always hit the bull's-eye. I'd only stop when my shoulder got too sore. Later on, in my early twenties, I briefly dated a security consultant, and sometimes we'd go to the shooting range on the weekend. He took photos of me one time and they wound up on the cover of a gun magazine. These guys set up a target for me so I could practice drawing and firing my .357 Magnum and my snub-nosed .38. They were impressed with my aim: I could put a shot dead through the center of my previous one. They all roared when I shot a dummy in the balls—twice.

After a couple of hours, Leti and I walked back to the house, and there was a message from the mayor's office: Some of the neighbors—Oscar Gutierrez's bodyguards, as a matter of fact—had called and reported gunshots out at our ranch. I told him we'd been target practicing. He said the police were on their way and asked if our guns were registered. I said yes, which wasn't entirely true: Cielo was using some of Eduardo's antique guns we hadn't gotten to yet. Luckily, Cielo spotted the police approaching, grabbed a backpack with the offending weapons, and bolted into a field, using the cacti and mesquite trees to camouflage his retreat. When he reappeared, he was zipping up his Levi's like he'd been heeding nature's call. The cops were suspicious and started snooping around, but they never found anything. The next day, Cielo got all the guns registered in his name (since I was technically a foreigner), and Michael showed me how to unload a .38 with one hand while I was driving. From there on out, I carried my snubby in my purse, and in a gun holster whenever I was alone at the ranch.

Cielo was being fantastic. The kids were really taking to him; I was so glad he was there with us. He and I had had our ups and downs in the past. The divorce had been very hard on both him and Aurora, as it would on any teenager—complicated by the fact that his mother had come out as a lesbian and his father had married a woman only slightly older than his children. That can't be easy for anyone. But we had developed a real bond over the years, and he had dropped everything to come to my aid, hold down the fort, and help fight to get his father back. I was so grateful for that.

My other pillar during those first few months was Raul. He was such an easy person to have around. He was always content and always at task, intensely focused on his work. He felt like a perfect match for our family. It was like having an in-house psychologist for the kids and me. Once Nayah came over and asked him if she could play on his computer, and he set up a game and taught her how to play it. She was delighted. He told her not to click on anything else, though, because "there are some very ugly things on my computer that I wouldn't want you to see." I could only imagine. Thankfully, I could trust her to do what we asked.

Maybe she had an inkling. Raul was great with the kids. After working that intensely, he also recognized the need for us to blow off some steam. He asked me where he could buy a skateboard so that he could go riding with Fernando when he returned home in late August for the new school year. In quick succession, he brought home a basketball, a soccer ball, and a Frisbee so he could play with the kids. He took them to motocross races. In late July, he started training for a marathon to be held in San Miguel on El Grito, or Mexican Independence Day, September 16.

Raul blended into the ranch completely, even helping out with the chores. He learned to drive a tractor and helped bring in the alfalfa. I taught him the intricacies of harvesting prickly pears, or "cutting tunas"—extracting the sweet, delicious, juicy fruit from the prickly pear cactus that grew wild on our property, a skill at which I had become quite expert. (My technique: Always harvest in the mornings, when it's cool, so the fruit is firmer and the night rain has washed away the fine, hairlike thorns. Wait until it's a mottled green and yellow color, when it's at its ripest, then slice the top of the fruit and down the center in a vertical line, and slide your hand inside the incision, moving top to bottom. The fruit comes out whole, and the peel stays on the tree.) We ate prickly pears every morning that summer, and I would harvest and sell them by the crate.

Raul told me early on that the investigation per se would be fairly low-key until Eduardo got back, so as not to endanger him. Whenever he was out with me, he was very careful to blend in, as if he were my driver. But on occasion, Raul would slip into town on his own and take the temperature of the street. He would talk to people but always told them he worked for a cell phone company and came here frequently on business. Occasionally, at the gym or a taco stand, he would randomly ask people if they knew about the guy who was kidnapped locally and what they had heard. People would tell him all sorts of things. That's how he found out that people believed we were getting eight million dollars from the Cal Wimberley deal—coincidentally, the same amount demanded by the kidnappers.

There was some initial speculation that the kidnappers knew of this secret land deal with Cal Wimberley and somehow overestimated our net worth because of it. They had obviously researched our routines and habits—how else would they have known I got up every morning and exercised? The kidnappers' original asking price was roughly a ballpark assessment of our ranch and holdings plus the amount of money we stood to make. Their first e-mail to us even chose the term "Austin chow chow"—not a recognized breed of dog but incorporating the Texas city that Wimberley hailed from. But if they had any inkling of our impending windfall, then the joke was on them. The deal was contingency-based, and our first money wasn't due for months. Wimberley hadn't even secured his financing yet. And more than simply complicate the transaction, it was the kidnapping itself that queered our deal with Cal Wimberley.

Six weeks after the date that Eduardo was kidnapped, we were supposed to receive the second part of the down payment—roughly four-fifths of the amount we had agreed on. During that period, Wimberley was supposed to complete his due diligence—that is, secure permits for development, water usage, land and house inspections, and so forth, all of which Eduardo was supposed to sign off on—which he was unable to do and I couldn't do for him because I did not have power of attorney. After Eduardo was kidnapped, Wimberley secretly flew down to see me and we met with lawyers—it was all very furtive, in case the kidnappers were watching us. There we determined that legally, since Eduardo had been abducted and I could verify that with authorities, Wimberley could sue Eduardo for nonperformance; because Eduardo would not be there to defend himself, a judge would allow the sale to go forward without him. But it was during that six-week period that the credit crunch caught up with most pending financial deals, a ripple effect from the collapse of the U.S. subprime housing industry of the previous February and March. By the time this solution presented itself, his credit source, Prudential Latin America, was no longer willing to loan him capital, and the deal collapsed. Wimberley made one additional trip to see me in October in a last-ditch effort to salvage the deal, but we could never surmount these hurdles.

Almost from the beginning, I took what measures I could think of to curtail costs and raise additional funds. We had eight full-time employees plus Gustavo, who worked part-time, so we paid out a sizable amount of money in wages alone. There were Christmas bonuses coming up, equal to another week's wages, legal fees, car and property taxes. I had to have the tractor repaired for four thousand dollars, reseal the leaking roof, pay for water filters, cover a monster electric bill. I was paying Cielo's rent on his apartment and other expenses for the first couple of months while he and his family stayed at the ranch with me. And we had hired a teacher for the seventh and eighth grades at the school, and we had already committed to his salary beyond what school tuition would cover. Eduardo had handled the finances, and I was astounded to learn what it took to run an operation of that size. Not to mention that I was trying to raise an additional eight million dollars.

I was extremely careful with our expenses. I bought only what we couldn't raise ourselves. We ate eggs from the hens. Most of our food came from our garden. I cut off the Dish TV subscription. When the housekeeper quit, I didn't replace her. Almost immediately, I began to sell off the horses, sheep, and the rest of the farm animals. I sold rabbits; I sold puppies (Nayah was especially sorry to see them go but promised me she understood). Eventually, I had the workers collect scrap metal from around the ranch, which we sold by the kilo to be recycled. There had been a lot of old metal machinery that was rusted and no good, so all of that went. I never ate out, or even left the ranch except when I had to, for school functions or the like. Cielo even sold two of his own paintings to a woman in New York. Every little bit helped.

At the same time, I was trying to borrow money from family members, some of Eduardo's wealthier friends, and eventually everyone I knew—a process that was both awkward and infuriating. Most people would say, "Sure, let me talk to my banker and I'll get back to you." Of course, then I never heard from them again, and they wouldn't take my calls anymore. There was even an extremely rich cousin who had been very close to Eduardo as a child, whose father had been helped in business by Eduardo's father, and who herself had been kidnapped at fifteen (by amateur college students who were quickly caught without incident), and still she declined to help, claiming her financial advisers recommended she not get involved. Two of Eduardo's friends finally stepped forward and promised me money when the time came—and then actually followed through. Both were successful businessmen whom I won't name here, as the AFI has advised that disclosing their identities could be dangerous. But I wish I could.

And it wasn't just raising the money (or not raising it)—we also had to arrange all the logistics that go along with having or moving large amounts of money. Cielo and I made preparations for an armored car to deliver the ransom money to the ranch when we were ready, as the bank refused to be responsible for the money after it left the building. In the end, we bought a safe to keep at the ranch. At the advice of the AFI, we asked Gustavo and his brother Coco if they would deliver the ransom, and they accepted. (If a family member makes the delivery, they run the risk of a victim exchange—merely substituting one family member for another. We asked both because we wanted two options in case one of them backed out at the last minute. We asked them again in September, just to be sure, but both remained committed.) We even asked Richard Leet if we could have his private plane on call, since there was a possibility Eduardo could be released at some distant, remote location. Another friend of Eduardo's in Mexico City lined up a helicopter for us.

But as the summer dragged on, my energy for this kind of thing waned. I didn't want to talk to anyone or explain anything; in fact, I just wanted to retreat inside myself as far as I could go. Everyone was an expert; everyone had a theory. Very few people understood the decisions I made. This didn't help my morale. It was constantly like swimming upstream to have to repeat the same story again and again to try and convince people I was doing the right thing. It weakened me. I stopped taking phone calls. (After the first couple of days, the phone stopped ringing, since no one wanted to tie up the line in case the kidnappers were trying to call.) When I could help it, I stopped receiving visitors. It was wearing me out.

Then Cielo was succumbing to the pressure. He started drinking a lot and missing meetings at which we had to make important decisions that could affect what happened to Eduardo. There was just an immense amount of pressure on all of us, all the time. Cielo was working as an artist and as a deejay at night. Many times he never made it back to the ranch after work, and we all spent several nights awake and worried. Then he started having trouble with Leti, and they almost split up. Leti is supermodel gorgeous and now a successful fashion designer, and they were always the most striking couple. Raul and I both told him that he couldn't afford the luxury of letting himself crack up; we were all hanging on by just a thread. He needed to have his wits about him, and he needed to watch his back. Then he started pressuring me to loan him money, and I couldn't. None of this was helping. It was becoming a burden. Raul had a talk with him and told him he had permission to move back into his apartment and concentrate on his own life for a while but that for now he was out of the inner circle. To my surprise, he took it well—he actually seemed relieved.

At one point, I called Lynda, Eduardo's ex-wife, and asked her to come. She was a counselor in the U.S. (who worked with Spanish-speaking people), and more important, she was Cielo's mother. Lynda and I had always gotten along. She's a beautiful woman, with high cheekbones, striking green eyes, and a very kind, gentle demeanor. The divorce with Eduardo was a friendly one, and although the circumstances of it were foreign to him, he harbored no ill feelings. She was nothing but kind to me from the very beginning, and I knew that she must have mixed feelings about my presence in his life. But we all got along very well. We went to the movies or out to dinner, and once to a Gipsy Kings concert together at Wolf Trap.

When Lynda arrived, Aurora was also there. I don't think this was on purpose, but I quickly started feeling like an outsider in my own home. Everyone wanted to make sure we were doing the very best we could for Eduardo, but I was having to explain and reexplain every decision I had made along the way. They wanted to know all about our finances, how much money we had available to us—things I was uncomfortable with sharing. The whole thing was a drain on my energy. I know they wanted to help—and they did—but I was glad after a long weekend when everyone went back home.

With Cielo gone, there was one less layer of experience between me and this untenable situation I found myself in. I lost a lot of weight. I had never been much of a drinker and never took drugs, but after a doctor friend wrote me a prescription, I took a tranquilizer that knocked me out for three days. I had been taking passionflower extract to calm me down so I could sleep at night, but it gave me head-aches, so I started taking chilled shots of vodka from the freezer right before bedtime. Martin Peña brought me two bags of Eureka lemons from his brother's farm in León, and I made two big bottles of limoncello—vodka, fresh lemon, and simple syrup—which I started sipping as an aperitif at lunch. (My motto became "When life gives you lemons, make limoncello!") I started drinking every afternoon, then all afternoon, and it was easy to see where this was heading.

Finally, Raul told me that I had to snap out of it—not just the drinking but all of it. He asked me one day if hanging around the house and never seeing the light of day was what I typically did before he arrived. When I smiled uncomfortably and told him no, I used to be very active, he said, "Then you need to do that again. This is going to be a long haul, Jayne; you need to get back into life or you're not going to make it." I knew the thing that would breathe life back into me and provide me with a source of joy was to be able to dance again, but the mere thought of it made me feel guilty—dancing at a time like this. Raul explained to me it was just the opposite. There was a deep hole inside me now that was filled with sadness, and the only way to displace the sadness was to fill it with something else. It didn't matter what people thought, because it wasn't their problems I was trying to solve.

"If Eduardo could see you right now, and could think with a clear mind, he would want it that way," said Raul. "He would not want to see you suffer like you are now. You will best serve your husband by getting a grip on yourself. It is very hard to fathom, but Eduardo is nothing but merchandise to them. Disconnect as much as you can and negotiate dispassionately, based on your realistic options. We will get him back, but until then you have to keep it together—do you understand?"

So I started taking dance classes again, calling up my old friends, and basically pulling myself up by the bootstraps. There was a lot to organize. I would sit and make elaborate belts or headpieces for my dances. I did research online about ransom negotiations and the EPR. I gardened.

I worked on getting the junior high class together; I spent time promoting it and pulling the parents together, getting the kids registered, and taking payments so that I could partially fund the desks, chairs, materials, and so on. I took furniture out of storage. I started to go to the school board meetings again. The new teacher arrived in August, and I started to do all of the things that were a part of my life before the kidnapping. It was a lot of pretending, really, but it did make it all much easier.

Another thing I did was to start keeping a journal. We had reached the point in the negotiations when Eduardo was forced to write letters, and it became clear to me that the kidnappers were lying to him about what I was doing to resolve the situation. Raul told me that eventually they would brainwash him through his isolation, and that he could even end up with Stockholm syndrome, developing a sort of empathy for his captors. I decided to document what was going on in the outside world so I could show it to him later. I wrote it as a kind of letter from home, as if he were traveling abroad. Eventually, it became too hard to relive everything before I went to sleep, so I stopped. It was just too painful. I picked up again later when I felt strong enough.

Here is my first entry:

Saturday 21 July 2007

Dear Eduardo,

I never imagined in my wildest dreams that we would ever count this one as one of our life experiences. I awake each day wondering how many more I will have to endure without you. Today was one of the many days that I could do nothing more than think of you and contemplate every angle of the situation we are in. Every second of every day, I think of where you are, what condition you are in, if your needs are being met, are they harming you. With every bite of food I eat, I wonder what they're feeding you. I worry so much about your sleeping. We've worked so hard toward your health, and now this. It's all too impossible for me to comprehend. Why you? Why us?

We are more than one month into this, and I am only now able to concentrate enough to put my thoughts to paper. I am completely devastated. I feel so lost without you, yet I am pulling out all the strength and courage I have in me to do what you would do if in my shoes. I meditate several times a day, sending you my love, light, and strength so that you may get through this and come home to me and to your children, who need you and miss you desperately. This is all so unfair. How could we ever have generated such a thing?

I pray for you to find the strength to escape. I pray that you can stay clear-minded and use your people skills to keep them from harming you. I pray for justice when this is all over. I need you so badly. It shatters me when our babies ask me when you're coming home and I can't tell them. The mesquite pods have come and gone and you weren't here to enjoy them, as you always do so much. This morning Nayah and I got up early and picked the first tunas of the season. We discovered a peach tree we didn't know existed and shared a peach. Everything is green and beautiful. We're having a good rainy season so far. I know you love the rain so much, especially when it rains all night. We had two storms with hail and the roof started to leak. I had to have Tavo reseal the whole roof. I'm trying to do everything that you'd be doing if you were here. I went to the U.S.A. on July 1 for my checkups but only stayed ten days. I canceled my surgery; I'm too weak to take an operation right now. It's been too hard to eat and to sleep. It took

*a long time for my hand to heal from grabbing the
barbed-wire fence the day of the kidnapping. I knew that
surgery wasn't a good idea. I sent Nando to Miami with
Aurora's ex-husband and their boys. I left Emi with my
mom. I wanted to distance them as much as I could from
this whole experience. Nayah is still too attached so
she's with me. Guero and I have formed a tight team in
this and are doing everything humanly possible to get
you back . . . So many people have shown us support in
this. I'm going to try and start from the beginning to
keep a journal of all that is happening.*

On August 1, the EPR claimed responsibility for bombs
at a Sears store and a Banamex bank in Oaxaca. The second
bomb failed to detonate, and no one was hurt in either
incident.

The e-mails continued, as did Eduardo's handwritten
pleas. He began to write Cielo, saying the kidnappers were
threatening to kill him outright or cut off a finger, and
subtly suggesting that I had not done enough to meet the
kidnappers' demands. Raul told me this was highly unlikely, especially at this level of negotiation. It still gave me
a horrible feeling in the pit of my stomach. I remembered
when we had spent the afternoon with a wealthy businessman Eduardo knew in Queretaro to watch him work his
bulls and horses. When he took his hat off, I noticed that the
tops of his ears were missing. I asked Eduardo about it later,
and he said the man had been kidnapped twice by the same
kidnappers, and each time they cut off the top of one ear. I
remember looking at Eduardo's ears that evening and then
his fingers and thinking how he had such beautiful hands. I
couldn't help thinking that I would be absolutely horrified
to have something like that happen to my husband.

In late August, the boys returned for the new school semester. My mom came back with them to lend an extra pair

of hands. Then on August 29, another e-mail arrived, the last of the summer:

Jayne's second (middle) name.

Marie.

Taking care of him is your job, by paying.

It seems you're still betting on a notion that's incorrect.

But as for your offers, we're willing to accept 7,850,000 USD . . .

In case you're interested, Eduardo is sending you an incentive for your work. You will find it buried on the side of the highway to Guanajuato. Get off from San Miguel toward Celaya. Once you get to the fork toward Guanajuato, take that road. Pass the Allende Dam and keep going until you see the 19km sign. Stop on the right-hand side just at the sign. Search beside the fence until you find a patch of black dirt. There may be a green plastic container just on top of it. A few centimeters under the surface you will find a smaller package, wrapped in plastic.

Cielo and I were sweating bullets. Raul told me that neither of us could go retrieve it, as it could be a trap. Although all e-mails were forwarded to Benito Roa at AFI headquarters in Mexico City, this time Raul called him immediately. They decided Coco should be the one to collect the package. He had to wear plastic gloves (which I had for cutting tunas), and he called from the roadside, with the rest of us breathlessly circling the speakerphone at the ranch. He found the green plastic container, just as they'd said, and then dug down in the soft black potting soil to find a package wrapped in Saran wrap. As he carefully unfolded it, he reported that it was a stack of documents—IOUs, signed by Eduardo, addressed to potential donors who could loan us money. We breathed a collective sigh of relief.

Or rather, momentary relief—relief as a placeholder for some other emotion, unformed as of yet, that I could feel was on its way. This deep repository of sadness inside me that I had worked so hard to dislodge was now draining out of me, carrying with it the corroded residue of blocked, half-digested feelings—all the things I'd been force-fed and couldn't stomach at the time. Taking its place was a new emotion, scalding in its clarity, one that imbued me with a new, profound sense of purpose:

Rage.

ELEVEN

Cardon Cactus

SEPTEMBER: ANGER

I felt like I hit a turning point that day in August. After feeling so out of control, devastated, and weak for so long, I moved into a whole new psychic space. Who the hell did these people think they were? What right did they have to my husband, my family, our money? How in their twisted minds did *we* become the enemy? Our privileged, pampered, entitled, inconsequential lives were perfect fodder to be made examples of? To expose the upper classes in their decadent, hollow death-brays as imperious leeches, preening bloated ticks on the body politic, powerless to turn back the rising tide of history—all for the illumination of some idealized masses?

Screw that.

I felt like that day I unsheathed a sword and prepared for battle—one I planned on winning. A few days later, I sat down with Raul and asked him, "What would happen if we told them they can go ahead and keep him, that I'm done negotiating. If they don't want what I can give them, they can go fuck themselves." He laughed at my sudden spirit and change in attitude.

"These are criminals, Jayne," he told me. "You have to treat them like kings. They have the upper hand because they have Eduardo. You treat them as if they are the boss and you'll do anything they say. Meanwhile, we carefully negotiate based on your circumstances, trying to protect him as much as possible. You're the weak, trembling housewife desperate to come up with their demands. They could kill him otherwise."

The problem was, the shivering housewife act wasn't feeling right to me anymore. I was overcome with dark scenarios of revenge, and now I had a loaded gun in my purse everywhere I went. I wanted so much to tell them what I really thought of them. "Wanted: Chow chow puppy. Take what I have and give me back my husband, you miserable rat-fuck bastards. $FU.00USD!" This was a different person in response mode now. The old me was gone forever. Hear me roar.

September 5 was my birthday. Ever since my flirtation with cancer at thirty-eight, I swore that I would never let another birthday go by without a celebration—not even this one. I had a belly-dancing gathering at the house and dedicated it to Eduardo. We all circled up and sent him positive energy. And regardless of its momentary drawbacks, I gave thanks for another year of life. Five days later, another one of Eduardo's letters arrived as an e-mail attachment. It began:

> *It's a miracle that after three months I am still alive. I have a serious infection in my eyes and I could go blind at any moment because I'm not taking any medicine, and still you haven't reached any satisfactory arrangement. I don't know how to tell you anymore, but I feel destroyed, sad and deceived that you can't get me out of here. Be aware that if you don't come up with the rest of*

the money immediately, you might as well forget about
me forever . . . [Otherwise,] they are going to inject me
with the AIDS virus from contaminated blood from ho-
mosexuals and drug addicts.

Whereas just weeks before, this letter would have left me
blindsided—catatonic in a fetal position—now I was literally vibrating with rage. I had to keep telling myself that
they were working from a playbook, designed to produce the
most visceral emotions in me they could manage. Emotions
were their allies, spies within our house, whispering their
sordid logic in our ears, sabotaging our will and ability to
reason. I was fairly certain they were dictating these letters
to him or having him copy them over in his own handwriting. They didn't sound like him. He would never say some
of the things he said to me. But more than that, it was the
tone: They were desperate, but it was a very calculated desperation. "I'm screaming—can't you hear me screaming?
Do something to stop my screaming!" That's very different
from screaming.

At the end, in English, he wrote, "Happy birthday." That
part made me cry. It was his way of telling me the rest was
just a charade. This was the Eduardo who still loved me. I
had tried to harden myself inside in preparation for doing
battle, but this just melted away my resolve. I sat at the dining room table with my face in my hands and wept.

That week Plata, a Neapolitan mastiff, killed one of our
ratoneros (a kind of Andalusian rat-catching terrier) and
one of the Akitas. She lost her mind after the kidnapping
and started killing the other dogs one by one, and I finally
had to have her put to sleep. The same day, six bombs exploded disabling Pemex pipelines in the states of Veracruz
and Tlaxcala, forcing the evacuation of over twenty thousand people and causing damages in the millions of dollars.
The EPR claimed credit for the bombings.

With the new school year under way, the boys were suddenly plugged back into the hyperactive hive society that passes for civic discourse in San Miguel de Allende, after three months away from facing our slow-motion tragedy on a daily basis. On the face of it, Emiliano, who was eight, was the lesser influenced by outside events. He's the self-sufficient kind of child who will get involved in his own play and may not seem aware of what's going on. But, of course, he's hyperaware. He takes in everything. He would go about his business, and I'd think he was okay, but then he'd offer me the contents of his piggy bank or ask me if Eduardo was cold or if they were feeding him. And every once in a while, he would snap. Things came to a head in mid-September, just before his birthday.

Some of the kids at school were obviously repeating what they had heard at home, telling Emi that his father had to be dead, saying, "Your mom just isn't telling you the truth." One of the kids actually went as far as to report that Eduardo had been killed and they had found him chopped up in a trash bag in the park. When Emi came home that day he was pale, and he went straight to his room, his eyes never leaving the floor. When I went in to talk to him, he exploded at me.

"Why don't you just tell me the truth? I know you're lying to me! I know he's dead and you're just lying! I'm never going to see him again! He's dead and he's never coming back!"

He was completely hysterical. It took me a long time to calm him down. I explained to him that we had to be secretive about everything we were doing, and so no one knew any of the details but us. When people don't have information, they make things up based on fear and ignorance—they make assumptions and jump to conclusions that are groundless, once you apply logic to them. This wasn't just true for kids either—they were obviously repeating what they were hearing from their parents. I showed him that if Eduardo were dead, then why would Raul be with us? Why would we be putting ads in the newspaper and being careful how we answer the phone? Not only would I never lie to him, but he could prove these things to himself if he applied deductive reasoning to them. I told him that he had to be strong and simply tell the other kids that those things hurt his feelings and then set them straight in a kind way. I talked to the teachers at school about it and they were extremely supportive, although deep down inside, they and everyone else in San Miguel were starting to think that I was completely out of my mind. No one had ever heard of a kidnapping lasting so long. This was very unusual. "Eduardo is dead and Jayne has lost her mind and is bringing the kids down with her." My friends reported that this sentiment was widespread among the parents at the school. Many, many people tried to set me straight. I found myself constantly reassuring those around me that he was coming back and that he was very much alive.

The second week in September, I volunteered to speak at a shopping center to promote enrollment at the school. This was only my second appearance out in public, and some of the administrators seemed uneasy about it, but I was fine. Everything went fine—no glitches—except during my speech, I noticed a strange man standing in the back of the crowd of about fifty people. He had the same kind of look as the kidnappers—hat, sunglasses, mustache, khaki pants—and he never broke eye contact with me as I rattled off our growth plans for the coming year. I stared him down for about five minutes, and he disappeared into an alley behind the mall. After I got home, Raul said it was common for kidnappers to keep tabs on the victim's family. Cielo had sensed the same thing in his own daily rounds. We were being watched.

Emi's birthday was September 18, and we had a big party for him that Friday. When I started dancing again and the kids saw me leave in my outfit for dance class, I think they felt like things were at least partly back to normal, so I

decided to take Raul's advice and start doing all the fun
things we used to do—one of the few variables within my
control. So for Emi's birthday we rented one of those blow-
up jumping tents that make the kids go nuts. I jumped too.
We also had sack races. I went head-to-head with Raul; little
did he know I was a ringer, and I'm proud to say I smoked
his ass. All of his wind sprints and marathon training were
no match for my natural hopping abilities. He confessed
he'd always been skeptical that I could have hopped to the
road in record time and flagged down a city bus with my
hands and feet bound, but now he was a believer.

We planned to have a piñata like we always did. It turned
out that Raul's family in Guerrero were piñata makers, and
he spent several days in his room making Emiliano a knight
piñata. It was really good, and when it came time to blindfold him and take a whack at it with a stick, Emi wouldn't
hear of it and locked it in his room instead, treating it like
an absolute treasure. (Luckily, I had a backup piñata on
hand, just in case.) Emi couldn't stop thinking of Eduardo
all day long—at one point, Raul and I had to calm him
down. We recorded everything on video for Eduardo to
watch when he got home.

Cielo showed up at the party unannounced, claiming
he had heard a rumor that Eduardo was being held at a safe
house in La Colonia Guadalupe, a neighborhood just off
the central plaza. Earlier in the week, a friend of his had
been in a late-night convenience store when he saw two
policemen stop a local drug dealer known as "El Michoa-
cano." Michoacán was a nearby state to the southwest of us
where the local drug gangs were indulging in beheadings
and all kinds of crazy things, and "the Michoacan" was a
large-scale drug trafficker with reputed ties to La Familia.
To keep from being arrested, he offered information on
Eduardo's kidnapping, a high-profile crime that he had
knowledge of but was not involved in—describing the
street, the safe house, and even providing an address. Cielo

had taken it upon himself to stake out the neighborhood to see what he could find out. He was certain he was being followed, and had taken to carrying a pistol, as had I. He'd been out searching for Eduardo for three days, and he looked it.

Cielo had been out of the loop with his drinking and late-night deejaying—he was starting to doubt the theory of the AFI and was still seeing this as some small-time revenge scenario involving Oscar and Norma and the local drug gangs. We were no longer on the same page. Whoever was behind this had spent tens of thousands of dollars setting it up—it was neither random nor small-time. But instead of reporting this lead through channels, Cielo went tearing around with a nine-millimeter pistol, going undercover on the streets, playing junior G-man and exposing himself to some dangerous people. Raul was really pissed.

As if that wasn't enough, I got into a fight with Fernando a couple of days after Emi's birthday. Ever since he had gotten back from my mom's, Nando had been hanging around with a new boy from Canada who is kind of a wild kid. He started lying to me, getting into trouble at school, and doing dangerous things to test my authority. When I saw him doing daredevil tricks on his four-wheeler without a helmet, I made him promise to be more careful. The next day, when I came back from doing errands, my mom told me she'd seen him shooting BBs and scaring the horses (the few we hadn't managed to sell yet) and being reckless again on the four-wheeler. I had another talk with him—I thought more forcefully. I told him all I needed right now was more trauma. He acted like I was being overprotective but said he'd watch it. Then the very next day, while this Canadian kid was over, he came in holding his mouth funny and told me he had to talk to me. He'd broken his front tooth down to the gum line. They had dumped a gallon of shampoo onto a polished cement ramp on the basketball court, making it fantastically slick, and then gone skateboarding on it.

I lost it, and I came down on him like a ton of bricks. He broke down in hysterics and started screaming, "I hate you! I hate you!" Three months of tight smiles and repressed fury came pouring out of both of us in one gushing swoosh.

I threw him in the car and drove him to Queretaro, both of us silent and fuming the whole way there, where luckily the dentist saw him on an emergency basis. By evening, we had both calmed down enough that we could talk. We had a long discussion that night about his need to indulge in dangerous behavior. I grounded him for a month. I took away his motorcycle, his phone, his skateboard, and his Xbox. And with Raul's help, I started reeling him in. Within a week, I had enrolled all three kids in tennis lessons, and that seemed to help. Nando also started hanging out more with Raul, who was exerting some much-needed masculine influence on my twelve-year-old burgeoning teenager.

Nando started tagging along when Raul went to the gym in the evenings. One time he called me on Raul's cell phone and asked if he could have the corn on the cob the street vendors sell—boiled in suspect water and slathered in mayonnaise that goes unrefrigerated for days. Once before, he had eaten one and gotten violently ill, so we had a rule against it. But he begged and pleaded, and I finally gave in—he could have corn on the cob, but no mayo. The next thing I knew, Raul showed up with Nando in tow—violently ill and barely able to stand. Raul and I quickly got him to the hospital, where he spent the next three nights incapacitated with extreme vomiting and diarrhea. I stayed by his side for most of that time, and it gave us a time to talk, be silly, and undo some of the damage from the week before.

When we brought him home, Fernando had to take this horrid medicine they gave him—an anti-parasitic that was so rancid, it could even kill the kind of life form that could live in unrefrigerated mayonnaise. Nando hated it, and as a result, he kept telling me he felt fine and didn't need to take it anymore. This turned into a standing joke, and as I was chasing him around the kitchen table one morning, trying to spoon-feed him his medicine—laughing but not really—Raul happened through and put him in a mock chokehold with lightning speed. While Raul restrained him, I held his nose until he opened his mouth to breathe, then gave him the prescribed dose. Nando couldn't help but laugh, but from then on, he was lying in wait for Raul.

One morning a few days later, I had just come in from picking tunas and was making breakfast for everyone. Fernando came into the kitchen to see what smelled good just as the phone rang. I was flipping pancakes when he said, "You might want to get that." It was Raul, who was locked in his room. Nando had bolted the door shut from the outside, and he had to call me to let him out. This happened several more times. From there on out, Nando never missed an opportunity to play a prank on Raul. When they were going to go play tennis, which Nando was showing a real flair for, he told Raul he'd meet him there with their rackets, then showed up with Nayah's hot-pink children's racket with Minnie Mouse on it for Raul to use. And once he figured out that Raul liked a girl at the gym but wasn't going to do anything about it (out of deference to his job and the situation), Nando surreptitiously stepped in and got her number for him, then, producing it with a flourish, loudly proclaiming Raul a wuss.

As the month wore on, I tried to focus on lighthearted moments like that, which were few and far between, as I kept up with running the ranch and trying to line up money for Eduardo's ransom. But as the weeks turned into months, I couldn't understand why none of the leads we had provided the AFI home office were bearing fruit. If they didn't have the technology or the expertise in forensics to follow up, then let's send the evidence to the FBI, which most certainly does. Even Raul seemed frustrated at times.

One of the things my mom did to keep busy while the kids were in class was to take Spanish lessons at a local school. One day she came home and said that one of the teachers there, the mother of one of our students at the Waldorf school, had told her a fantastic story.

A few days before the kidnapping, this woman was on her way to the school one morning from her home in El Nigromante when a man offered her a ride in a black pickup truck with tinted windows. He said he was on his way to nearby Dolores Hidalgo, where he had to tend to some agricultural properties. He was stocky, about fifty-five, with dark hair, wrinkled olive skin, and a mustache. He wore a gold ring and gold chains, as well as some kind of hat, and looked like he smoked. He said he was from Michoacán in the southwest but spoke with a northern Mexico accent. At one point during their conversation, he received a call on his cell phone, but in the middle of it a second call came in on a different cell phone. All in all, he had six separate cell phones in his truck. When she asked to be let off at the school, he said he was interested in enrolling his kids in the school and asked who the owners were. As they pulled into the parking lot, she pointed out Eduardo and me as the school's founders. He wrote down everything she said in a notebook, at one point claiming, "Notes are money these days." When she asked him if he wanted to meet the school administrators, he declined.

She saw him again the morning of the kidnapping. She was waiting under a big mesquite tree on the road from the ranch to the highway, talking to another parent, when three vehicles drove by in quick succession, all coming from the school. His pickup was one of them. (Neither Eduardo nor I remember a black pickup.) He had the window partway down and she recognized him. This happened between 8:45 and 9:00 A.M., exactly when we would have been going by, moments after the kidnapping. She noticed that he turned to the right, toward Dolores Hidalgo. She hasn't seen him since, but other people in her neighborhood know him and have shown her where he lives. He is reportedly often in the company of other men with mustaches, and their pit bulls often get loose onto the neighbors' property. Neighbors also claim to have seen trailer trucks empty their contents into the large house. On another occasion, she received a ride from the man's nephew who lives with him in the house. When she asked him what he did for a living, he told her it was private and he couldn't talk about it, but that he made a lot of money. She claims she told the authorities all of this at the time, and that only last week AFI agents came and questioned her for several hours, showing her photographs of men she didn't recognize. She was overwhelmed with guilt for not having told me at the time of the kidnapping and was anxious for me to know this. It seemed to correspond to what I'd heard at the time from Lucy Zavala, and I asked Raul why the AFI hadn't questioned me about it—especially if they had photographs. He said there must be a reason.

Once again, I was frustrated with the pace of forward momentum and began chafing at the restrictions that I felt were being put on me, supposedly in my best interests. So I decided to take matters into my own hands. We knew people—Mexico is a small place, really—so I decided I would just write a letter to the president. Always start at the top.

Fortuitously, Rafael Loret de Mola—the well-known Mexican writer and father of Carlos Loret de Mola, the famous journalist and news anchor, and the son of Eduardo's mentor—stopped by unannounced, brand-new bodyguards in tow. He agreed that this could be the handiwork of the EPR, and he was very concerned about Eduardo and asked how he could help. I told him I was writing a letter to President Calderón, and he offered to hand-deliver it at the end of the month, when they were scheduled to meet. That evening, Richard Leet was passing through town (he also sported a retinue of armed bodyguards), and he and his wife invited me to dinner. When he asked me how the school was doing, I told him that between Eduardo's kidnapping and the crash of the land deal, we could no longer afford to subsidize the purchase of a new school bus. Renting a bus was currently draining the school's savings, and without a bus, we couldn't have a school. Leet, who had lost a fortune after his enterprise with Oscar and Norma combusted, had a foundation that still had a little bit in its bank account. He sent me a check the next day, as did two of the creative people on Cal Wimberley's team. Between them, we were able to buy a full-scale used Blue Bird school bus, a real beauty. Gustavo picked it up for us in mid-December in Oklahoma and drove it back to Mexico.

As we were walking to our car after dinner, my cell phone rang. It was Raul telling me that tomorrow the AFI would be sending a sketch artist to the house to take a *retrato hablado*, or spoken portrait, of my perception of the kidnappers. This is something I had requested months ago, which now was finally happening the day after I made no secret of my plans to write a letter directly to the president of Mexico. Interesting. Beyond that, in the days and weeks ahead, the AFI seemed much quicker on the draw: If I requested a document, they got it to me overnight; if I had a question about some arcane point, they called me back within the hour.

The following day, I made a formal statement about what had happened to a visiting AFI stenographer, and then a police artist sat down with pencils and a sketch pad and asked me to describe in detail the kidnappers I had gotten a good look at—principally the Thin Man, who was blocking the road near our front gate the night before the incident. It was amazing how accurate he could be with only a few simple leads: He asked me the shape of his face, his coloring, his age, height, weight. He would make a line, and then he would erase it and move it a millimeter based on my comments. We did the eyes, the mouth, the nose, the ears—

longer, flatter, rounder, thinner, the eyebrows a little thicker, a dimple in the chin. It was fascinating and more than a little creepy to see the face of this man once again as it took shape before me, based on the shadowy image in my mind. I later found out that after he was done with me, he did the same thing with my friend from El Nigromante.

Loret de Mola was supposed to return a week later to retrieve my letter, but he never showed up. I called him and sent it overnight via Estafeta, the Mexican equivalent of FedEx. He said he'd deliver it as promised. But I decided not to put all my eggs in one basket. Luis Alberto (our senator from Guanajuato) and his wife stopped by to check on me, and I gave him a second letter to hand-deliver, which he promised to do when he returned to Mexico City in a week, as he and the president are very close. Like Rafael and others with inside knowledge, he agreed this sounded like the EPR. He told me furtive stories of EPR training camps in the mountains of Queretaro. When I shared what the AFI had told me, that ETA members from the Basque country in Spain had allegedly shared their knowledge of explosives with the EPR on a freelance basis—something I felt safe telling a senator and close friend—he said that three Spanish men had lived in the San Antonio neighborhood of San Miguel for several months earlier in the year. He had seen the men several times, and the rumor was that they were ETA members. Of course, there is no shortage of speculative rumors in San Miguel—including about me—but after the kidnapping, supposedly no one ever saw them again. We dutifully sent a *tarjeta* to AFI headquarters, as we did with everything else.

My plan was to keep finding people to hand-carry my letters to the president until he took notice of my situation. But after the letter sent through Luis Alberto, I received a letter from the Office of the President—signed by Felipe Calderón, but obviously written by an underling. It wished me well in this difficult time and promised to do everything in the government's power to bring this matter to a successful resolution.

And still it wouldn't stop—not just the kidnappers terrorizing us or the frustrations of the bureaucracy surrounding it but also these ill-considered and often destructive rumors and gossip loose in the community.

Michael French told me one of his friends who went shooting with us had dinner with one of the senior police officials, who delivered some rant to the effect that Eduardo had faked his own kidnapping to point the blame at Oscar and Norma, or else he was scared of them and wanted police protection at the ranch. He labeled Eduardo *auto-secuestrado*—self-kidnapped. What a clown.

Eduardo's next letter said that in addition to injecting him with HIV-tainted blood, they would also cut him up into little pieces. I spent hours lost in dark reveries of becoming a sniper and dispatching my enemies—swift, painless, not a sound or sign left behind. I suspect I wasn't the only one.

Then a few days before the end of September, I returned home from dance class and Tina told me a *citatorio*, or legal notice, had arrived in Eduardo's name. It turns out that Maru, one of our beloved housekeepers, was suing us, claiming Eduardo had terminated her without cause and demanding more than a year's salary plus severance.

This was all I needed right now. She claimed Eduardo had fired her without provocation, that she never received a bonus, and on and on. I was livid. She had *really* picked the wrong time to try this with me. Generally, since the legal costs are prohibitive, employers settle out of court. I went a different way. I hired a lawyer, and in the end the case was thrown out and she got nothing.

But by that point so much had happened. My feelings for this beautiful country had been hollowed out like a honeycomb, leaving me brittle and exposed. I felt like our family was a fallen tree that everyone wanted to make firewood out of. I'd had it.

That Sunday, I gathered the kids and told them we were going to play a new game I had invented. It was called Cardon Cactus, which is a kind of cactus that grows wild like a weed, with limbs that look like reptilian claws and big jagged thorns that are like fishhooks to get out of your skin—*cardo* means spine or thistle. It's like a plague. I gave everybody paper and crayons and told them to draw the face of a bad guy—"like the ones who have Daddy." They really got into it. Nayah's had worms crawling out of the forehead, nose, and mouth. Emiliano's was scary, with big jagged teeth, and Fernando's was dark and menacing. Even Vera, Cielo's eight-year-old daughter, drew one with green bulging eyes. We went outside and attached them to these cacti that I had already picked out—the ones that scratched the Jeep when I parked too close to the edge of the driveway, or that I ran into whenever I went outside at night. We all wore goggles, hats, gloves, and layers of protective clothing. Then we smashed the cacti into pulps with baseball bats. We took turns beating them into the ground. Then we took what was left of the drawings and burned them in a pile. Then the boys peed on the ashes and the girls spit. The kids loved it! It went a long way toward relieving this crushing stress that was weighing all of us down.

Very therapeutic.

TWELVE

Black Widow

The Colonel used to have a saying he instilled in Eduardo growing up: *Es mejor una mala direccion que dos buenas.* It's better to go in one bad direction than in two good ones.

It means to decide on a course of action and see it through. That was how I looked at the AFI. Whatever its political agenda, however its members interacted with the machinery of government at the very top of the chain, it was extremely adept at this slow-motion hybrid of chess and chicken that constituted hostage negotiations.

At this part of the game, our side broached the subject of *estar comprometido*, a practice whereby you reach a compromise and agree to follow through with it even after the situation is resolved. Prior to this, it was all about expressing how the kidnappers had overestimated our ability to pay. At this stage, we suggested they release him, and then either we would renegotiate a settlement, give them an additional amount at an agreed-upon date, or leave the country. It's also a form of onetime protection money, in that the kidnappers promise never to target you again—the implied second kidnapping is a common downside to meeting the kidnappers' original demands. Psychologically, it was a way to change the subject—to segue from their ongoing threats when we couldn't raise the kind of sums they wanted, to a new discussion based on what we could afford to pay.

But even as we were negotiating, I knew I couldn't honor any kind of deal like that. Over these past five months, I had come to the conclusion that there are humans who are lower on the evolutionary chain. They have not developed a conscience. They go through life without feeling love, empathy, or reverence for life. I could not be party to letting them exercise control over us for even a second longer. I preferred to move to the farthest corner of the earth rather than give these bastards another dime once I had Eduardo back. (In fact, without telling us, Eduardo's kidnappers did present this option to him, and he agreed to pay an astronomical amount if they would release him.)

At the same time, Cielo and I were both undergoing intensive rehearsals with Raul for what we would do in the event of various contingencies. Cielo was no longer with me on a daily basis as in the beginning, but he did come by and participate when we needed him to. We role-played scenes and ran dialogue for the inevitable phone calls from the criminals, or the ones they certainly would force Eduardo to make, once his lurid letters no longer had the desired effect. Luckily, my acting training played right into that. I could read a situation pretty well, and I could think on my feet. But there was something else going on that dovetailed as well.

After I spoke at the shopping center on behalf of the school in mid-September and recognized that the kidnappers were always watching me, I realized that I had a stage on which I could perform whatever role I wanted. In the classified ads in the back of the newspaper, I would be whatever they wanted me to be—the scared little rabbit, the ingénue in jeopardy. I would say or do whatever my AFI handlers instructed me to. But I was free to live my life any way I wanted. It may sound a little sick, or slightly unhinged in the cold light of day, but I wanted to punish the kidnappers— these sadists who were so certain they held all the cards. I wanted to make their world a little less secure, and the easiest way I could do that was to mess with their most basic assumptions about me. When they threatened to start injecting Eduardo with AIDS-infected blood, it only strengthened my resolve. If they were going to be watching me, then I would put on a show for them. This is what I was trained for, where my confidence resided, and where I could exercise some power over my circumstances. It was incredibly liberating.

The first thing I did was to carve out a small emotional place with my kids where the burdens of the outside world had no effect on us. I was like a thermometer to them: If I was running hot—desperate, panicked—then they were the same way. Conversely, when I was despondent and distraught, they felt sad too. I came to see that the time I spent reveling in my own misery was a luxury I could no longer afford. So I made the decision we were all going to proceed as if everything would be fine. We would put our positive vibrations out into the universe and wait for them to be revisited upon us. Joy was now the part of my emotional palette I defaulted to, a goal to be obtained in every possible setting. I learned how to disconnect emotionally from my reality as a survival mechanism. It was acting, and it was passive-aggressive, but it allowed me to be in control of my environment—to dictate its tone and mood. And I wanted the kidnappers to see this as well. It was my way of manipulating them like they were manipulating me. I was happy. I was getting along just fine. It was tough at first, but now I was through the worst of it. Maybe I didn't want him back that badly. Maybe if you play your cards wrong and push me over the edge, I'll pack it up and take it all with me. You can keep Eduardo; you won't get a dime for his corpse. Such was the image I was projecting. They had their double lives they were leading—this was mine.

People who saw me out and about were certain I had lost my mind. On the one hand, I was rock solid in my certainty that Eduardo was alive and was coming back to me. And then, I didn't even seem all that concerned about it anymore. I was happy, positive, beaming. They thought I had snapped.

It's a cliché, but you always find out who your friends are in a situation like this. Some people were afraid to come around for security reasons—one family didn't even send their kid to school anymore, and several more kept their kids home during the first week, until the police established a regular presence during school hours. Most people were supportive or tried to be anyway. But almost everyone assumed that Eduardo was already dead. For security reasons, I did not leak any info, so there was never any news about the kidnapping—just my resolutely sunny disposition. They didn't know Raul was embedded with me, so they didn't see any contact with the authorities. There was nothing in the papers. People would come up to me on the street and say, "I am so sorry—is there anything I can do? Can I send a casserole or something?" Or the best was "We loved Eduardo so much—we really did." I would have to stop them and say, "You don't have to apologize. My husband is coming back."

Others found it offensive that I wasn't in constant mourning. When we were practicing for a performance with our belly-dancing troupe, a friend of mine gave me a look that I will never forget. At school functions, there were a lot of stares and whispers. Finally, one of my good friends called and told me another mother at the school said that I needed a talking to, that enough was enough, and that we needed to move on as a community. Eduardo was dead. I had kids, for God's sake. I at least owed it to them.

These were not bad people—I'm sure they had my best interests at heart. They were simply wrong. How could I make them understand that and not appear mad? It was this ridiculous situation in which I was constantly trying to instill hope in the very people who should have been doing that for me.

On October 11, the kidnappers sent me a photo of Eduardo holding the morning newspaper posed against a floral blanket. He looked gaunt and haggard, probably from having lost so much weight. Two days later—Eduardo's birthday—my carefully crafted facade failed me, and I collapsed in the middle of my dance class. It was all I could do to drag myself into a corner of the classroom and curl up in a little ball with my head on my knees, wracked with sobs. Try as I might, I couldn't quit crying. Everyone just huddled around me with their hands on my shoulders or back or head to transmit their energy and emotional support, and I wept like I had needed to for months. That night, our dance troupe performed at a local theater and I dedicated the performance to Eduardo. It was Michael French's birthday as well, and at his gallery afterward he had two cakes— one for him and one for Eduardo.

A few days later, an e-mail from the kidnappers announced:

On Tuesday, October 30th, Eduardo is going to receive his first gunshot in his left leg unless there's a change in the total amount offered to seven figures, in the millions of dollars.

If you don't publish, same consequences.

If you keep offering ridiculous and unacceptable proposals, same consequences.

Our "consideration" leads us to demand $6 million dollars today (7 figures).

Although he found it unlikely, Raul prepared Cielo and me for the possibility that they could actually shoot him. They'd done it before.

Somewhere in the middle of this, I filed paperwork against Oscar Gutierrez, which extended his jail term. It was for the crime of displacement, or removing someone from their property, since he still refused to allow us access to our train car. He refused to budge, even though it was clear this would happen. I guess he thought that eventually we'd get sick of the continued legal battle and sell them the land at rock-bottom prices. But to me it just appeared insane. Then one day, I looked out the kitchen window to see Oscar's wife and her bodyguard emerge from her SUV. She had her hands folded in front of her like a librarian or a nun. She looked thin and very frail. I probably should have listened to what she had to say, if for no other reason than to report it here. But I had the cook inform her that she was trespassing, and that whatever she had to say, she could say it to my lawyer. I resisted the urge to greet her with the shotgun.

This was during a period when I was planning my annual Halloween party. Halloween is not a traditional Mexican holiday—the Mexican version takes place on November 1, the Day of the Dead—but the kids loved it, and I'd already made the commitment that I wasn't going to let our dire circumstances ruin things for them. This could be the last Halloween we ever spent at the ranch, and they had a right to experience the traditions we had always celebrated. But the closer we got to the party, the more it became part of this elaborate drama I was staging. If the townspeople believed I was the Madwoman of Chaillot, then I would give them a performance to remember.

As I usually do, I harvested all my Mexican pumpkins and use them to carve jack-o'-lanterns. I roasted corn from our fields and gave it to the kids on sticks, along with corn tamales and a black bean salad from the beans we grow. For the party, I hung goblins made of old white sheets with black felt faces from all the trees and organ cacti, all strung with fishing line so that they would blow in the wind. We had about eighty people there, with a hayride, music, a huge bonfire, and trick-or-treating all over the ranch. I dressed as the Black Widow—partly to make fun of the way I was being perceived. I served a drink called the Black Widow as well—vodka and black Sambuca over ice with a stick of black licorice as garnish. There were also Gummi worm cupcakes with ground Oreo "dirt."

The next day the kids and I made an altar for the Day of the Dead. Traditionally, you put photographs of dead loved ones on the altar and place their favorite foods or items beneath it so their spirits can return and enjoy these earthly pleasures once more. I couldn't help but imagine the possibility that next year we would have a picture of Eduardo. I felt like I should somehow make a drawing or painting of my old life that was now long gone, and for which it seemed like I was in perpetual mourning.

Later in the day, an e-mail arrived from the kidnappers:

Sirs:

Here is proof that we followed through with our warning.

You didn't follow through and you continue with your ridiculous excuses . . . WE DON'T GIVE A SHIT ABOUT YOUR EXCUSES, just like we didn't give a shit about Eduardo's plea to write you another letter in order to save his leg.

This is what is going to happen: Another spin of the roulette wheel . . .

If you don't publish numbers that are satisfactory, Eduardo will receive a gunshot in his left arm.

If you don't publish, same thing.

If you keep making ridiculous proposals, same thing.

Attached to the e-mail was a photo of Eduardo, his face not visible, lying naked on his side on gray industrial carpet partially covered by a white sheet. His hands were hand-cuffed behind his back. He had been shot once through the thigh with what looked like a .45-caliber bullet. There was a small amount of blood where the bullet had entered and much more down the back of his leg where it had exited. From the placement of the wounds, it looked like they had taken special care to avoid the bone. The sheet also held a significant amount of blood, partly obscured by the day's copy of *El Universal* to establish the timeliness of the photo. In the lower left corner, a man's hand wearing a yellow and orange glove held Eduardo's left ankle. It reminded me of paintings of St. Sebastian, pierced by arrows.

I was predictably devastated. I went to my room and got under the covers. I didn't want any part of a world in which this was possible. My head was flooded with images of Eduardo in a wheelchair, helpless, unable to talk, to feel anything. Raul had to remind me that this had always been a possibility, and that as little consolation as it might seem right now, the kidnappers were professionals and knew what they were doing.

Raul had to travel to Mexico City to sign paperwork as part of a structural overhaul of the AFI, which was being reorganized under the title of Federal Police. While he was there, he had a doctor and forensic specialist inspect the photograph. The doctor confirmed that this was essentially a flesh wound: The bullet had entered the muscle midthigh and apparently made a fairly clean exit. At such close range, the bullet would have had a cauterizing effect, searing the flesh and sealing it to prevent excessive bleeding. There was little chance of lasting damage or the loss of function-ality, and any necessary antibiotics would most likely have been provided by a medic who was standing by, if past cases were any indication. As Raul told me, "He's their merchandise. They won't let him die; he's too valuable for that." An Italian victim of the EPR living in Mexico had been shot twice and returned home to his family, apparently none the worse for wear.

If this was understandably putting me more on edge, then it seemed to be reflected in the world around me. The dogs were unusually nervous and kept me up all night on a regular basis. The coyotes were encroaching on our territory, killing our sheep and leaving behind a bloody mess. And there were signs of them having ventured closer to the house, as if the bond between predators and their natural feel for any kind of weakness had somehow translated across species. When I began to hear strange noises at night, I often would go out alone in the Jeep with my .357 Magnum and patrol the perimeter, raking the fields with a spotlight. Raul begged me to wake him up so he could go with me, but I rarely did. The night was an alien landscape, especially when I was wrenched awake from half-devoured dreams, and it seemed only logical that feral beasts should be coming for us, chewing through the border between worlds like a porous membrane. Besides, if the kidnappers really were watching me, they needed to expect a fight. But all I ever saw was fields of jackrabbits—more than I could imagine existed. Their startled expressions indicated I was as improbable a presence in their world as they were in mine. Eventually Raul and Fernando camped out all night to shoot the coyotes that ventured too close, and the threat subsided.

I kept a suitcase packed by the front door with Eduardo's clothes and personal items for when he returned, so we could leave this place immediately. In mid-November, I unpacked his summer clothes and repacked the suitcase with his winter clothes, to keep up with the changing seasons. I knew his jeans would no longer fit him, but I included sweatpants with drawstrings. I was overwhelmed by the smells trapped in the folds of his clothing, Eduardo's scent encircling me like a phantom lover. In the middle of the day, I would find myself standing in his closet and holding his shirts to me. I missed his kisses, being held by him, the way he would steal up behind me when I was cooking and slip his arms around my waist, inhaling the aroma of the impending meal. I was starved for these simplest of experiences. I slept with his favorite bandanna under my pillow, so I could breathe him in as I drifted into dreams. I felt like a widow who still clings to the last of her husband's possessions. It felt pathetic, but I couldn't stop.

Sixteen days after the first photo, another photo arrived. This was just a close-up of Eduardo's arm, neatly pierced in two places halfway between the shoulder and the elbow by what looked like a .22-caliber bullet. A brown discoloration on his upper arm could have been iodine, indicating he had received some kind of medical treatment. An attached letter from Eduardo sneered, "Thank you for your useless efforts and empty words, and besides, it's my money. You could have prevented this . . . Everything has a limit. Tell my little kids I say good-bye; I adore them. Tell my kids, grandkids, friends, and relatives that I could have lived, but that you preferred the money, and I was left thrown on the floor, abandoned, infected, without being able to move, like a vegetable, an invalid, a product of the torture and pain on my path towards death."

Right after this, *El Universal* became suspicious of the classified ads we were placing in their newspaper and refused to accept any more. Apparently, this is a preferred way for kidnapping victims' families to communicate with their assailants, and so the major papers are constantly on the lookout for patterns that fit the profile. Raul got on the phone with them and they allowed us to place one last ad. Soon after we switched to *Reforma*, per the kidnappers' e-mail instructions.

Then, as I was preparing for Thanksgiving dinner, which I decided to go ahead with regardless of our circumstances, a taxi driver named Tobias contacted me after giving Juanita Otero a ride in his taxi. He claimed to have worked for Oscar and Norma as a guard. He said that he had witnessed the kidnapping as well as the second getaway car that took off with Eduardo. That seemed impossible: No one who hadn't been in the car with us could have witnessed both—that was the whole point. When he showed up at my door, Raul had wired me with a surveillance microphone and sat listening in the other room. I asked Tobias a handful of questions—a little quiz—that he failed. He told me he saw Norma in a black car on the highway by La Cabaña, along with other guards who used to work for her as well. He was off on everything he said. He then volunteered to work as an undercover agent for me. As a taxi driver, he could blend into his surroundings, and he knew where all the safe houses were in San Miguel—one of which might actually hold Eduardo. Of course, he would have to be paid for this, but he was sure we could make a deal. I couldn't believe what I was hearing. By the time he left, Raul was fuming.

"*Que gente*," he said. "I can't believe these people."

Exactly. *Que gente*. I'd had about enough of playing the victim for one run. Meanwhile, I felt like I was in exactly the same situation as twenty years ago: I had an agent—Raul—whom I spent most of my time arguing with about line readings. I had a director—Benito Roa—who was generally out of pocket and emotionally unavailable. I had a script that was forced on me and a character who was chafing at the constraints. And my audience and harshest critics blamed me for everything they saw and didn't like, even though my hands were tied.

So I decided to do something about it.

One day, sometime during the week before Thanksgiving, without apparent plan or provocation, I started packing up the household items as if I were getting ready to move. Everything we didn't use—furniture, boxes, things that we previously had in storage in the room that now housed Raul—went into a huge warehouse where we kept the farm machinery. I left the doors wide open so anybody who wanted to could see what I was doing. We wrapped everything in Bubble Wrap and duct tape and carefully stacked and labeled all of it. Everybody pitched in, including the kids. The movers worked for two days running, patiently carting our lifetime of possessions from the house to the barn, like the army of leaf-cutter ants that strips everything in its path.

They knew I was an American. I took insidious delight in the chain reaction that I imagined this would set off in their minds. Was I giving up and moving back to the United States with my kids? Had the pressure finally broken me? Everyone I knew thought so. Was I really after his money— all those horrible things they had forced Eduardo to write in his letters? What if they had been right all along and never knew it? All of their finely crafted bluster and logic had been field-tested on Mexican women used to the macho posturings of their men. But maybe I was a different animal entirely—an American trophy wife on an open-ended foreign adventure who never signed up for this and was going to take a slow boat back home, leaving them covered in the blowback of their own best-laid plans.

Of course, my plan was that when Eduardo came back, we'd have to go somewhere, just to give him time to recover. That certainly meant closing up the house and probably leaving the country. I simply dragged everything out into the open. Just imagining they were watching me somehow lifted my spirits. They had their weapons; I had mine.

That year, we had Thanksgiving like we always did with family and close friends. I left an empty place at the head of the table where Eduardo always sat. We said a prayer for him and sent him our thoughts and our energy.

Later in the day, an e-mail arrived with six separate letters from Eduardo attached. Each one took a different tack, and all appeared written in a hurry.

Whatever I had done, it seemed to have gotten their attention.

THIRTEEN

Bloodsuckers

EDUARDO IN CAPTIVITY REDUX

For the duration of his time in captivity, Eduardo constantly clutched at any hard fact with which he could begin to reconstruct his worldview. Since he was always wearing a black hood that covered his entire head and was only blindfolded a couple of times, he learned to identify his captors by their sounds and smells, and how to assess their mood, and along with it his own safety, like he would as an animal in the wild. But living in fifty cubic feet of contained space, his senses mediated by bright lights, blaring music, soiled carpet, stagnant water, and a lack of sustenance, while constantly besieged with an overwhelming and irrational terror, it was often impossible to find even a toehold from which to reclaim his bearings.

One small way he was able to do this was to exact revenge on the tiny, almost invisible parasites known as *chinches* that infested his environment. Like nearly microscopic ticks, these foreign creatures would slip in through the airholes at the top of the box and burrow into his flesh while he slept. Over weeks and often months, he would hunt them down, tirelessly combing through the fibers of the gray industrial carpet that covered every interior surface of the box, forcing them into a corner where he could finally trap and crush them. This became an obsession, a way to fight back against the constant torment he was subjected to, as well as to exercise some kind of control on his environment that would not result in physical repercussions. Over time, he became adept at learning their ways, and he was able to find and kill them in a matter of days.

After a fair amount of time in the box, Eduardo heard what must have been a small fireworks demonstration. He deduced that this must be in honor of the annual Independence Day celebration on September 16 and that he must be on the outskirts of a small town within driving distance of San Miguel. He had isolated the sound of a city bus that ran Monday through Saturday and stopped at a bus stop near where he was being held, indicating the house was located near the street. This way, he could keep track of the days of the week. Now with a fixed date, he had a working calendar. He also heard the kidnappers regularly practice target shooting near the house and noticed that the men who held him frequently came into the box with dirt or mud on their boots (he would discover dirt and mud when he cleaned up his box after they left). All were clues with which to someday reconstruct a map of his whereabouts.

Everything Eduardo learned from his captors, or thought he learned, was also the opportunity for disinformation— encouraging through subterfuge what they wanted him to believe. By the same token, he found it almost impossible not to attribute meaning to every new connection, no matter how random. For instance, his captors incessantly played *narcocorridos*, the story-songs performed in the *norteño* tradition that celebrated drug traffickers and their lawless exploits. Was that out of an enthusiasm for the music, identification with its subject matter, or merely a ruse to make him think they came from the ranks of the *narcotraficantes* who were otherwise ravaging the nation? At one point, out of the blue, El Jefe asked him, "Why are you fighting with Oscar?" Eduardo explained that he wasn't fighting with Oscar—he was merely trying to access his train car. Then a few weeks later, El Jefe said, "A while back, your friend Oscar gave me two million pesos [roughly US$150,000] to take two people out of the country"—presumably to smuggle them into the United States. Who exactly? And for what reason? He didn't say. Was El Jefe suggesting that Oscar was involved in all of this—that they had a long-standing relationship, and he could make people disappear at will or send those who were involved to someplace out of harm's way? And why would the kidnappers, who were so careful about every detail, tie themselves into another case in which the authorities were already involved? Or did El Jefe merely read about their feud in the local paper (one of Oscar's full-page ads, maybe)—or learn about it from his emissaries on the street—and dump more lies into Eduardo's churning mind?

More than halfway into Eduardo's captivity, his captors started using the pejorative phrase "people of your class." Did that suggest sympathy with the revolutionary philosophy of the EPR—and if so, why did it take them five months to vocalize it? Did they call themselves blood brothers out of a political or a paramilitary loyalty, and was this gesture authentic or ironic? By the same token, was the hammer they left at the kidnapping scene a symbol or an anti-symbol—a calling card or a false flag? They asked for eight million dollars and clearly expected to get it, as evidenced by their frustration as negotiations dragged on. Did this indicate a financial stake in the outcome, making them more mercenaries than zealots? Or were they hired hands, part of the semipermanent contract army that was trained at the War College and has been caravanning around Central America for the past fifty years—possibly with a bonus built into their deal? Did their apparent brainwashing attempts even make that point—were they reading out of the same psychological operations field manual as the folks running Camp X-Ray in Guantánamo, Cuba?

But for eight million dollars, you don't need a motive to commit a crime. Eight million dollars *is* a motive. It was criminals who were doing this—organized crime, which could afford whatever expenditures were required. Possibly in collusion with law enforcement, which was just another arm of the same group. Or the same corrupt forces within the government that Eduardo had been railing against his whole life. Or his father before him—an entire century's worth of entrenched enemies. With the help of various nefarious elements, any of whom might have fingered Eduardo as part of some other agenda entirely.

Any and all strange bedfellows were worthy suspects. Anyone could have done this, and there was always a chain of logic leading backward to prove it. A person could go mad thinking like this—even one not confined to a living coffin.

As I suspected, the kidnappers wrote many of Eduardo's letters for him—printing them in a careful script that he was forced to copy in his own handwriting. The letters were always presented to him after one of his beatings, while he was still bleeding, presumably when his resistance was at its weakest. If he changed even so much as a word, El Jefe would hit him again and force him to do it over again. Eduardo went through a dozen ballpoint pens during his months in captivity—at least two a month—endlessly writing and rewriting these letters. Some of them were never sent. At times, as an exercise, he was forced to make his plea in no more than a hundred words—if his note stretched to a hundred ten, they would tear it up and make him try again. Or they would highlight sections and force him to expand on just that part, intensively copyediting him under threat of violence. Interestingly, whenever the letters contained references to specific amounts, he was instructed to seal those letters in envelopes marked "El Jefe" before slipping them under the door of the box. This suggests that the guards who would collect those messages were not aware of the amount of money at stake.

After their beatings, the kidnappers often left Eduardo notes like the following one from El Jefe:

> We are definitely going to kill you, and your fucking family is not even going to see your body. If they want to see your body, they are going to have to pay for it. I'm thinking about how to start. I don't know if I'm going to cut off your fingers first—I'm going to talk to my associates about where to start. But one thing I promise you is that you are never going to get out of here alive, and your family is never going to be together again. We are going to cut some body parts off, that I assure you.

At one point, after making repeated threats, they entered the box, forced Eduardo onto his stomach, and brandished a large pair of branch cutters. They doused his hands with rubbing alcohol and placed his index finger between the blades, before disintegrating in laughter and exiting. Another time, they sent a note saying that they would bind his wrists so tightly with handcuffs that it would cut off circulation, in order to cut off one finger at a time. They threatened to kill our dogs by beheading them and hanging the carcasses from a fence post, and they actually injected Eduardo like they told me they would, telling him it was AIDS-contaminated blood. The mental torture was as bad as the physical torture.

When the beatings or threats no longer instilled the requisite amount of fear, they used anticipation of these things to magnify their effect. They would interrupt whatever schedule or stability had been implied, telling Eduardo they would be back in three days to deliver a beating, then not show up, only to appear on the fourth or fifth day, blaming his family's failure to come through with some offer.

But all of this paled next to the shootings.

The kidnappers told him every day for three weeks they were going to shoot him in the leg: First they would shoot him in the left leg, then the left arm, then the right leg, and finally the right arm. By that point, the left leg would have healed enough so they could start with it again. They claimed that by staggering the shootings like this, they were ensuring that he could still lift himself up onto the makeshift toilet.

Finally, at the end of the third week, on a morning redolent with the smell of strong coffee that always prefaced something bad, they stripped him naked and bound his hands and feet together. Then El Jefe, who was wearing his mask, placed a .45-caliber automatic pistol against his upper thigh, taking care to adjust the angle so that the bullet wouldn't pass through the bone, and pulled the trigger. The bullet easily exited through the fleshy part of the back of his leg and lodged in the wooden floor beneath the carpet. With the gun held directly against the skin, it gave the sensation of the explosion coming from inside his leg, the pain expanding from the inside out, like a large air pocket suddenly dislodged from the bottom of a lake. This was followed by the smell of black powder mixed with burning skin. There were powder burns on the front of his leg, and loose flaps of skin hanging open, which they immediately cut away with scissors—an act that may have been more painful than the shooting itself, if that were possible. The first time, Eduardo went into convulsions and almost passed out. His captors refused to give him anything for the pain.

Eduardo was convinced he was never going to get out of the box. His greatest fear was that he would permanently lose his sanity—that the pounding music would break his mind or spirit or that these horrible images in his mind of violence and revenge would never leave him. In fact, the only thing that gave him strength was that he was free to take his own life at any time. In the beginning, when they gave him slivers of Valium to help him sleep, he tried to hoard enough to take them all at once and overdose, but he could never save enough. Now, if he could just dislodge one of the industrial staples in the corner of the box, sharpen a chicken bone, hone the edge of a fingernail just right, he could open a vein and bleed out before they ever found him. By not giving them the satisfaction of deciding whether he lived or died, and knowing at any moment he had the ability to subvert their plans for success, it gave him an immense sense of empowerment over his situation. Contrary to what his letters said, every time they told him that his family wasn't cooperating, it filled him with a secret joy, because it meant he had allies in this war against his enemies. In an odd, circuitous way, it was the possibility of suicide that somehow kept him alive and sane.

This private war of attrition finally reached its culmination when El Jefe—frustrated, angry, and desperate—told Eduardo once again that he was going to kill him, that he was useless, a waste of time. Finally, Eduardo shouted back at him, "I don't have eight million dollars. I just don't have it. You should go ahead and kill me." Eduardo could see that El Jefe's hands began to shake, and he quickly left the room to get his gun and load it. When he returned, he entered the box and put the gun up to Eduardo's head, his hands still shaking. They stayed that way a long moment, each one staring at the other, neither one blinking, until finally El Jefe broke. That's when Eduardo saw him mouth "motherfucker" in English.

Like his father, Eduardo is a street fighter. It's a skill he has rarely had to use, but many times he has told me that he easily could have become a gangster if he had been born into other circumstances. Like me, in ways that perhaps he didn't realize beforehand, Eduardo had been blessed with exactly the skills he needed to survive something like this. It was the ability to go all in, to make it personal and not back down. It's what made him a defender of the poor, in defiance of his class. Whatever would come afterward, something about the balance of power between them shifted that day. Whatever elasticity there was in this horrible sequence of events that had spun our family so totally out of control, this was the point at which it stretched as far as it was going to. From that day forward, Eduardo was on the road back.

Right after the first shooting, El Jefe wrote Eduardo a letter: *In sixteen days, I'm going to shoot you again.* In exactly sixteen days, he repeated the same actions, down to the smallest detail, with the exception that this time, as announced, they shot him in the left arm, just above the elbow. Because Eduardo was so frail at this point and had lost so much weight, they used a .22-caliber pistol, whose bullet makes a much smaller hole (and is considerably less painful). El Jefe promised to return in another ten days and shoot him in the other leg. But when the tenth day arrived, Eduardo was mystified to find himself completely calm and relaxed. His body had adjusted to the trauma and prepared for it accordingly. El Jefe failed to show that day and in fact never came into the box to beat or threaten him again. Soon after that, El Jefe approached Eduardo to ask his advice. This would have been right after Thanksgiving, when I packed up all our possessions and put them outside.

"I need you to tell me what I should do," El Jefe said to him. "Your wife just doesn't react. What do you suggest?"

From that point on, things began to happen very fast.

FOURTEEN

Bargaining

DECEMBER: BARGAINING

Right after Thanksgiving is when everything started shifting. Instead of the eight million dollars they had intractably clung to, even as Eduardo tried to negotiate unilaterally, suddenly the kidnappers cut their demand in half and appeared willing to bargain from there. Eduardo's letters, although still containing flashes of anger, were now much more pragmatic—endlessly detailing how I could raise the necessary capital to appease his captors. They started to send copies of the letters to Cielo and Aurora as well, in an effort to open up a second front in their campaign. They would send multiple copies of their e-mails but include passwords that only Cielo or Aurora would know, thus ensuring their participation whether I liked it or not. Eduardo also asked me to prepare whatever forms were necessary from our banker to liquidate our assets.

In our negotiations to date, I had walked a tightrope with a bundle in each arm. One bundle was that of Eduardo's life and well-being, and the other was our family's finances. I would have given or done anything to have Eduardo home with me, but unfortunately, that wasn't especially relevant. A kidnap for ransom is all about the negotiation. It is a careful dance, with the prescribed steps set out ahead of time. To those who participate in it—by choice, not by consequence—it is an act of precision and formal beauty. Make it too easy for them—pay too early or too effortlessly—and you prolong the ordeal by becoming these people's private ATM. Make it hard—offer to pay too little or fail to pay the proper respects—and you risk losing everything, increasing or prolonging your loved one's suffering many times over. But worst of all, fail to acknowledge the rules of the game, and for lack of a better word, you offend their sense of aesthetics: The only thing worse than playing poorly is not understanding that you're playing at all.

And so I did my best to make myself a worthy adversary. Part of that was recognizing the theater of what we were engaged in.

They decide: "We will make ourselves look big and scary. Now make your move."

Okay, I get that, so here are my circumstances: This is how much I can realistically pay.

"Oh yeah? Well, that's not enough. Look at this—*this* is how big, mean, and scary we can be."

Okay, now I'm scared. But it doesn't alter my situation. And no matter how loud you roar, my finances will not change.

It's a rabbit hole and a mind trick and a chess game. Welcome to the Terrordrome.

The week after Thanksgiving, I returned to Maryland alone for one of my semiannual cancer checkups. Mom stayed with the kids in San Miguel. The constant stress was taking a toll on me. I started feeling really tired in the afternoons; I even told Raul I was worried about my health. He assured me I was going to be fine. So when I flew back to Maryland, I was careful to get thoroughly checked out.

Sometimes, it seemed impossible not to have a relapse, with all that was going on in my life, and I was trying to stay on top of my diet, steal a nap here and there, and make my private deals with God. Even if I hadn't had cancer, I began to think I would have gotten it from this ridiculous, relentless state of agitation and anxiety.

But I was fine. My breast MRI and blood tests were normal, and the doctors couldn't find anything wrong. If I was tired all the time, well, who wouldn't be in my situation?

One night in early December when we were getting the kids off to bed, the phone rang. The protocol we had established was that if we didn't recognize the number on caller ID, then one of the employees would answer, and if it was important, Raul and I would get to our assigned stations and Raul would tape it. Raul was away in Mexico City just then checking in with headquarters, which he did on a regular basis. But when I caught sight of Raquel on the second landing as I was coming up the stairs, she was deathly white, and I braced for the worst. She told me that Eduardo had just called asking for Cielo. When I got to the phone, there was no one there.

Later, I found out that the kidnappers were using a technique known as "palming" whenever they would call us—like placing one palm over the other until they line up perfectly. Eduardo would be on speakerphone inside his box. They would use that cell phone to dial an intermediary in Puebla or Oaxaca—it didn't matter—and that party would use a second and third cell phone to call us. Both phones in the middle were on speaker so we could hear each other. They knew that it took at least three minutes to trace a call to the nearest cell tower, so they used a stopwatch and always hung up before then. They would stagger their calls ten or fifteen minutes apart throughout the evening until the conversation was complete. Even if the AFI could identify which cell tower, it wouldn't matter, because they couldn't pinpoint where the call was coming from, and next time they would use a different location. And it was suspected that after each series of calls, they'd toss the cell phone microchips in a Dumpster.

But this was completely out of the blue, even though we had planned for it in the abstract. I immediately got Raul on my cell phone. He told me to stay on the line and he would talk me through it, but I could tell he was freaked out too. I was shaking uncontrollably. And then—the phone rang again, and it was him, Eduardo, on the other end of the line, like he'd stopped at the grocery store and was calling home to see if I needed anything. His voice was robotic, he obviously had a gun to his head, and he was reading from a prepared script, but it was unmistakably my husband. He asked for the contact number for our banker, and I told him it was in another part of the house. Then I went into my prepared script. Meanwhile, I had Raul on my cell phone in the other ear, feeding me instructions.

Suddenly, I remembered what this felt like: my semester at the University of Maryland studying broadcast journalism. It's like I was in the anchorperson's chair—reading from a teleprompter, receiving directions in my earpiece and trying to sound natural—serious but not morose, personable but never flippant. In a matter of seconds it all came back to me. The words were second nature to me because I had already practiced this dialogue. I could cry at the drop of a hat. I had a wellspring of emotions at my disposal. I could repeat what the kidnappers needed to hear from me, find the exact emotional timbre in my voice, and still slip in what I wanted him to know—that I loved him and that I had never stopped loving him—in a way that made him believe me. I was there in the moment, living it as it happened, and I was also outside myself, watching myself act, making mental notes, handicapping my performance. As soon as Eduardo told me he loved me, the line went dead.

The banker had always been our good friend. Eduardo has a way of bringing that out in people, and this was no exception. And I greatly appreciated his offer to help when Eduardo was first taken. But as the months dragged on, I noticed a subtle change in his tone as we spoke on the phone and in his e-mails. I sensed that he was growing uneasy. His wife was disturbed that they were somehow getting pulled into this, and it was very upsetting to his children.

As soon as Eduardo hung up, I called the banker at his home, even though it was late. He was out, so I had to coach his two little boys not to answer the phone until their mommy and daddy got home from dinner. If Eduardo got a message to the banker before I could talk to him, there's no telling what he would do. I would have had to pull the banker out of a business dinner to debrief him.

Five minutes later, Eduardo called back. Along with the banker's contact information, he wanted the numbers of some of his wealthy friends. Whenever anyone's name started showing up in Eduardo's letters, I took the precaution of calling them and warning them not to try and negotiate or give in to his demands. If the kidnappers could extort money from Eduardo's family and friends, there was no reason for them to continue negotiating with me. I had tried to alert everybody from the beginning. One of Eduardo's sisters became so unnerved that she changed her telephone number. Cielo hadn't paid his phone bill and it had been cut off, so I didn't have to worry about that. That's why Eduardo had called the house looking for him in the first place. Eduardo had sent both Cielo and Aurora, who lived in Veracruz, separate e-mail letters from the ones he had sent me, saying things like, "Jayne is a bitch, I married the wrong woman, you have to realize she's going to kill me, don't let her do this to me, you're my children and you have to stand up for me"—nasty, horrible stuff. They would try to pit us against each other, but luckily we saw that coming ahead of time and were ready for it. Cielo, although he had dropped out to a large extent, saw the AFI operate up close and shared my faith in them. With Aurora, since she wasn't part of the day-to-day activities at the ranch, it was hard sometimes keeping her in the loop. The first time the kidnappers sent her a letter from her father, she actually tried to open it and read it without contacting us, even though both Cielo and I had been very clear that she should forward any letters unopened and hang up on any calls. Luckily, the kidnappers had misspelled the password, effectively blocking her access. Everyone else was on the lookout and successfully managed to avoid contact.

From the start, the bank had told me that a transfer of funds was impossible without what is known as a callback. If you want to transfer money via verbal request over the phone, the banker needs to be able to call you back at your registered home phone number to verify that it is indeed you. But knowing this, the kidnappers had devised a way around it. Utilizing the same system they employed for calling the house, they instructed me to go out and buy a speakerphone and a separate cell phone with a speaker on it. I was to have the banker call the house, have Eduardo call the cell phone, and put them together as if Eduardo were really there—a polite fiction that the bankers would presumably overlook in the interest of expediting a resolution to this situation. The day came and I dutifully followed their instructions to a T, but the system broke down when Mexico's spotty phone monopoly failed us and I couldn't get cell phone reception at the ranch. (After this endeavor, this particular bank subsequently changed its policies, no longer allowing just one person to have control over an account, in order to prevent something like this from happening again.)

As a fallback, the kidnappers were familiar enough with international banking laws to know that the bank, if it wished, could legally transfer the money from one account to another one that I could access. Soon after, Eduardo began calling the banker at work and threatening him, saying, in effect, "If you do not wire the money into Jayne's account immediately, you are signing my death warrant, and I will sue you for killing me." This so unnerved bank officials that at the eleventh hour of negotiations, they relented and announced to me that they would release Eduardo's money after all. This looked like a decision solely to protect themselves from legal exposure if something went terribly wrong.

The problem was that at this stage, since we were well on our way to reaching a settlement, by flooding the negotiations with a much larger pool of money, we ran the risk of capsizing our work to date and having to start all over again. The AFI was dead set against it; it felt that with what I had been able to borrow, we soon would be able to close the deal. The EPR usually kidnapped its victims in June and released them sometime around Christmas. If we upped the amount so substantially this late in the game, we could prolong Eduardo's time in captivity—something we weren't confident his health would tolerate. We needed the bank to cooperate. I begged the banker not to take Eduardo's calls.

He didn't for a while: The secretaries all claimed he was perpetually in meetings—a level of subterfuge the bank had not signed up for. The kidnappers were effectively holding the bank hostage as well.

Eventually, the banker told me, "We cannot do this anymore. I have an office to run, and it's being terrorized. If Eduardo calls again, we will be forced to make the transfer to your account in order to not be held liable." He sent me a formal request for the necessary account information in order to transfer funds to our joint accounts in the States. I tried to stall. But the longer I did this, coming up with increasingly implausible excuses for why I couldn't send him a simple account number, the banker began to suspect that my motives were less than honorable. If Eduardo died, I stood to inherit much of his estate. He began to treat me like a suspected criminal, one who quite possibly could be the biggest bitch on the face of the earth. It was the impression I had wanted to give the kidnappers. Now here it was coming back to bite me but through no efforts of my own. Very quickly, I imagined this attitude metastasized throughout our tiny community, borne along on gossip and idle chatter. An eyebrow raised here, a look askance there. Suddenly, I felt like I was vilified, met with dark stares and furtive glances everywhere I went. This chess game had become three-dimensional, and I was one of the living chess pieces—the ice queen, imperious and unpitying.

This was all getting to be a little too much.

To be fair, from the banker's point of view, he had seen a lot of me at first, when I emphasized that I alone would make all decisions affecting our financial future. Then he hardly saw me those long months when I internalized this trauma and had to learn how to guard against it. When things reached a critical flash point, he dutifully found a way around my problem for me, offering to transfer my funds to a U.S. account I could draw from, only to have me rebuff his offer for reasons that seemed murky at best. No wonder he had his suspicions.

But I really felt like I was coming to the end of my rope. I had used all the tricks in my bag to avoid the obvious and stave off the inevitable, and I was fast running out of road. Eduardo's family was either too far removed or too overwhelmed to be a source of strength to me. Any number of people thought I was out of my mind, and now I ran the risk of being seen as quite possibly evil. My kids were a source of emotional strength to me but not one I wanted to lean on too heavily, since they were like litmus paper to my fluctuating moods. And although Raul and the AFI were resolute in how to deal with this situation, for me it amounted to an enormous gamble: If they were wrong, they would go on to the next case and hope to do better. But I would always live with the guilt that I'd had the power to resolve this and had failed miserably. My kids would hate me, Eduardo's friends

and family would hate me, and most of all, I would hate
myself. I didn't know if I could live with that. Now the cu-
mulative pressure was causing me to buckle. I felt like I was
on the verge of a nervous breakdown. I worried that after all
this, even if the experts were right, I was going to somehow
lose it and undo all our months of careful planning.

My salvation came from the unlikeliest of sources.

Since midsummer, Cielo had been largely missing in action. He was drinking, staying out late; he and Leti had
separated, and he was putting himself in unnecessarily dangerous situations, in what I felt was a misguided sense of
survivor's guilt. But around this same time, in ways I wasn't
even aware of while they were happening, Cielo had started
to pull it together. He stopped drinking. He and Leti, although they had already reconciled, started legitimately
working through their problems. He started spending a lot
of time with the kids, taking them places on Sundays, filling
the emotional void left by Eduardo's absence. Whereas before he succumbed to the pressure, I always saw in Cielo
the eager young man he had been when I first met him, now
I saw a grown man hardened by the worst the world had to
offer—one who had withstood its blows and now come
back to finish the fight. I could see in his eyes that he
wanted to destroy these people in the worst way. So did I. I
guess we had both changed, for better or worse.

Cielo got on the phone with the banker and explained in
no uncertain terms that his participation was absolutely
crucial: He had the power to undo seven months of intensive negotiations with one ill-considered phone call. He
told the banker, "Look, man, this is my father's life, and
you are about to ruin everything. We will lose all credibility
with the kidnappers and we will be back to square one.
They won't believe a word we've said about anything now,
and we'll prolong the whole ordeal for my dad. He's been
shot twice, they're threatening to shoot him again, and he
can't survive like this for much longer. Just follow our in-

structions and don't fuck it up." As a follow-up, I wrote a confidential letter to the banker carefully outlining our strategy and taking full responsibility for these actions as Eduardo's wife. He agreed and successfully avoided Eduardo's calls for another week. By that point, the kidnappers had given up their back-channel strategy and things returned to some semblance of normal.

One of my biggest fears was that Eduardo would return to me so bludgeoned and brainwashed by his captors that he would believe these things he had been inundated with for months. His phone calls continued, even as the negotiations seemed to be bearing fruit, and every emotion you can think of flickered across his voice in the course of those conversations. When a call came in now, someone else would answer, and the kidnappers would hang up and call back. All the employees and children had to clear out immediately. I would grab my dialogue folder with my notes, Raul would get the whiteboard and markers, and we would quickly connect the recording device to the phone. The phone would ring, and I was on. I didn't know if Eduardo even knew me anymore—it was hard to glean his silhouette in those recited monologues—and I was honestly afraid that he had lost touch with reality. He knew the state of our finances as well as I did or better, and yet for months, in the cramped handwriting of his frantic letters, and now in his borderline hysterical phone rants, he relentlessly hammered home just the opposite.

I wished Eduardo could be somehow more circumspect and resist the kidnappers' demands to reveal every nook and cranny of our financial infrastructure. At times, I felt like he was working against me, and it gave false hope to these criminals, who desperately wanted things to be how they were not. I might as well have wished he could withstand torture, which ultimately no one can. It's as if the kidnappers thought that if they convinced him it were true, that we actually had the kind of money they imagined, then he in turn could convince me, and I could will it into being. If Eduardo believed that, then he could easily believe the rest of what he was saying—that I was killing him, that I prolonged his agony, only wanted his money, was turning his kids against him, and reveled in his pain.

I told Cielo, "You know, when Eduardo walks through that door, it's quite possible that instead of coming to embrace me, he's going to go for my throat. And I'm going to need you to defend me." I even thought about how I could restrict his ability to move money so that I could get him some psychological help first. The practical, dispassionate part of me had always prepared for the possibility he could die; in the back of my mind, I knew how I would get past it and what I would tell the kids. It was my way of controlling my fear of the unimaginable. But I could never imagine a world in which he hated me—in which he actually believed the horrible things he said to me, that I was his enemy, and that he would want to divorce me. I was able to set aside my emotions and replace them with emotions of my choosing, because essentially we were both reading from a script. Take away the script and all that's left is real life, and that was too profound to contemplate. That could destroy me.

Just before Christmas, the AFI received information from an EPR defector about a victim being held in the state of Morelos, near Cuernavaca. They staged a daring late-night raid, expecting to find a wealthy man known as the Tortilla King of Puebla, as well as clues as to where they were holding Eduardo. Instead, they found a third victim they didn't know about, whose name has never been released. They also discovered printed EPR propaganda, grenades, armaments, and stacks of hundred-dollar bills. This was a different EPR cell; six or seven people were arrested, but none of them had any knowledge of the group that had Eduardo. The Tortilla King was released just after Christmas; he had been held in an empty cistern for six months.

Lynda, Aurora and her two youngest kids, Eduardo's

sister Lupe, Cielo and Leti, their daughter, Vera, my mom, and Raul all spent Christmas with us. Christmas was always an experience at my house—one that Martha Stewart would envy. I baked gingerbread houses and figures with the kids, decorated the tree with edible ornaments, chose and wrapped each gift with care. The whole house smelled wonderful. I was determined to make this Christmas the equal of any other.

I bought Eduardo a pair of winter boots that he'd been wanting and I made him a card. I put them under the tree along with the presents the kids made for him, in hopes that we'd have him back before Christmas. But as the day approached, I realized that wasn't going to happen. We were making progress with the kidnappers, but it was slow going, having to place our counteroffers in the daily classified ads, and the thing with the banker had set us back a couple of weeks. The kidnappers weren't going to let us close the deal until they'd played all of their cards, and calling our banker was the last of their cards. The kids didn't want anything but to have their daddy back, although Emiliano asked for a big bag of play money to see if he could bribe the kidnappers with it. Eduardo had missed Fernando's graduation, school plays and concerts, Father's Day, Nayah's first day of school, Emi's birthday, my birthday, his own birthday, and Thanksgiving. But we never thought he'd miss Christmas.

As we counted down the days on the Advent calendar, the younger ones were full of existential questions I couldn't answer: If Santa Claus has magical powers and can fly around the world in one night, then why can't he tell us where the kidnappers are? Should we write him at the North Pole and ask him? If he knows when I've been bad, he must certainly know the kidnappers and where they're hiding, since they're very bad indeed. Emiliano had just turned eight and wasn't sure he believed in Santa Claus anymore. I told him about the time when I was ten and becoming a disbeliever. I was awake in my bed on Christmas Eve, tossing and turning, and my dad opened my door to tell me to look out the window. Just up the street, there was something that sure definitely looked like a sleigh, sans reindeer, parked at the curb. Five minutes later there was a knock at our door. My dad came to my room again and told me there was someone who wanted to see me. I very nervously went to the front door and there he was: Santa Claus—real beard, real hair, red velvet suit, roly-poly belly, rosy cheeks, turned-up nose. He let out a big laugh and called out my name. It cured me of my crisis of faith. And I could tell my children with conviction that at the end of the day, I may not have all the answers about Santa Claus, but I know what I saw that night. They seemed satisfied. Good thing. We needed a little Christmas magic right about then.

On Christmas Eve, we made a fire in the big fireplace in the living room. We all sat around the tree and had hot *ponche*, the traditional Mexican holiday punch, and a light dinner of soup and hors d'oeuvres. There weren't many smiles. We tried to be merry, but this was the first Christmas we had to try. The emptiness in the house that night was like a ragged hole where Eduardo used to be. No one could pretend that it wasn't there. There was a full moon outside that cast a silvery hue over everything. Fernando came into the living room where we were all seated, looking like he'd been crying. Lupe said that we should all go outside and send our energy to Eduardo. We grabbed our coats and headed outside and got in a big circle and held hands, just like we'd done at Thanksgiving and on my birthday. One by one, underneath this intense full moon, we all said a prayer out loud with our wishes for Eduardo. We hoped that somehow the moon would transport our messages to him. Everyone cried as they spoke—everyone, that is, except for

Nayah and me. I was over crying a long time ago. I had lost that internal trigger that turns real feelings into tears. And Nayah was okay as long as Mommy was okay.

After everyone went to bed, Raul helped me put all of the gifts under the tree. With so many kids in the house, it looked impressive. My living room floor disappeared under it all. I had three gifts for Raul, one from each of the kids—a couple of Nike sports shirts and a gym bag that Fernando picked out. Raul told me that once Eduardo was back, Raul would purposely start to distance himself from the children so that they could start transitioning back to having their father again. They had bonded so much with Raul. He said he felt more hospitality from us than on any other assignment. He also enjoyed playing Santa Claus for the first time.

The next morning, there were ribbons and wrapping paper flying, and we all forgot our problems for a little while. When the melee was over with, the only packages left under the tree were the ones that read *To Eduardo, with love.*

Things were quiet the whole week between Christmas and New Year's. Apparently, even criminals spend the holidays with their families.

FIFTEEN

Extraction

JANUARY: RANSOM PAID

In San Miguel, it doesn't really get cold until late December, which means you just need a sweater sometimes during the day and maybe a jacket at night. There is no snow, but the landscape turns to shades of amber and beige, once the trees have lost their leaves from the freezes. It's much more barren looking and often reverts to desert. Once the weather had changed, it finally seemed like change was possible, maybe inevitable.

In the first days of the new year, things began to move very quickly. E-mails arrived from the kidnappers in which they apparently were negotiating in earnest. Their numbers began to drop precipitously, and the usual lag time of several days to sometimes weeks became almost nonexistent. Eduardo's letters took on more of the tone of a cheerleader standing on the sidelines, cheering us to victory. It looked like we were finally getting somewhere. I began to call in loans to cover the amount we had committed to in anticipation of closing the deal. The banker advised me that when the time arrived, I would have to transport the cash myself and put it in a safe at the ranch. We would have to keep this transaction extremely secret—even other bank employees couldn't know, lest we risk a break-in at the ranch. We discussed having it transported by armored car, but the bank wouldn't cover the cost, and in the end it seemed like it would just draw more attention than it was worth.

And so on an average midmorning, I walked into the local branch of my bank, just off the main plaza; waited my turn to see the manager; repaired to the back room where I watched him count out what to me was an enormous amount of money in hundred-dollar bills; put it all in my yoga bag, which I slung over one shoulder; and walked out into the noonday sun and dusty streets of our sleepy little town, where anyone could have conked me on the head and lived the rest of their lives in modest luxury. I had my yoga mat and water bottle sticking out the top as a decoy, but if you see someone walking out of a bank with a duffel bag over one shoulder, you don't have to be a genius to guess what's in the bag. When I was leaving, I ran into a friend of mine with her kids and stopped to talk after giving her a hug. I even set the bag down on the sidewalk between my feet. After a few minutes, I said good-bye and casually sauntered down to the corner, where my "driver" Raul was waiting for me in the Jeep. He was watching his rearview mirror carefully as we drove away. Despite my performance—"Girl on a Winter's Day"—I found the whole thing incredibly nerve racking. Once at the ranch, we videotaped each and every bill, according to AFI protocol. There were piles of cash all over the living room. For what wasn't the first time in the last seven months, I felt like I was living in a movie.

Then, on Wednesday, January 9, there it was—an e-mail from the kidnappers: "We have a deal: Follow the enclosed instructions in Eduardo's letter and be ready to deliver the money by the 16th of January." An attached letter from Eduardo contained the heading "Seize dynamite and rocket launchers from Zetas"—a headline from that morning's newspaper, included as a kind of informal proof of life. In it, he instructed me to choose two emissaries to deliver the money from the following list: Cielo, Aurora, Gustavo, or me. With any GPS system removed, the approved emissaries would be prepared to drive our Jeep to wherever they were instructed, carrying the agreed-upon amount of cash in new series, nonconsecutive, unmarked hundred-dollar bills, avoiding any police presence, tracking devices, or tricks of any kind. If they were injured, killed, or detained en route, Eduardo would be terminated immediately. I was to await further word within the week.

We had already lined up Gustavo and his little brother Oscar, known as Coco, to deliver the ransom, so we formally submitted their names. As per AFI guidelines, they weren't family members and didn't have any real money of their own—not ransom-sized money anyway—so they didn't run the risk of being kidnapped themselves. One of our main benefactors asked to deposit the balance of his loan through a third party, so as not to arouse the suspicions of bank employees and possibly put himself or his family at risk. Gustavo agreed to have the sum deposited into his bank account, since he already would be privy to many of the ransom details, with the understanding that he would immediately transfer the funds into my account for withdrawal, since I had already verbally committed to that amount with the kidnappers. He agreed.

Instead, he left for the United States the next day without making the transfer.

We were in a panic. His office assured us he'd be back within the week but said he'd left no instructions for the transfer of any funds. I felt the blood drain from my face. I thought it must have been some kind of mistake. Before I transferred the ransom money to his account, I had asked Gustavo to come over to the house. I looked him in the eye and explained the importance of what we were doing and that if I told the kidnappers I had a certain amount, I actually had to have that amount. I couldn't say I had it and then suddenly ask for an extension. Eduardo's life was hanging in the balance of all of this. I had his promise. I had the money put into his account, I called to let him know that it was there, and he said that he would go to the bank immediately to make the transfer into my account. And then he was gone.

While Gustavo was away, the kidnappers proclaimed our choice of couriers acceptable. From now on, there could be no changes to the plan as they had approved it, which meant we couldn't replace Gustavo and Oscar with someone else to transport the money. Numb became my new default emotion. I became like a circuit breaker that just shut down at the slightest provocation. It was at these moments that I usually went upstairs and crawled under the covers. I couldn't cry, I couldn't scream, I couldn't do anything but feel empty. I'd hear the kids come in from school and the color would start coming back into my face. I'd take a deep breath, and then it was showtime.

Gustavo returned ten days later with a used Ford Expedition. I was ready to strangle him. He was extremely apologetic, claiming he had left explicit instructions with his secretary to make the deposit and couldn't imagine why there had been a mixup. I told him, "I can't *believe* you just did this to me! They're going to kill my husband! You're going to make this transfer right now, and I'm taking you there myself." Again, he assured me he would handle this but then managed to elude me for another couple of days. When he finally did make the transfer, it was approximately ten thousand dollars short. He continued to deposit money into my account a thousand dollars at a time almost right up until the moment I had to make the withdrawal. It was actually a race against the clock to see if we would have enough to pay the ransom.

My feelings for Gustavo had changed ever since he first

went into business for himself two or three years earlier. Before that, when he worked for us full-time, he was like family—practically his whole family was employed by our family. There is an extraordinary side to Gustavo—he is charming, kind, funny, and has a contagious laugh. He is extremely street-smart and a very quick study. He is resourceful and skilled at so many different things. He had really earned our trust over the years. I'm not sure where it all went wrong. Perhaps we trusted him too much. More than just an employee, Gustavo had become one of Eduardo's closest friends. Whenever Eduardo had important business decisions to make, he always consulted Gustavo first. He was born and raised locally, knew everyone, and had a great deal of common sense. He was an important ally.

He told Eduardo how happy he was working for him. He had a house in El Nigromante, a wife and two lovely little girls, a classic Mustang he'd restored himself with parts he found in junkyards. Yet he was constantly asking for raises. It reached the point where we couldn't pay him any more, so we started recommending him for other construction jobs. Whenever one of Eduardo's friends asked him who our ranch foreman was, Eduardo would talk him up. As long as it didn't interfere with his duties at the ranch, it seemed like a way we could help him out. But the more outside work we got him, the less we saw of him at the ranch. He formally shifted from full-time to part-time employment with us, and Coco stepped in to take up the slack. But still he couldn't seem to meet his responsibilities.

From the beginning of when he started working for us, he often borrowed things without asking, only admitting it when Eduardo would bring it up. It was never anything of value or even anything that would likely be missed: One time Eduardo went to get the shotgun when a pack of feral dogs was venturing onto our land, only to discover there were no shotgun shells. When Eduardo confronted him about it, he

admitted that he had taken them, saying he planned to replace them. He claimed his wife was pressuring him about
money. (I once saw her smash her old car into a boulder on
the ranch when she was pressuring him for a new car.) A
major cultural difference separated Eduardo's and my reaction to this. He considered it a form of "tipping"—to be expected from the people who work for you. I felt that trust and
loyalty were the most important assets in an employee—
in people, really.

Just before he was abducted, Eduardo and I had gone
over what bills needed to be paid, so I felt like I was up to
speed on our finances. Gustavo continued to work for us
part-time as a kind of ranch foreman—dealing with the employees, monthly expenses, and the logistics of running a
ranch. He had power of attorney to collect rent on a building we owned downtown and then deposited that to cover
the ranch expenses. But several months into the kidnapping, I noticed that our operating expenses were fluctuating
wildly. I asked Gustavo for receipts for everything, but I
never seemed to get them. Gradually there was less and less
money coming in every month, and when I'd ask him about
it, he'd cite some overdue bill or unexpected expense he
had to take care of—some of them things I knew Eduardo
had already paid or that he didn't intend to: At one point,
Gustavo deducted five thousand dollars for a water pump
for the filtration system—which never showed up—a system that retailed for eight hundred dollars. My feelings
toward him went from sentimental to anger at his misman-
agement to horror at his willful disregard for a life-and-
death situation.

What finally pushed me over the edge—and made Cielo
literally want to kill Gustavo—was when I ordered material
to close up an area of the fence where the dogs were getting
out at night. This was after he had disappeared with the
ransom deposit. Gustavo had placed the order with a company out of Celaya. The delivery came late in the day, after

Coco had left. Once the driver had unloaded the truck, I asked him for a receipt, and he told me he had specific instructions not to leave a receipt at the ranch. I told him I was Gustavo's employer and finally managed to get the receipt out of him, only to discover that Gustavo had charged me much more than he should have. He denied this over the phone and once again said there must be some misunderstanding, but it was painfully obvious that he had been taking advantage of me at every turn for some time now. This would be distressing enough in the best of times, but now I had put my husband's fate in the hands of someone I no longer trusted, and I could only hope for the best.

My months of resistance to this ridiculous, insane situation suddenly gave way. Whatever makeshift fortifications of the spirit I had erected to see me through this thing started to shift and crumble. I completely lost it. I was hysterical. Raul told me not to worry; he would talk to Gustavo and Coco. With the AFI monitoring them this closely, they would be fools to try to take any of the money. This could also put Eduardo's life in danger, which would make them accessories after the fact if the worst happened. I don't know what he said to them exactly, but I saw Gustavo afterward, and he looked like someone had just instilled the fear of God in him.

Along with their approval of our choice of couriers, the kidnappers included explicit instructions for delivering the ransom: Gustavo and Oscar were to take the money in a soft black bag and drive our Jeep to Mexico City with a *T* formed by duct tape on both rear passenger windows. They were to check into the Holiday Inn on Revolution Avenue on Monday, January 21. On the day of the drop, Coco should wear a pink shirt and white pants and Gustavo a white shirt and white pants, both with their shirts tucked in. They were warned not to carry guns, transmitters, or money of any kind. We also had requested and received a proof-of-life photo. I told Raul that I didn't think I could look at it.

He convinced me that I had to or we couldn't pay ransom; I had to provide a positive ID. He pulled the photo up on my computer screen. I was afraid to lose eye contact with him and shift my eyes to my own screen. Before he let me see it, Raul warned me that Eduardo looked very, very thin, but that he would recover. But even that wasn't enough to prepare me for the image before me: The healthy, vibrant Eduardo I had last seen on the day of the kidnapping was gone. In his place was what looked like an eighty-year-old man, staring back at me with a lifeless, expressionless gaze. His face was so gaunt that his nose now dominated his face. He reminded me of one of those shriveled apple-head dolls that I used to see at flea markets in southern Virginia. I stared at the photo, off and on, for what must have been fifteen minutes. No matter what angle I looked at it from, there was no way I could connect this scarecrow figure with the handsome, vital man I knew as my husband. Cielo had the same reaction. Eduardo had thick, shiny hair. This man was much older and so frail, he looked to be in his eighties. We even seriously discussed the possibility that this was a forgery and that the person in the photo was not Eduardo. After staring at the photo for several minutes, I could tell it was him by his eyes, but even the look on his face was one I had never seen before. He looked like a caged and dying animal, weary from abuse and neglect, that no longer even knows how to respond to anything. By the looks of him, I didn't know if he would ever recover.

The headline of the newspaper he was holding in the photo read UN AUTOPISTA DE NUNCA ACABAR—"The Never-Ending Highway."

For good or bad, I wouldn't have long to dwell on it.

On January 20, we left in two cars: Gustavo and Coco drove the Jeep, and we followed them in our Ford Explorer—Raul drove, Cielo rode shotgun, and I shared the backseat with the bag full of money. Cielo in particular had risen to the challenge here at the end and was shouldering much of the burden of pulling off what had to be a precision-crafted plan. One slipup, the slightest missed cue or miscommunication, with tensions riding high and paranoia simmering at a low flame, and the dominos could topple too fast for us to stop them. At times, I felt like one of the walking dead. My emotions were shot and flared up at inappropriate times; in other moments, it was all I could do to physically go through the motions. In retrospect, I probably should have been sedated, except that I wouldn't place this situation in anyone else's hands. Whatever was going to happen, it was going to be my responsibility. Without Cielo there for me, I don't think I could have gotten through it.

On the four-hour drive to Mexico City, we stopped at the guys' favorite *cabrito* joint that featured a variety of barbecued baby goat. It was a carnivore's delight. Looking around at these farmers and their families, I wondered how many of the restaurant's patrons had ever left a car out in the parking lot full of hundred-dollar bills. Probably more than I imagined.

When we arrived in D.F.—the Federal District, which is how most people refer to our nation's capital—we parked in front of the Holiday Inn on Revolution Avenue, and I checked Gustavo and Oscar into their room and put the duffel bag in the room safe. Since it was likely we were being watched, we had to leave them there and drive directly back to San Miguel de Allende to await word from the kidnappers. When it was time to go, Raul went over to the Jeep with them and gave Gustavo and Coco a last-minute pep talk. I felt such a huge responsibility for these men. Yes, I was saddened and disappointed by all that had happened. But they were both people we had known for years, they had wives and small children, and I was concerned for their well-being. They had volunteered to do us this favor—one that was both stressful and dangerous—and to their credit, they were going through with it. I hugged them both and asked them to be really careful.

Back in San Miguel, we waited helplessly for some sign of movement. Gustavo and Coco were not allowed to leave the hotel, so they watched TV and ordered takeout. Finally, on the second day, an e-mail arrived from the kidnappers instructing them to leave the hotel at 5 P.M. with the money packed in twenty-thousand-dollar bundles. Coco was to drive and Gustavo was to carry the bag with the money. They were to follow a fixed route and park in a Kentucky Fried Chicken parking lot. While Coco went in and bought a soda, Gustavo was to cross the street to a phone booth, where he would find an envelope containing the final set of instructions. They were to leave their cell phones behind.

The envelope in the phone booth sent them to a convenience store a half hour away, where they found another note on the back of a phone booth, and then to another phone booth and another note. They kept this up all night—a latticework of directions back and forth across the city and a wild goose chase that kept them busy until 1 A.M. They finally were directed to park at the opening of a long, dark alley. The final note had contained a photo of a skinny man with the face cut out, and Gustavo was instructed to walk down the alley and release the duffel bag only to the person who provided the missing piece of the photo.

So while Coco watched from the Jeep, Gustavo walked to the end of the corridor of light cast by the high beams from the Jeep, the duffel bag slung over one shoulder like a soldier headed off to war, and then disappeared into the inky blackness beyond. As he sat there, Coco noticed a police car that circled through the area every fifteen minutes. It was unclear which side they were there to protect and serve.

At 3 A.M., Coco called us from a pay phone in a panic. His brother had been missing now for two hours. He had waited in the car as he'd been instructed, fighting off the rising tide of fear, but there was no sign of Gustavo, Eduardo, the kidnappers, or the police. He didn't know if it was a setup, if something had gone horribly wrong, if they had decided to cut their losses and bury the evidence, or what. He didn't know what to do. We told him to go back to the hotel and wait for our call.

Eduardo had promised from inside the box that he would come out and make another payment to them since they had not been able to get what they wanted. The kidnappers considered what we paid to be an amount not really worth their time and exposure to getting caught. They wanted more one way or another. They told him that if he handed over the now $4.5 million he was supposed to somehow magically come up with, they would leave him alone and he could still continue living in San Miguel. If not, they would hunt us down wherever we were and kill us all. They told him that it didn't matter where we went, no matter where in the world we tried to hide, they would find us. Of course they repeated this message to make sure it sunk in. It was fear, after all, that was their insurance that Eduardo would come out and pay.

A week earlier, not long after El Jefe had put his gun to Eduardo's head and failed to pull the trigger, after the beatings had stopped and their treatment of him had suddenly grown more civil, his kidnappers came for him without warning and moved him to another, even smaller box in a different room of the same house. This one was approximately six feet long and not quite two feet wide, leaving him no more than an inch clearance when he lay down. While they were moving him, El Jefe threw him over his shoulder and Eduardo felt a gun in his shoulder holster. There was a moment when he could have grabbed it, but he was too weak to do so. He was afraid that the effort required might have shattered his bones.

Eduardo had little contact with the kidnappers in his new box. They still would play rock music on the speakers at earsplitting decibels, but there were no more beatings and no more abuse, so on balance he considered it an improvement. He had just settled into this new routine when he was awakened one night around midnight. They made him take off all his clothes and left new clothes for him to put on. Then they took everything but his shoes and burned them in a pit in the yard. He had several tiny notes he had managed to slip into his socks containing key dates and random clues he thought might help identify the kidnappers, but they found them and destroyed these as well. He was informed in writing he was to be released in the cemetery on the highway to Queretaro, across from a seafood stand popular with long-haul truckers. They carried him downstairs and laid him out on a long mattress, where he waited three and a half hours. He was handcuffed and his eyes were covered with duct tape, which caused his face to break out in an allergic rash. At roughly 4 A.M., they carried him outside the house for the first time in seven months and placed him in the backseat of a car.

Contrary to expectations, Eduardo was not happy about this turn of events. He had been living like a rat for over a half year at the hands of people who physically beat him, reveled in psychological cruelty, and lied to him about almost everything. In fact, every human interaction he'd had during that time was designed to either break down his mental resistance to make him more easily manipulated or else to convince him of half-truths and outright lies in order to obscure his tormentors. Good news in this context was very likely bad news, and so he was prepared for the worst. He rode the entire forty-five-minute drive with his head shoved down in the seat. He tried to keep careful count of how many minutes he was on pavement and how many on dirt roads, with special attention to speed bumps and entrance and exit ramps to the freeway. By the time they arrived at the cemetery, he had an elaborate map constructed in his head and was convinced he had been held at a semirural location near Dolores Hidalgo.

At the cemetery, he was forced to get out of the car, and

the duct tape was removed from his eyes. One of the kidnappers, whom he was explicitly warned not to look at, escorted him fifty yards to the perimeter so that he was facing a stone wall. He was told to count to two hundred slowly and then start walking until he could find a taxi. They gave him three hundred pesos for bus or cab fare.

"Until you get to your home, you cannot talk to any person about anything," he was told. "Once you get home, you can talk to your family about whatever you want, but not until you get home, and not to anyone before that."

They had left him with two apples and three hard-boiled eggs, which he quickly devoured. It was pitch-black, and all he could see was the moon and stars, which he had been deprived of for months and which threatened to overwhelm him once he had taken in their immensity. Everything was like that until he regained his equilibrium, the simplest things suddenly made wondrously complex simply by their prolonged absence. He started to walk—blindly and haltingly at first, his limbs still stiff from extended confinement, his body ravaged and weak. He had no idea which way San Miguel was but thought it imperative to keep moving. Dogs barked at him, but he was afraid of nothing. It was an unseasonably cold January, and he was shivering so hard he was scared he would chip a tooth or fracture a rib. It was now close to 5 A.M. and the morning was beginning to stir. His feet found pavement, and he picked up speed. A Honda slowed as it passed, the driver obviously contemplating giving him a ride, but he was weaving severely and looked drunk, and the car sped away.

He passed three tiny old women in serapes and asked them, "Which way to San Miguel?" They pointed straight ahead. "Where can I catch a bus?" he asked, and they pointed in the opposite direction. He started walking back the way he had come, until he reached the bus stop. An old man was seated on the broken bench and Eduardo asked him when the next bus was due.

"Six A.M.," the man said. "Where are you going?"

"Los Charcos," Eduardo said.

"You're fine," the man said, explaining where he should tell the driver to stop. "Do you work there?"

"Yes, sir," Eduardo told him. The man said he was on a religious pilgrimage, in search of a miracle. They sat there in silence together, making intermittent small talk, Eduardo perhaps the unspoken object of his quest.

Eduardo's bus companion worked for a rich family in Queretaro. We knew them well: His employer was the man who had been kidnapped and had the tops of his ears cut off.

"When you work for these rich people, it makes me happy I am poor," the old man said to Eduardo.

"Why is that?" Eduardo asked him.

"Well, I go home after work, I'm with my family and I enjoy simple things," the man said. "These rich people are always paranoid; they have to take care of so many things. I would not like to live like that."

"Me neither," said Eduardo.

When the bus came, Eduardo only had three hundred-peso notes for a thirty-peso fare, so he told the driver to keep the change. The driver let him out about a mile from the turnoff to our ranch. By this point, Eduardo was so weak that he was walking sideways. A car passed and offered him a ride—a teacher from a nearby school who failed to recognize him. He let Eduardo off at the dirt road that ran in front of our ranch—the same road where I'd spotted the Thin Man, El Jefe de los Jefes, the night before the kidnapping. The same road that the Yukon had spirited us away on seven long months ago. The dogs were in their pens in the yard, and they recognized Eduardo and began to howl and scratch at the fencing. He stopped to pet them, his first contact with unconditional love in what seemed like an eternity. When he came to our front porch, he wasn't strong enough to climb the front steps, and so he stood there in the yard, seemingly vexed by this final hurdle.

The whole family had been waiting feverishly for any word of him. Fernando had canceled his thirteenth birthday party—something he had been planning literally for years—in hopes that his father would make an appearance. When he blew out the candles on his cake, just immediate family in attendance, he looked at me and I knew what his wish was. It was now January 23—one day after the delivery of the ransom. That morning, an e-mail had arrived from the kidnappers:

The money was complete—so far, without fake or marked bills.

We will comply with our end: Eduardo will be freed in the next 48 hours and will arrive home in good health.

As soon as he arrives, publish a message in *Reforma*, the same section as last time, so that we can know the deal we had with miss Jayne went through satisfactorily.

They want me to call and let them know that Eduardo got home safe? That's twisted.

But at the bottom, almost as an afterthought, there was a sentence that took whatever hope we had that this ordeal was almost over and sent it crashing to the ground.

Mr. Gustavo is with us, enjoying excellent health. Upon his arrival home, Eduardo will explain the deal he has with us. We hope Mr. Oscar wasn't too distressed.

Mr. Gustavo is with us. The one thing the AFI was most certain would never happen was now a reality: The kidnappers had merely exchanged one victim for another. As soon as we got over the initial shock of the e-mail about Gustavo, and Raul had pulled himself together enough to talk, we had a meeting. He said that we would be starting over, negotiating just as we did before—the whole saga again from square one. I called Luis Alberto, our senator, and told him I didn't know what to do. This was beyond what the AFI could deal with. I asked him to call President Calderón himself. I didn't know what good that would do, but I felt beyond desperate at this point. He told me he would try to come to the house so that we could meet in person and come up with a plan.

Raul said that Cielo and I had to go with him immediately to break the news to Gustavo's family. All of the siblings and both parents were there. Juanita—Gustavo and Coco's mother and my longtime seamstress—wasn't easy to get along with. She was a stubborn, headstrong woman, sometimes more like a bulldozer. She and Eduardo had always had a mutual understanding, but not everyone was so lucky. The assembled family sensed that something was wrong as soon as they opened the door. Raul led the meeting. I told them we would do anything necessary to get Gustavo safely home and that we would be paying ransom, just as we did with Eduardo—as much or more, if necessary—to guarantee his safe return. Juanita was pale and shaken but didn't cry. She had worked her way up from nothing and owned quite a bit of local real estate. She was a rock. One of Gustavo's other brothers said he knew something like this would happen and had advised Gustavo and Coco not to get involved. He blamed the AFI for not having seen this coming.

Raul handled the situation very well—he always said his job title was "situation control"—and by the time we left, we felt like they were okay.

The AFI told us that kidnapping victims are always released in remote regions so that it takes them a long time to get home, thereby allowing the kidnappers time to cover their tracks. Raul, Cielo, and I were packed and ready to go at a moment's notice whenever we received word—

somewhere in Oaxaca or Chiapas, we guessed, in the heart of rebel country. I had a helicopter standing by just in case there was a medical emergency. I didn't leave the house, and I bet my mom didn't leave my side but once or twice. It was 7:45 A.M., and we had just finished breakfast. I was at the sink and my mom was clearing the table when she said, "Honey, there's someone at the front door." When I turned around, all I saw was the flash of a fluorescent baseball cap and a figure in dark clothing. I thought it was one of our workers, the only person I knew who was that thin. As I was going to unlock the glass side door from the kitchen to the patio, I suddenly saw him framed in the doorway.

He was disheveled, gaunt, draped in loose dark clothing, and looked like he might be a beggar. It was at least five seconds before I recognized him. The force of the realization nearly knocked me on the floor. I said, "Oh my God, it's him." I yelled for my mom to take Nayah into the boys' room. I could barely get the door open, and then he could barely get up the steps because his muscles had atrophied so dramatically. The boys were in the back brushing their teeth, so only Nayah saw him. Luckily, she didn't recognize him either. The AFI had recommended we get Eduardo shaved, showered, and looking somewhat normal before the kids saw him, in order to minimize the impact on them. I was crying and kissing him and trying to breathe all at once. I just kept saying, "I love you so much." His face was impassive, and he could barely lift his arms; it was like holding on to a dead body—he was just skin over bone. He seemed confused and could barely speak, and he was dizzy and had to sit down. He looked like he was weeping, but no tears would come out.

The first thing he said was "I have been through so much." It was like the enormity of trying to fit it all into words was just too daunting. All the things I had feared the most—that he would hate me, resent me, want to divorce me—just melted away in a heartbeat. The thing he was most shocked by was that I had never been in captivity at all. Until I told him, he had no inkling. He was anxious to see the kids, so I dressed him as much like the old Eduardo as I could and then made them promise not to hug him too hard, and they all came in and just held on to him on the couch. Fernando especially was shocked at how he looked, but the younger ones were happy just to have him back. I called a doctor who was on standby and Dr. Bev, my psychologist, and both agreed to come over right away. Eduardo didn't want to go to the hospital. Instead, he asked me to make him banana pancakes. And scrambled eggs. And yogurt with nuts. He kept calling out the meals he'd been fantasizing about in captivity. I started to laugh. It was just so comical—I feared that when he saw me again, he would hate me, and here he was working his way through the menu at a diner. I told him to prioritize, since I couldn't make them all at once. He was so hungry he couldn't get the food down. I was afraid his body would go into shock.

Eduardo told me that just before they had released him, they put him on the phone with Gustavo, whom they were now holding, contrary to what the AFI told us was likely to happen. "We have to give them everything," he said. I agreed.

"But there's someone you have to meet," I told him. "A man has been staying with us—a federal agent—monitoring this from the beginning and advising me on every move. We will negotiate like we did before. But we have allies. We're not in this alone." Raul had been hovering in the main room, to allow us a private reunion and to wait for the appropriate time to make himself known.

Eduardo had a quizzical expression on his face, and then he struggled to his feet and gave Raul a tremendous hug. He thanked him over and over again, and then when he finally released him, I could see that a change had swept over Eduardo. A flicker of the old him was suddenly back—frail but filled with a ballooning spirit, this life force that affects everyone he meets. I could see his mind racing back over the last seven months, suddenly reframing everything that had happened in light of this stealth campaign. The old smile appeared on his lips, and a warm glow settled high in his cheeks.

"Let's go," he said. "We can take the Jeep. I know more or less where they are. Get your guys, get some guns, and let's go kill these motherfuckers!"

SIXTEEN

The Never-Ending Highway

FEBRUARY–MARCH: AFTERMATH

We made plans to leave within forty-eight hours. A team of AFI agents was standing by in Mexico City to debrief Eduardo on anything he might remember that could lead to the capture of his kidnappers. There were also doctors who would be able to examine Eduardo in detail. And the AFI advised us not to be accessible when they started the negotiation process all over again, which might further infuriate Eduardo's former captors. After that, we planned to leave the country as quickly as possible. No one could realistically advise us on how much danger we were in, and even if they could, the last professional advice we got was that whoever delivered Eduardo's ransom wouldn't be seized in his place. Better safe than sorry.

I spent much of that first afternoon calling up our friends and putting Eduardo on the phone for two or three minutes at a time. It was very emotional—perhaps even more so because for a lot of them, it was like having Eduardo suddenly return from the dead. I could listen in as they covered in fifteen seconds the same emotional distance I had traveled over the summer, fall, and into winter—from despair, to a twinkling of hope, to courage, to optimism, to confidence Eduardo would come back to me, to elation when he finally did. It was like a rocket taking off, this rush of feelings, and every time it happened, I relived all of it with whoever was on the other end. It was exhilarating.

Late in the afternoon, Juanita came to the house. Eduardo was extremely frail and was resting in bed. I had given him the leather boots I had from Christmas, and he insisted on wearing them, but they were too heavy for his legs to lift. He could only walk in them with Raul and I supporting him on both sides, and he looked like a skinny little boy trying on his father's boots that were way too big for him. I told Juanita that Eduardo was very weak and needed to rest, but he would be glad to see her for a short visit. We brought Eduardo out into the living room. They embraced, but she was clearly shocked at his appearance. Unlike the rest of us, whose horror at first seeing him was mixed with a muted joy that we finally had Eduardo back, Juanita must have seen him through the scrim of what these monsters were likely to do to her son. Especially when you first encountered him, Eduardo was barely recognizable.

Both Eduardo and I reiterated to Juanita that we were completely dedicated to getting her son back unharmed. We would pay whatever ransom we had to. Moreover, for the past seven months, unbeknownst to any of our neighbors, we had been conducting just such a (now successful) negotiation with these same people: We knew firsthand what they were like, we knew the routine, and the AFI agents who had been advising me had both a successful track record and a solid idea of what we could look forward to. As before, we believed strongly that we should place this matter in their hands. Raul assured Juanita that the kidnappers would not be treating Gustavo in the same manner they had treated Eduardo, and they would probably not keep him for nearly as long. But nothing seemed to appease Juanita. This wasn't what she wanted to hear. She wanted us to write a check to the kidnappers for whatever they were asking, right now, and she wanted her son home tomorrow.

I finally had to excuse Eduardo; he would make sense in waves, but then he would go off on a tangent that made me realize he was still somewhat delusional from the trauma and malnutrition. He would start saying things that Juanita shouldn't be hearing at a moment like this—his need to talk to people and express himself overwhelmed any common sense in the moment. Juanita left saying a friendly good-bye, but I could tell there was trouble brewing. She didn't climb down off the back of a donkey and into the driver's seat of a shiny new car, a successful businesswoman who had worked her way up from nothing, without moving quite a few mountains along the way. She had never been a quitter, and she wasn't going to leave this alone until she got what she wanted.

Since we were the ones being extorted, the kidnappers continued to deal with me over the weeks and months ahead, and Raul served double duty advising me like he had and keeping the Otero family informed. As before, we had a fixed amount of money to work with and made offers and counteroffers accordingly. Eduardo and I had loans that had to be covered immediately, and the bank would only release what it legally could. And although we now had access to the rest of our money, the worldwide financial crash had occurred in the interim, so our money wasn't worth as much (since we hadn't been able to reinvest)—not to mention the Cal Wimberley deal that had fallen through. At one point, we owed the bank more than what we had in the bank. Nevertheless, what we offered in the beginning for Gustavo was far more than we had initially offered for Eduardo. And although we resolutely refused to comment in the press, since the AFI told us it ran the risk of endangering Gustavo, there were several leaks in the local newspaper—a mix of fact and rumor—including that the AFI was now involved.

I wasn't surprised the next morning when Juanita showed up at the house again with her family in tow. Luis Alberto was there—he'd driven all the way from Mexico City to be with us. We were meeting in the master bedroom, since Eduardo was still extremely weak. Raul sensed trouble from the second she arrived, and so did I. She was beyond pushy and demanded to know all kinds of things.

How much did the kidnappers want?

How fast could we get it to them?

What were we waiting for?

As we had twice before, we patiently explained that the kidnappers were asking amounts that we simply didn't have. You can't put in a duffel bag what you don't have in the bank. When Cielo arrived and joined us, she called him a coward for allowing Gustavo to walk down a dark alley in his place. She demanded to know why Raul would have allowed her son to do this when it should have been the AFI's job. She insinuated that we had sacrificed Gustavo to get Eduardo back, promising to pay the kidnappers more money after Eduardo's release and then reneging on the deal, leaving Gustavo behind as now worthless collateral. Eduardo tried to explain that he had only learned they had taken Gustavo long after he had agreed to pay them an additional amount. Since they now were actively negotiating with us, this strategy obviously superseded any previous fixed agreements. But she wouldn't have any of it. She said that she would do *anything* in order to protect her son. Raul, for the first time since I had met him, did not have the situation in control. Juanita began to verbally attack Eduardo, who was barely able to speak above a whisper. She was hurling insults left and right, and no one else could get a word in edgewise. I could feel the blood rushing to my face.

I told her that she was attacking and alienating the only

people in the world who could help get her son back, as well as the ones who best understood what they were going through. I informed her that she had just interrupted a meeting with a senator who had driven from Mexico City this morning to help us come up with the best possible plan. I reminded her that Eduardo hadn't even been back for twenty-four hours yet, he was still extremely weak, and this was no time to be threatening his life. No one had set her son up. This latest development had been orchestrated by hardened criminals to exert maximum leverage in order to increase their haul. If she needed someone to hate, they were right there for the taking. Join the club.

The entire time, she kept shouting over my words, accusing and threatening and name-calling. The two decades we had known each other were gone in a flash—everything Eduardo and I had done for her and her family as employers, clients, friends, and benefactors: how he had defended them and the people of El Nigromante and allowed them to keep their homes, how we had set Gustavo up in business and gotten him his first clients, their attendance at our wedding, even that we were paying all of Gustavo's and his ex-wife's household expenses for as long as Gustavo was away. I didn't even bother to mention our other problems with Gustavo, which we would deal with at the appropriate time, after this latest nightmare was over. But none of that mattered now. She was facing a life-altering moment—the same one I had faced seven months ago and had been dealing with ever since—and she was lashing out at anyone within reach. For all I knew, the kidnappers were inflaming her with private e-mails, and she couldn't see that she was being manipulated. She just kept yelling.

That's when I lost it.

I pointed my finger in her face and told her in Spanish to go fuck herself. I told her she was out of her mind. I came very close to physically attacking her. I told her to leave, but she wouldn't. I left the room before I did something we would all regret. Raul joined me out in the kitchen, at a loss for words. He asked me if I was going to be okay, and I nodded. He went back in to see if he could salvage the situation. After I left the room, both Cielo and Luis Alberto tried to reason with her, but to no avail, each in turn joining me in the kitchen, shaking his head. Eventually, there was no one left to yell at but Eduardo, with Raul at his side as a silent bodyguard, ready to mix it up if necessary.

In one of our meetings, Benito Roa had told us that no amount of security could keep us safe at our ranch: The EPR was an army with many members and no profile. Its people were invisible; we were not. Juanita was going to keep coming by, as would many friends and well-wishers, once word spread that Eduardo had been released. He asked if we had someone in Mexico City we could stay with who wasn't a family member. A friend graciously provided his palatial estate. Roa told us he would meet us at the Guanajuato airport with armed guards and a military transport plane to transport us there. There would be no log or registry of our destination; we would simply disappear. Cielo and Leti would drive to Mexico City with Raul and meet us there; no one else was to know where we were going—no exceptions. It was tough for the kids to know what to pack. They asked when we would be back and I said several months. I wasn't sure if I was telling the truth. We left early the next morning.

In Mexico City, we had lunch at our friend's house, where we planned to stay for the next ten days incognito. I had to warn him and his wife to brace themselves before they saw Eduardo. Our friend had taken the kidnapping especially hard; he had stopped smoking years ago but started up again while Eduardo was in captivity. At lunch, I had to stop Eduardo from eating the chicken bones, reminding him that he didn't have to do that anymore. It was moments like this that hammered home how far he had to go to undo the brainwashing of the past seven months.

That evening, we met with Benito Roa, Federal Police Commissioner Facundo Rosas Rosas, and other higher-ups in the AFI to begin our debriefing. When he was introduced to Genaro Garcia Luna, Mexico's director of public security—the head of law enforcement in Mexico—Eduardo apologized for wearing a sweatsuit that barely stayed on his body and boots he could hardly walk in.

"I'm sorry, sir," Eduardo told him, "but I'm so skinny that nothing fits me."

"I am the one who should be apologizing to you," said Garcia Luna. "I'm very sorry for what happened to you. Nobody trusts the police, but we deserve it—we did this to ourselves. We've been working hard on trying to rebuild our image, and who knows how long that's going to take . . . Nobody chooses the police forces in Mexico because of the horrible corruption."

The debriefing consisted of hours and hours of questions on every single detail of the kidnapping and captivity—smells, sounds, colors, impressions, what the kidnappers ate, their habits—the whole seven months, frame by frame. They separated us so we wouldn't influence each other's testimony. They had psychiatrists on hand and were shocked that we were so willing to cooperate. They said that almost never happens. People are afraid to talk; once they get their loved ones back, they're reluctant to expose themselves to further risks.

Over those first few days, the debriefing process was interspersed with visits to various medical specialists. When Eduardo's personal doctor first saw him after we landed in Mexico City, he was visibly shaken—even outraged—at the injustice of what he was seeing. Eduardo was suffering from liver damage, severe starvation, malnutrition, multiple infections, hearing loss, and a host of other maladies that could be traced directly to his months in captivity. He had multiple broken ribs, and his legs and feet would swell up at night. He looked like a concentration camp victim. When we stopped at a Japanese restaurant for lunch afterward, the waiter was impressed with the amount of food Eduardo could eat.

After several days of declarations—our official statements—it became apparent that Eduardo couldn't continue. He had a hard time sitting up and talking for any length of time, and he eventually lay down on one of the black leather sofas in Rosas's office while three female agents took turns recording his answers in shorthand. If he had to sit for even a short amount of time, his feet would balloon to twice their size from malnutrition. After a couple of days of this, Roa said that Eduardo needed to recuperate before we could continue. He asked if we had access to someplace to stay near the beach, so that Eduardo could relax and let himself repair. We drove our car to Acapulco, where our friend offered us his place right on the water. Eduardo was anxious to lead the AFI to where he thought the kidnappers' house was and still felt confident he could find them. The AFI promised that when he was stronger, agents would take him out in the field with them, protected by bodyguards and bulletproof cars.

The house in Acapulco already had very high security. About five days into our stay, my mother took the kids back to the United States with her. Cielo and Leti had already returned to the ranch—they were given forty-eight hours to pack up their living quarters and could see or talk to no one—and would soon be on their way to the the States as well. After another ten days, Eduardo had recovered enough and put on sufficient weight for us to return to Mexico City. We wrapped up our work there in another couple of days and returned to San Miguel de Allende in a police convoy. About a half hour outside of San Miguel, very near to where Eduardo was released, we were met by Raul, Coco, and three AFI agents who were to be our personal bodyguards for the next forty-eight hours, all carrying machine guns. We were transferred to a decoy car at the rear of our motorcade, an unassuming, nondescript compact, along with the bodyguards, and Raul and Coco drove the other two cars. The AFI agents who accompanied us had some major firepower with them in the front seat. They asked me if I knew how to handle a gun. I said yes. They said that if we got into any kind of trouble, they would be handing me one, so be ready.

The AFI told us we shouldn't linger at the ranch, so we made plans to fly to the States as soon as possible. Once back at the ranch, the bodyguards quickly took control, laying trip wires on the grounds and setting up a rooftop sentry post. They were trained for nothing short of warfare and approached our circumstance accordingly. They carried with them several huge three-ring binders that held the assembled evidence of our case. I asked early on if I could look at them, and they said no. But we invited them to join us for every meal, as we do with all visitors in our home, and before we left, they let me take a peek. I remember the artists' renditions of the suspects, some of which came from others and were extremely detailed and quite accurate, and I saw there had been an investigation into Norma's two brothers who were ex-AFI agents, which turned up nothing. At the end of forty-eight hours, they drove us to the new airport in León and escorted us to the head of the security line, where we said good-bye to Mexico. The AFI told us to be on standby, since it had twenty-five agents collecting information and they were hot on the trail of the culprits. We had to be ready to return to identify them at a moment's notice.

While we built a new life back in the United States, a place that held memories for us both, although not together, negotiations continued with Gustavo's kidnappers. They followed roughly the same pattern as Eduardo's negotiations had, although in a sped-up fashion; it was like fast-forwarding through a movie a second time. In our absence, the kidnappers had started having Gustavo write letters to his friends, family, employees, friends we had in common, the school board, school officials, and anyone else they could think of, saying that we had abandoned him to the kidnappers after trading him for Eduardo in order to save what was left of our money. We were offering them nothing and had fled the country to hide. He begged people to pressure us to pay his ransom. Juanita also went to the press with information that was often incorrect. Unfamiliar with the details of the last seven months—and often surprised that Eduardo had returned alive—people appeared willing to believe almost anything. Even people at the school who had known Eduardo and me for years now doubted our character and integrity. It was amazing. I started getting e-mails from the school, people Gustavo had worked with, his family, and second-party e-mails threatening that if we did not pay for Gustavo's release, we would not be allowed back in the city. We had been through a kind of hell that most people could never imagine, and yet even people who knew us were suddenly treating us like criminals.

I had to write many of them back and say, "You are becoming unwitting accomplices to these criminals. Stop and think for a second who we are. Put aside the kidnapping. Do you think we are capable of doing the things they are claiming? With this school we have created, the crusades against civic injustice Eduardo has spearheaded through his TV show, and all the things we have done for this community, do you think our character would allow it? You are believing exactly what these people want you to believe. You are part of the problem." They would invariably e-mail back and say, "Of course, you're right. We're so sorry." But I didn't know everybody, and so this sentiment spread unchecked.

To be fair, we had disappeared to another country, for the sake of our safety and that of our children, and all Juanita had was a single cell phone number where she could call and leave a message. We purposely had no contact with the Otero family. They got regular updates from

Raul on the state of the negotiations, but in their minds they couldn't understand why we were negotiating in the first place. Only Coco remained sympathetic to our plight. He had a clearer mind than his mother, and her behavior really upset him. He even continued to work for us and ended up in the hospital with ulcers at one point. The whole thing obviously took a toll on him.

What changed Juanita's mind was when she was forced to take over Gustavo's business in his absence. She went to collect on money she thought was owed him, only to find out that it was the other way around. Juanita soon discovered that Gustavo had mismanaged his and our businesses.

Of course, he wasn't the only one, as far as we were concerned. Merchants, carpenters, electricians—they all thought Eduardo wasn't coming back, so they could cheat or overcharge me because I'd never be able to ask him about it. Eduardo was like a once majestic fallen oak, and they all wanted their little pile of firewood for the winter. We finally had our accountant do a full forensic audit on our finances, and he was able to prove much of this. It was a completely awkward, unnerving situation.

And then one day, about halfway through April, six weeks after we had returned to the the States, we got a call from the AFI telling us that Gustavo had been released. The kidnappers didn't demand a ransom—not even the amount we had agreed to so far. The AFI said the kidnappers had finally decided to cut their losses: Exposing themselves to another handoff for less than seven figures simply wasn't worth it. In the kidnappers' eyes, unlike us, Gustavo was a working man, a member of the same class they purported to champion. He wasn't the enemy. Killing him could be a public relations nightmare. It was easier to move on to the next victim. So they put him on a bus to Queretaro, and he called the police from the bus station. They had kept him in a box slightly bigger than the one that held Eduardo, and outside of his first day in captivity, they never beat him or treated him poorly. When Eduardo talked with him by phone, Gustavo said the kidnappers had started to get very nervous. There was a rumor in town that President Calderón had taken a personal interest in the case, owing to our handful of mutual friends, and they could have felt the heat closing in. Gustavo was held in captivity for two and a half months. After he was released, Gustavo told us that the kidnappers had held a gun to his head to make him write those letters to the community. He also told us the kidnappers had given him a message for us:

> Tell Eduardo it's a good thing he kept his money. He's going to need it to bury his whole family.

After Gustavo's release, Roa confided to us, "If I were you, I would remove the Otero family from my life. Who knows what kind of conditions the kidnappers put on his release or what information they demanded in return?"

According to Roa, in almost every case, there is someone—either an employee or a member of the family—who serves as an informant, either voluntarily or involuntarily. Many times, they had no idea what they had done until much later. There were, for example, the potential buyers Gustavo brought to my mother's house who seemed more interested in Eduardo and me than in the house. Similarly, as much as we were drained emotionally by our battles with Oscar and his wife, Norma, there was never any evidence connecting them to the kidnapping.

None of us will ever forget that Gustavo and Coco selflessly offered to carry the ransom payment for Eduardo. They did this out of love and loyalty, and we will always be profoundly grateful for that and deeply sorry that Gustavo was victimized as well.

While we were recuperating in Acapulco, I noticed that my bones were constantly sore. I had been running on adrenaline for so long that I had become desensitized to my own body. I had willed myself not to get sick, and once that external pressure was no longer holding me intact, I could feel my body start to collapse from within. Four weeks after we returned to the States, I started feeling really bad. I made an appointment with my oncologist. He ran tests and performed several biopsies. When the results came back, he told me that not only had my cancer returned in the other breast, but it had now also spread throughout my entire skeleton. I was diagnosed with Stage 4 breast cancer with widespread bone metastasis that was considered early onset. I really wasn't even that surprised. It was almost like I had granted myself permission to disintegrate. If you keep reaching deeper and deeper into yourself for the resources to carry on, it's like anything else: Eventually you have a deficit that somehow must be repaid.

So that was it then. This was the lesson I would take from this ordeal: Surmount the hurdles that life has in store for you, and life will find you bigger hurdles. There is a house advantage built into the game, and anyone with the temerity to think they can outwit fate has a surprise in store. The Never-Ending Highway, indeed. I had spent almost a year now trying to put myself in Eduardo's place, to stay strong and vigilant in deference to the sacrifice he was making, which was so much greater than mine, and now I had finally gotten my wish: I wasn't at the end of a terrible journey after all. My own terrible journey was just beginning.

I was done. I had reached my limit and then kept walking, until I was so far over the edge I wasn't even sure of the way back. I seriously considered ending it all right then. Except, exactly like Eduardo, I began to focus on the faces of my three beautiful children. I spent two weeks of the most intense self-reflection I have ever experienced. I was on a dark river, floating out to sea, borne along on the light of my children's smiles. We come from darkness and we return to it, but in the meantime we leave behind particles of light in the lives that we reproduce. That was the best I could come up with.

And so I started chemo. I was bald—I had been through this before, so I knew what to expect. One day, my mom dropped me off for chemotherapy—I had on my little hat and was trying to be as cheerful as I could. It was near the first day of spring; I remember feeling a twinge of sadness that the world would soon be in bloom again for another cycle, and I wasn't sure I'd be making this trip. I should have recognized that as a sign.

When I got to the doctor's office, someone had left a book on top of the sign-in sheet so that I had to move it out of the way. On the cover was a beautiful woman with shoulder-length blond hair; she was wearing a cowboy hat and was standing in front of the Grand Canyon. The title of the book was *Crazy Sexy Cancer Tips* by Kris Carr—a title that was both cheesy and funny, just the sheer audacity of it. Although I didn't know it at the time, this was the author who had survived her "terminal" cancer for five years. But it was the look on her face that caught my attention— knowing, like an advertisement for surrendering to the moment. Or, rather, like we shared a secret—that this was a carefully placed clue in a murder mystery—and she was doing her best to hide a smile of recognition. I opened it to the title page, and someone had handwritten a note saying this was for the chemo room and whoever could get something out of it.

Aha. My instincts were correct—this was a clue. So I asked the nurse if I could borrow it.

I started reading it right there in the chemo room. I usually fell asleep from the Benadryl, part of my chemo treatment (it's supposed to keep you from having an allergic reaction to the poison). But this time the book kept me wide awake. The author reminded me of myself. She had been an actress in New York; we had similar backgrounds. After she developed a pain during yoga class, she discovered she had liver and lung cancer that was diagnosed as 100 percent incurable. So she turned to a diet of raw food and wheatgrass juice and underwent a major lifestyle change. She sold her condo and started on a quest that took her through the world of alternative medicine. Within a couple of years, the cancer went into dormancy; it didn't disappear, but it stopped dead in its tracks.

That's all I needed to hear. It was like a crack in my world, a hairline fracture through which I just barely saw a brilliant white light. If there was light on the other side, then I could get through this wall. That was the easy part.

I told my doctor about the book. As gently as he could, he tried to make me see that the odds against this were astronomical; these were the stories they put in books because they were so amazing—the modern equivalent of miracles. He was right—this was not the kind of thing rational men of science needed to lavish their time on. I left his office that day and never went back.

Now I was on fire: Stand back and let me at it. Possibility started to bubble up inside me, and soon it became infectious. Anyone who couldn't recognize that and support me was part of the problem. Like the kidnappers before it, cancer had picked the wrong girl to mess with. I found another doctor at the Cancer Treatment Centers of America who combined traditional therapies with acupuncture and many other complementary therapies and who thought I could get well—at least in his mind there was a possibility. And he was willing to let me explore all the tributaries of alternative medicine I wanted. So while I completed conventional therapies, I read rafts of books on what was out there. Later, I augmented my treatment at the Hippocrates Health Institute, where I learned about raw foods for healing—wheatgrass, ginger, garlic—and that helped me develop a special regimen based on my case history.

Within months—between the new chemo regimen, my new drug schedule, the strict raw food diet, my newfound enthusiasm and redirection of purpose, divine providence, karmic rebate, and who knows what else—I was completely cancer-free. My PET scans—full-body X-rays down to the bone, which had previously detected hot spots of cancer all over my body—were now completely clear. The doctors told me they couldn't guarantee it would last, but for now they couldn't find anything wrong with me. Once again, as men of science, they chose to interject a note of sober caution into my understandable elation.

"You know, Jayne," they told me, "we're thrilled with what is happening to you, but more than likely, we'll be managing this for the rest of your life."

I said, "Well, we'll see about that."

They cautioned me not to remove my Medi-Port—the valve in my chest where they administered chemotherapy so that it didn't disintegrate my veins—since they assumed I would relapse within six months. But I'm two years past chemo now, and they can't detect any return of the disease. I had scheduled a mastectomy after the cancer appeared in my other breast, but the surgeon who had performed my original operation told me he couldn't justify it merely as a preventive measure. On my last trip back to my doctors, the oncologist told me, "Not only can you take out the Medi-Port, you're completely in the clear, and I'd like to know what you're doing. I wish I could take credit for it."

When I first approached the clinic, I was scheduled for a "forgiveness intervention" with a pastor and a psychologist—a nondenominational routine part of their treatment process. During the session—more psychological than religious—Dr. Michael Barry, the pastor, asked me if I had anyone I needed to forgive. It was then that I decided forgiveness would have to be the first stage of my recovery. I had been so angry for so long, not just as a natural reaction to what had happened to my family—this bomb that was dropped on my private Garden of Eden and that decimated the plenitude I had grown accustomed to—but as the actual engine that kept me moving forward. If I believed in a holistic worldview—the interconnection of all things in seen and unseen ways—and I was gambling everything on it, then it seemed like no accident that I got cancer after the kidnapping. Every inner resource I had went toward fighting something outside of me. My molecules were in a constant state of agitation; there was a hostile energy seeping out of my pores, staining every decision and calculation I made. It was like swimming upstream against the natural harmony of the universe, the state of things at rest. My rage had become my life force. Of course that should lead to cancer. How could it not? I was an engine running at high rev with no oil, and eventually the bearings gave out.

So I embraced forgiveness as a way to tame my inner anger. And after the toxic cloud had passed, I could see very clearly, in a way that could only be by design, that this had been my salvation. The cancer and its aftermath had been a spike driven into the side of my life, and it acted as a vent for this enormous pressure that had built up inside me. The universe—fate, destiny, God, Gaia, the organizing intelligence that runs through everything and is not without a sense of humor—could see that what I personally needed to escape this cage, to find my own way back, was exactly this kind of challenge. In a self-correcting system, this was merely the most efficient means for my recalibration. And once it had all played out, once I came to the reveal in the third act, with only the slightest push from an unseen hand—a sly look from a woman on a book jacket, a clue left in plain sight, a sudden clearing in the forest that emerged from off the beaten path—then all was once again right with the world.

I still keep a close watch on my health. Now that I have it back, Eduardo and I advocate for justice for my family and the swift apprehension of the kidnappers—not out of revenge, but because we adamantly believe that until people start coming forward to shine a light into the recesses of fear and corruption that have overtaken Mexico, it will only continue to eat away at the body of this once-vital country—every bit a growing, unchecked cancer. And in ways that I couldn't have predicted, I now feel closer to my husband and my family. These ordeals have bonded us, and our respective paths through them have brought us a kind of grace. And if I'm not exactly grateful for what has happened to us, I'm grateful that we have come through it intact and that the effort has made us recognize ourselves in each other.

Grace is where you find it. And paradise is where you make it.

EPILOGUE

While Mariachis Play

As I write this book, it's almost two years now since Eduardo came home to me. We've only been back to Mexico once—to film a two-hour episode of *Dateline*, the NBC primetime news program, devoted to our story and ordeal. We were there only for a couple of days, and we were protected by bodyguards the entire time. Eduardo is adamant he will never again travel to the country of his birth.

People ask me why I'm doing this—telling our story, drawing attention to the dark side of recent Mexican history. From everything I hear, or that people go out of their way to tell me now, there is a great deal of animosity toward us in San Miguel de Allende. They say that the attendant negative publicity has destroyed the tourist trade, depressed property values. They say we have focused on a few isolated incidents either to foment panic or revenge or else to prosper at the expense of our former neighbors. There have been newspaper stories or blog postings that have said some terrible, hurtful things, some of them by people who ought to know better.

All I can tell you is that if I hadn't been sidelined with cancer, I would have done this a lot sooner. Forget for a second that we are property owners in San Miguel and that our property values have tumbled like everyone else's. It is exactly this attitude of denial that has allowed Mexico to rot from the inside, that has left it a hollowed-out shell, the value and spirit sucked out of it by corruption and greed, its tarnished veneer no longer able to gloss over the damage done by apathy and self-interest. Everybody's got the real story, which somebody heard at a cocktail party: We owed millions to some bad guys in an abortive land deal; Eduardo's a hothead and he finally pissed off the wrong people; this has to do with some political rivalry that goes back generations, as evidenced by the political connections of everyone involved. My favorite is that I sold the movie rights but demanded to play the lead myself. (Yes, there's a movie—at least a made-for-TV movie for the Lifetime cable network, with which this book shares a title, and hopefully it will draw attention to the book. I haven't seen it. A portion of the money we make from the movie and book will be used to finance a scholarship fund at the school we founded.) I've tried to be as detailed as I can in these pages, if for no other reason than to aid others in getting at the truth. As long as no one takes a stand—every citizen, in his daily life, who overlooks crime and tolerates inequity— then the meltdown of Mexico will continue.

And I don't just blame the Mexican government or the Mexican people. Without illegal arms by U.S. gun dealer sales, there would be no weapons to outfit Mexico's burgeoning criminal militia. Without the massive demand for marijuana and cocaine generated by the North American public, there would be no incentive for the *narcotraficantes* and drug cartels to wage their turf wars and public campaigns of psychological terror. Every college student or weekend warrior who buys a bag of pot or a gram of coke feeds this monster. And if these weren't exactly the people who brutalized Eduardo, it's the complete systemic breakdown of Mexican society—police you can't trust, a government you can't believe, class divisions stretched to the breaking point by municipal monopolies and predatory private enterprise, vast large-scale corruption—that enabled them and empowered them. If there aren't gunfights or decapitations in the streets of San Miguel quite yet—well, there are in Cancún and Acapulco and a lot of other places that once traded on their beauty and desirability. And there have been a half dozen lower-profile kidnappings in San Miguel since Eduardo's.

My guess is it's just a matter of time.

San Miguel de Allende is a tranquil, peaceful, enchanting community; it's not a rat's nest of sordidness or vice. And it breaks my heart that I am estranged from it and that I can no longer share it with my children, who were born there. But when they came for us, the police were powerless to do anything about it, and the people who perpetrated this against us are still out there roaming free, no doubt doing the exact same thing to someone else. If this can happen to us, then it can happen to anyone.

A case in point is Diego Fernández de Cevallos, a former senator and emeritus member of the conservative PAN (National Action Party) who was kidnapped in May 2010—the equivalent of a Newt Gingrich being kidnapped in America. Cevallos is an outspoken critic of the leftist movement in Mexico and a friend and colleague of Mexican president Calderón. I personally believe the same group that took Eduardo abducted him. It happened an hour away in Queretaro. Both kidnappings were carried out ambush-style by armed men with multiple vehicles. Both took place on a private road to the victim's ranch. Each occurred at roughly the same time of year—Eduardo's on June 13, Cevallos's on May 15. Blood and signs of force were left behind at both victims' abandoned cars. In both cases, the kidnappers used the same two newspapers—*El Universal* and *Reforma*—to communicate their intentions to the families. Accompanying the proof-of-life photo of Cevallos they sent to the press was the phrase *goza excelente estado de salud*—"he is in excellent health"—the same phrase the kidnappers used in early e-mail messages to describe both Eduardo and Gustavo. The list goes on. In private, former senior members of the AFI note the similarities as well. A more militant splinter group of the EPR, the TDR, who now identify themselves as "Red Por La Transformacion Global" (RPLTG) or "The Network for Global Transformation," has now taken credit for the Cevallos kidnapping.

When Mr. Cevallos was released on December 20, 2010, after seven months and six days in a box, and just days before this book went to press, the RPLTG released a formal statement to national and international media. The *Excelsior* newspaper in Mexico published their statement, where they called for an armed uprising of Mexican citizens to "take the country back" from the rich and from the multinational corporations, namely U.S. companies with investments in Mexico. This is the same group who didn't hesitate for a second to attempt to exploit Gustavo and his family—presumably the same worker class that all their efforts are for the benefit of—when they couldn't get what they wanted from us. I think they're worse than zealots or psychotics. I think they're hypocrites.

I was surprised at my reaction when Keith Morrison of NBC's *Dateline* asked me a leading question: "Jayne, what would you say to the kidnappers if you had the chance to tell them something?"

"I don't have anything to tell them," I said. What I feel is a strange kind of empathy. I would not want to be them, but I don't say that in an arrogant way. In my "forgiveness intervention," I needed to find a way to feel compassion for these people, to force myself out of my self-righteous mode. I pictured the kidnappers as infants—brought into this world as blank canvasses. And I tried to imagine what could have happened to them in their lives from childhood on to make them capable of doing what they've done. Did they believe so strongly in a cause that they could do this to a fellow human being? Did they hate anything enough to make Eduardo into a symbol and an object lesson? Or did they care so little for the world around them, or the consequences of their actions, that they could do this with a clear conscience? I know that I was pushed to the limit by the terror to which I was subjected. I carried a gun, and I would have taken pleasure in using it. I had constant thoughts of revenge and dreamed of torturing them just as they had tortured Eduardo. There's a saying in Mexico: *La burra no era arisca pero los palos la hizieron.* The donkey wasn't unfriendly until the whips made her so.

What I am passionate about is bringing these people to justice—not as revenge but simply because this cannot go on. They have taken something very precious from me: My husband, except I got my husband back. My family, but my family has survived. My peace of mind, mental health, a feeling of calm in the middle of the night. But all of that will come back to me, the more I seek it and find my way back to it. I'm one of the lucky ones.

What they took from me was Mexico—this place I fell in love with twenty years ago and gave my heart and soul to. This endless panorama that replays in memory, polished brighter by its absence, the birthplace of my children and my adopted home. The same shining ideal that's in danger of collapsing in on itself, as its citizens and inhabitants turn away from this emerging ugliness. The upper class lives like royalty, ignores the suffering all around it, and imagines it can do so forever. The poor shrug their shoulders as they have always done, chalk it up to the vagaries of privilege and fate, and ask themselves what they could do. The wine flows, scintillating aromas drift on the breeze, the lights of the fiesta swirl about them, and yet, even while mariachis play, the foundation is rotting beneath their feet.

While mariachis play. The reality of Mexico is so easy and comfortable to ignore, when life there is so simple and undemanding. This land of the siesta and sequined languor and carefree abandon. But sooner or later it catches up to you. There's still time left, before it slips away forever.

I don't have any way of knowing if I will remain cancer-free forever, or if this will indeed be something I will have to deal with on and off. I am not a super-woman, but I do know that where there is a will there is a way. However long I do live in this lifetime, I will always strive for the best possible health I can achieve. And for the record, I feel the same about justice.

Penguin Group (USA) Online

What will you be reading tomorrow?

Patricia Cornwell, Nora Roberts, Catherine Coulter,
Ken Follett, John Sandford, Clive Cussler,
Tom Clancy, Laurell K. Hamilton, Charlaine Harris,
J. R. Ward, W.E.B. Griffin, William Gibson,
Robin Cook, Brian Jacques, Stephen King,
Dean Koontz, Eric Jerome Dickey, Terry McMillan,
Sue Monk Kidd, Amy Tan, Jayne Ann Krentz,
Daniel Silva, Kate Jacobs...

You'll find them all at
penguin.com

*Read excerpts and newsletters,
find tour schedules and reading group guides,
and enter contests.*

Subscribe to Penguin Group (USA) newsletters
and get an exclusive inside look
at exciting new titles and the authors you love
long before everyone else does.

PENGUIN GROUP (USA)
penguin.com